Best
Restaurants
Chicago
& Suburbs

Revised & Expanded

BY SHERMAN KAPLAN

Illustrations: Roy Killeen

101 PRODUCTIONS
SAN FRANCISCO

Published by 101 Productions
834 Mission Street
San Francisco, California 94103

Distributed to the book trade in the United States by
Charles Scribner's Sons, New York.

Library of Congress Cataloging in Publication Data

Kaplan, Sherman, 1941-
        Best restaurants, Chicago & environs.

        Edition of 1977 published under title: Best
restaurants, Chicago.
        Includes index.
        1. Chicago--Restaurants--Directories. I. Title.
TX907.K37   1979   647'.95773'11   79-12230
ISBN 0-89286-151-7

Contents

CHICAGO   7

SUBURBS: NORTH   195

Evanston, Glenview, Highland Park,
Highwood, Lake Bluff, Lincolnwood,
Northbrook, Skokie, Winnetka

SUBURBS: NORTHWEST   222

Arlington Heights, Des Plaines,
Lake Zurich, Long Grove, Mundelein,
Palatine, Wheeling

SUBURBS: WEST   238

Cicero, Forest Park, Geneva,
Glendale Heights, Naperville,
Oak Brook

SUBURBS: SOUTH   250

Calumet City, Matteson

INDEX   256

Introduction

This revised edition of *Best Restaurants Chicago* is a natural outgrowth of the first, yet it is fundamentally different in several ways. First, it is more critical. While praise is offered and recommendations given, there are a handful of caveats put into the mix for leavening. Still, the book does remain a listing of those restaurants which I can, in good faith, recommend.

Secondly, this is an expanded compilation. Several restaurants from the first edition have been included in this book and scores more have been added. As a larger volume, it will be that much more useful to you.

Finally, the new *Best Restaurants Chicago* includes evaluated K/Ratings of all but a few listings. The K/Rating is my attempt to qualify in as simple a manner as possible, my overall feeling about a restaurant. Just as wines are rated on a 20-point scale, so too are restaurants in this book. I have taken four main areas of consideration and ascribed a numerical value to each: food represents 7 points; service 6 points; decor, ambiance and atmosphere 4 points; and overall value 3 points. Restaurants with K/Ratings of 15 to 16 points are good, ones with 17 to 18 points are excellent, while those restaurants earning 19 to 20 points achieve varying degrees of greatness. I hope that the K/Rating can help you form your own judgments about restaurants. Give it a try and become your own personal restaurant critic.

Perhaps most importantly, this book represents my personal value, tastes and choices. I accept the full responsi bility for those restaurants included and those left out. I confess to certain food prejudices; while my mother got me to eat all of my carrots as a child, she was not as successful with cabbage. In any case, where my personal taste or knowledge is lacking, I have made no attempt to review particular foods or cuisines.

Inflation has taken its bite out of the food dollar just as it has everything else. By standards of two or three years ago today's budget restaurants are not so inexpensive at all. Nevertheless, in an attempt to offer some guidelines, restaurants with $ offer dining for less than $7.50 per person, $$ are under $15 and $$$ are $15 and over. These prices do not include cocktails, wine, tax and tip. There are still some places where good food can be had for under $5 per person and you will find them listed in these pages.

Above all else, *Best Restaurants Chicago* should bring you pleasure. It brought me that in the research and writing. My thanks for its completion go to some superb restaurateurs; some colleagues at CBS where my career as a restaurant reviewer began some years ago; to friends who have shared tables, tastes and dinner checks; to the people at 101 Productions in San Francisco who have given me carte blanche to say what I want about the restaurants in and around Chicago; and of course to my wife Eileen, who shares not only my dinners, but my life.

February 1979   SMK

RATING SYMBOLS

To help you find a restaurant to match your budget for the evening, the selections are divided into categories of inexpensive, moderate and expensive, using the symbols shown below. The ratings are based on the price of an average meal in that restaurant, food only; cocktails, wine and tips would be extra. Unless the establishment is specifically a lunch spot, ratings reflect the average dinner cost. Prices quoted in this book were in effect at the time of publication and are subject to change at any time.

$ **UNDER $7.50** The food will be good as well as economical, but atmosphere and smooth service may be lacking at some of these restaurants.

$$ **UNDER $15** In this price range of $7.50 to $15 we expect some charm and atmosphere in addition to excellent food.

$$$ **OVER $15** At this price, we expect excellence in food, service and surroundings. Flaws should be minor.

K/RATING
The 20-point K/Rating system is based on:

FOOD	7 points maximum
SERVICE	6 points maximum
AMBIANCE & ATMOSPHERE	4 points maximum
OVERALL VALUE	3 points maximum

Chicago

Chicago
ABACUS
Chinese

$$

Dr. Phil Shen's initial restaurant venture remains a winner, even though his personal attention has been diverted to getting his new restaurant, Dr. Shen's, q.v., off the ground. Abacus is still a fine restaurant for those eager to learn about the culinary riches of the Orient. The menu is extremely explicit; waiters are knowledgeable and willing to help with suggestions. The menu lists dozens and dozens of selections, each with an authenticity rating. Shen and key members of his staff are frequent travelers to the Orient, always bringing back fresh ideas. I still have some favorites, including steamed pike in ginger sauce and all of the various vegetarian dishes. The Abacus egg roll remains a classic of its kind and definitely should be among your appetizer choices. Abacus offers a Sunday brunch that is exceptional; it is also served periodically, for such holidays as Chinese New Year or similar august occasions.

ABACUS, 2619 North Clark Street, Chicago. Telephone: 440-2311. Hours: Lunch: 11:30 am-2:30 pm, Monday-Saturday; Dinner: 5 pm-11 pm, Sunday-Thursday; until midnight, Friday-Saturday; Dim Sum brunch: 11 am-3 pm, Sunday. Cards: AE, MC, VISA. Reservations recommended. Full bar service. Casual, neat dress acceptable. Parking at nearby Texaco garage.

K/Rating 18.5/20 • Food 6.5/7 •Service 6/6•Decor 3.5/4•Value 2.5/3

Beef with Snow Peapods .... C 5.50

Mongolian Beef with Green Onions & Crispy
Bean Threads .... M 6.25

Tomato Pepper Steak in Black Bean Sauce .... C 5.50

Szechwan Home Style Shredded Beef .... Z 5.50

Szechwan Hot Diced Beef with Peanuts .... Z 5.50

The Abacus Steak on Sauteed Vegetables -
A House Special .... C 7.95

Beef with Fresh Spinach and Foo Yee .... S 5.50

Beef with Tofu and Chinese Mushrooms in
Oyster Sauce .... S 5.50

Beef Mandarin with Assorted Vegetables .... M 5.95

Hunan Beef with Tea Sauce on Watercress .... Z 5.95

Chun King Spicy Beef with Wood Ears & Hot
Pepper Sauce .... Z 5.50

Hunan Ginger Beef .... Z 5.95

Mandarin Hot Green Pepper Beef .... M 5.50

Hunan Orange Beef .... Z 5.95

Beef with Chinese Greens & Oyster Sauce .... C 5.95

Chicken Almond with Snow Peapods .... C 5.25

Chan Pow Mandarin Chicken Ding with Cashews ... M 5.25

Szechwan Hot Diced Chicken with Peanuts .... Z 5.25

Szechwan Empress Chicken with Vegetables .... Z 5.95

Cantonese Lemon Chicken .... C 5.95

Chicken Cantonese with Assorted Vegetables ...... C 5.95

Minced Chicken with Black Mushrooms, Water
Chestnuts & Bamboo Shoots on Crispy Bean
Threads & Rolled in Lettuce Leaves .... M 6.25

Squab Shanghai .... S 9.95

Crispy Home Style Smoked Tea Duck
with Hoisin Sauce .... Z 7.95

Peking Duck (With Peking Duck Soup,
1.25 Per Person Extra) .... M 20.00

West Lake Duck - Love of the Oriental Gourmet .... C 20.00

Dr. Shen's Omelet with Shrimp, Scallops &
Vegetables topped with Oyster Sauce .... C 6.25

Madame Shen's Shanghai Shrimp Patties
with Vegetables .... S 6.50

Braised Whole Fish with Chinese Greens .... C Seasonal

Braised Whole Fish with Hot Szechwan Sauce .. Z Seasonal

Shanghai Style Braised Whole Fish with Tofu ... S Seasonal

Sweet Sour Whole Fish .... C Seasonal

The Abacus Steamed Whole Fish with Black
Bean Sauce .... C Seasonal

Lobster Shanghai in Wine Sauce .... S Seasonal

Lobster Cantonese .... C Seasonal

Hunan Spicy Lobster .... Z Seasonal

Velvet Crab over Crispy Bean Threads .... M Seasonal

Scallops Saute .... S Seasonal

Abalone with Chinese Vegetables .... M Seasonal

ARNIE'S
Continental

$$$

Extravant decor, ambiance and a crowded bar are the big attractions here, although fortunately for people who take dining as more than a casual endeavor, Arnie's food and restaurant service have improved markedly in the past couple of years. When the restaurant first opened, owner Arnie Morton would say with a wink, "I'm a saloonkeeper, not a restaurateur." That somewhat cavalier approach cost Arnie's the respect of serious diners. More recently however, Arnie's has become a restaurant where the food is acceptable on its own merits. Among the appetizers I like the chilled trout in dill sauce and the beefsteak tomato with anchovies. A fairly broad selection of dinner entrées contains such peaks as pepper steak and veal Florentine. Fish preparations are usually competent. Arnie's also features nightly specials. Rack of lamb is particularly successful. Dining at Arnie's is probably as much a social experience as it is a culinary one. The restaurant bustles with "beautiful people," celebrities often among them. It has become the place to see and be seen in Chicago.

ARNIE'S, 1030 North State Street, Chicago. Telephone: 266-4800. Hours: Lunch: 11:30 am-2:30 pm, Monday-Friday; Dinner: 5:30 pm-midnight, every evening; Brunch: 11 am-2:30 pm, Sunday. Cards: AE, DC, MC, VISA. Reservations recommended. Full bar service. Jackets requested for men. Private party facilities available with special menus. Parking in Newberry Plaza Building.

K/Rating 16/20 • Food 5/7 • Service 5/6 • Decor 4/4 • Value 2/3

FISH

DOVER SOLE MEUNIERE   10.50   SAUTEED RED SNAPPER   8.95
With Lemon-Butter Sauce

FRESH WHITE GRENOBLOISE   6.95
Sauteed in Butter With Lemon and Capers

Above Served With Parslied Potatoes

VEAL

VEAL PICCATA IN LEMON BUTTER SAUCE   8.95

SICILIAN VEAL   8.95
Lightly Breaded with Garlic, Parsley & Parmesan Cheese

– ABOVE SERVED WITH LINGUINI –

VEAL FLORENTINE   8.95
Thinly Sliced Veal Over Spinach, Covered With Mornay Sauce

BEEF

PRIME RIB OF BEEF, WHIPPED HORSERADISH   9.95

SIRLOIN STEAK EL FORNO, SERVED WITH LINGUINI   11.50
Broiled with Parmesan Cheese, Butter & A Wisp of Garlic

FILET MIGNON, SAUCE BEARNAISE   9.95

SIRLOIN STEAK ARNIE'S   11.95
Broiled, Topped with Medallions of Lobster, Sauce Bearnaise Glace

Served With Baked, Au Gratin or ARNIE'S Special Baked Potato

VEGETABLES AND POTATOES

ARNIE'S SPECIAL BAKED POTATO   1.00

AU GRATIN POTATOES   .95   BAKED POTATO   .95

CREAMED LEAF SPINACH   .95

FRESH VEGETABLE OF THE SEASON   1.00

DESSERTS

BRANDY ICE   2.50   HOT FUDGE SUNDAE   1.75

CHEESE CAKE   1.50   STRAWBERRIES WITH WHIPPED CREAM   1.85

FRENCH ICE CREAM OR SHERBET   1.50

CHOCOLATE MOUSSE   1.50   MELON OF THE SEASON   1.50

COFFEE   .75   IRISH COFFEE   2.25   TEA   .60

ASK YOUR WAITER ABOUT OUR FLAMBING DESSERTS!

Chicago
ARMY AND LOU'S
Soul Food

$

Soul food comes from the heart as well as from the kitchen and when folks talk soul food in Chicago, Army and Lou's is one of the first restaurants mentioned. The greens, boiled beans and buffalo fish get traditional attention here. Fried chicken comes in large portions, steaming hot and crisp. Smothered chicken is real fixin's in soul kitchens and Army and Lou's serves it right, not only with giblet gravy but with a cornbread dressing, too. Right on the money are the barbecued ribs topped with a spicy sauce, the meat practically falling from the bones. One of the best selections not often thought of as soul food is Creole gumbo. This savory stew of crab meat, chicken, rice, vegetables and spicy seasonings is as perfect a gumbo as I have ever had. An extra cup of gravy can be requested for even more flavor and goodness. Army and Lou's uses separate deep-frying vats for chicken, fish and potatoes. That way flavors are protected from each other. All beef is prime. You could find a one-pound T-bone for less than $10 as of this writing. Dinners are complete and include soup, salad, two vegetables, fresh hot rolls and muffins. À la carte desserts such as peach cobbler and ice cream are worth the extra cost.

ARMY AND LOU'S, 422 East 75th Street, Chicago. Telephone: 483-6550. Hours: 9 am-midnight, Wednesday-Monday. Cards: AE, DC, MC, VISA. Reservations recommended. Full bar service. Casual dress acceptable. Private party facilities for 15 to 100 people. Ample parking.

K/Rating 17/20 • Food 5/7 • Service 6/6 • Decor 3/4 • Value 3/3

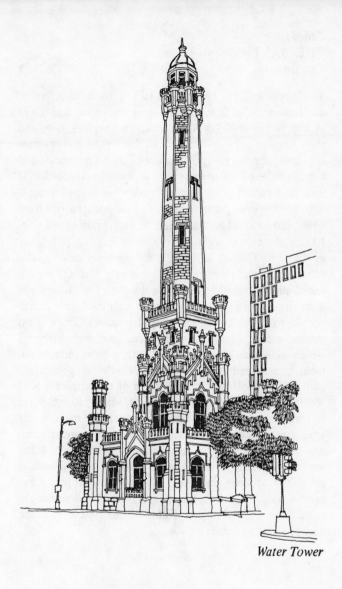

Water Tower

Chicago
THE BAKERY
Continental

$$$

The prix fixe dinner has gone up to $15 thanks to inflation, but basically The Bakery is the same restaurant that it was in 1963 when chef Louis Szathmary, his brother, Geza and their families opened the doors to this unique dining establishment. The Bakery is truly a one-of-a-kind restaurant and although there have been imitations, none has succeeded. If you are tempted to say that the quality has slipped some, it may be that your personal tastes and judgments about food have become more sophisticated. In fact, every time I visit, I know the cuisine will never rise above a certain point, but at the same time, it will not really erode in quality. The sameness of the place over the years may turn off experienced diners but there is no doubt that The Bakery has done more than any other single restaurant to educate people to tastes beyond steak and potatoes. There is no printed menu. Instead, waiters recite the day's offerings which include an excellent house pâté, a fresh soup, salad, main course and dessert. Often a chef's complimentary course is also offered. Most popular of the entrées is beef Wellington in a semi-sweet currant sauce. Roast pork, steaming hot bouillabaisse and the other fine main course selections each have their following. I was disappointed on one evening to see that men without jackets were being seated: Better restaurants should maintain a dress code. I am told that since that time, a jackets-for-men policy has been adopted. After all, if standards of food and service are maintained, mutual respect should be observed, even at the cost of losing a patron or two.

THE BAKERY, 2218 North Lincoln Avenue, Chicago. Telephone: 472-6942. Hours: 5 pm-11 pm, Tuesday-Thursday; until midnight, Friday-Saturday. Cards: AE, MC, VISA. Reservations required. Wines and champagne. Jackets requested for men. Private party facilities for 30 to 60 people. Parking at Children's Memorial Hospital.

K/Rating 16/20 • Food 5/7 • Service 6/6 • Decor 3/4 • Value 2/3

Chicago
BARNEY'S MARKET CLUB
American $$

West of the Loop, Barney's has been host to conventioneers, politicians and other visiting firemen for decades. Even local Chicagoans are regularly drawn by Barney's good food and "Yes sir, Senator" atmosphere. Steaks and seafood predominate, led by a 24-ounce giant T-bone. Lobster usually weighs in at 2-1/2 pounds or more, with recent market prices in the $20 range. Expensive, certainly, but thought of by many as the best steamed lobster in the city. Dinners include appetizer, salad, baked or delicious shoestring potatoes, soup, rolls and relish assortment. Barney's Market Club is one of the few places left where you can get a real feel of Chicago's brawniness.

BARNEY'S MARKET CLUB, 741 West Randolph Street, Chicago. Telephone: 263-9795/263-9800. Hours: 11 am-midnight, Monday-Saturday; 4 pm-midnight, Sunday. Cards: AE, DC. Reservations recommended. Full bar service. Valet parking.

K/Rating 16/20 • Food 6/7 • Service 5/6 • Decor 3/4 • Value 2/3

Chicago
BASTILLE
French Brasserie

$$

Although billed as a brasserie, Bastille strikes me as just a shade too posh for that description. The restaurant, which formerly housed the now defunct Le Bastille, has been redecorated from top to bottom, largely in shades of beige and cream. One section reminds me of a country dining room while the other looks like a Metro station. Food is generally well prepared, but not without some problems. For example, sometimes the mussels are a little gritty from insufficient rinsing. There is an assortment of house pâtés, including a fine goose liver forcemeat and an exquisite duckling. The onion soup leaves a warm, almost winey aftertaste, not at all unpleasant. Main course selections include daily specials plus such regulars as the satisfying and typically Parisian steak and *pommes frites*. The mixed seafood grill sounds better than it really is. Lamb and veal preparations fare better. Fresh pastries from the cart highlight desserts. Strawberry Napoleon and tarts are favorites.

BASTILLE, 21 West Superior Street, Chicago. Telephone: 787-2050. Hours: 11:30 am-10:30 pm, Monday-Thursday; until 11:30 pm, Friday; 5 pm-11:30 pm, Saturday; until 10 pm, Sunday. Cards: AE, MC, VISA. Reservations recommended; required on weekends. Full bar service. Casual dress acceptable. Private party facilities can be arranged.

K/Rating 16/20 • Food 5/7 • Service 5/6 • Decor 3/4 • Value 3/3

Chicago
THE BERGHOFF
German $

After a day of shopping along the new State Street Mall, The Berghoff is a great place for a quick and inexpensive dinner. At lunchtime the place is certain to be crowded with attorneys and judges taking a break from the busy schedule of cases at the nearby Dirksen Federal Building. Either time, lunch or dinner, you will find efficient service and some topnotch German-style foods. The menu changes daily but certain standards such as sauerbraten, German pot roast and kassler ribchen (smoked loin of pork) are available all the time. Some fish and steaks are listed on the menu at somewhat higher cost than many of the German preparations. A broiled strip steak at the current price of $6.25 could be one of the better values in this town of top quality steak houses. Many dinners include salad and potato or vegetable. You will find appetizers as exotic as French snails ($2.75) but Bismark herring for a dollar is more in keeping with the character of this sprawling restaurant. Waiters are of the old school: Black trousers, white shirts and aprons are their dress, service is efficient without familiarity until you become a regular. The Berghoff is noted for its special blended whiskey as well as house variety of beer, dark and light. This restaurant has been around for 80 years; I hope it is still going strong for at least 180 more.

BERGHOFF RESTAURANT, 17 West Adams Street, Chicago. Telephone: 427-3170. Hours: 11 am-9:30 pm, Monday-Saturday. No cards. Reservations taken for groups of six or more. Full bar service. Private party facilities for 75 to 200 people. Parking in Adams State Garage.

K/Rating 16/20 • Food 5.5/7 • Service 4/6 • Decor 3.5/4 • Value 3/3

Chicago
BLACKHAWK
American

$$

Don Roth's Blackhawk is one of the few consistently good places in the Loop. It may be living off its past in some respects, but it is still part of the Chicago experience and well worth an evening's dining. There is an almost clockwork precision about some aspects of the Blackhawk. Not a place to dawdle, it's a good pre-theater spot for dinner and always attracts sports fans during Bulls and Blackhawks season. Beef is the byword here, especially the perfect filet mignon. The spinning salad bowl is a tradition, and no matter how many times you have seen the performance and heard the speech that goes with its preparation, it's fun to hear it one more time.

Close to shopping and theater on North Michigan Avenue, Don Roth's Blackhawk on Pearson brings the famous Blackhawk dining to the Near North Side. The only difference is that the Pearson restaurant has a salad bar instead of the spinning salad bowl.

DON ROTH'S BLACKHAWK, 139 North Wabash Avenue, Chicago. Telephone: 726-0100. Hours: 11 am-10:30 pm, Monday-Saturday; 3:30 pm-10:30 pm, Sunday. Cards: AE, CB, DC, MC, VISA. Reservations recommended. Full bar service. Garage nearby.

DON ROTH'S BLACKHAWK, 110 East Pearson Street, Chicago. Telephone: 943-3300. Hours: Lunch: 11:30 am-2:30 pm, Monday-Saturday; Dinner: 5 pm-10:30 pm, Monday-Thursday; until 11 pm, Friday; until midnight, Saturday; 5 pm-9:30 pm, Sunday. Cards: AE, CB, DC, MC, VISA. Reservations recommended. Full bar service. Garage nearby.

K/Rating 17/20 • Food 6/7 • Service 5/6 • Decor 3.5/4 • Value 2.5/3

from the open hearth broiler

we're proud to serve you **u.s. prime beef**
you'll taste the difference.

u.s. prime sirloin steak (12 oz) —
the king of them all — thick, juicy, tender, closely trimmed... **12.50**

filet mignon (9 oz.) —
with fresh mushroom — everybody's favorite **10.50**

steak 'n lobster —
filet mignon and succulent lobster tail **13.25**

chopped steak blackhawk (12 oz.) —
broiled with onions & green peppers
or topped with bleu cheese **6.95**

half chicken
broiled or fried.................................... **6.85**

seafood of the day
could be scampi, whole brook trout (boneless),
bay scallops, etc. .... **7.95 - 9.50**

BEEF OSKAR — a tantalizing taste treat: filet mignon, crabmeat,
asparagus, and our own bernaise sauce.
11.25

Chicago
BOWL AND ROLL
American

$

The Bowl and Roll is one of those casual finds that dot Chicago. The limited menu of salads, soups, sandwiches and desserts has not changed since the restaurant first opened more than five years ago. As the name suggests, the specialty is soup and sandwiches. The chopped liver sandwich remains my favorite, being the kind of liver that sticks to the roof of your mouth. The smoked sausage is juicy and flavorful. Sandwiches are served on crusty French bread and, along with the soups, are among the few genuine bargains to be found in the Old Town area. Soup choices remain limited to three, although each is excellent. The chicken soup consists of a quarter or a half of the bird, depending upon your appetite, in a delicious subtle broth with chunk-cut vegetables and lots of noodles. Bean soup with sausage is heavier, not particularly to my taste. There are no flaws in the desserts which include deep-dish apple pie and pecan-raisin brownies. Since its first appearance in *Best Restaurants Chicago* the Bowl and Roll has obtained licensed wine and beer service.

BOWL AND ROLL, 1339 North Wells Street, Chicago. Telephone: 944-5361. Hours: 11:30 am-9 pm, Tuesday-Thursday; until 11 pm, Friday-Saturday; noon-9 pm, Sunday. No cards. No reservations. Beer and wine.

Chicago
BREAD SHOP KITCHEN
Vegetarian

$

There's nothing fancy about this neat little vegetarian restaurant where you go up to a kitchen counter to place your order. There is a daily listing of the menu on a large chalkboard. Each day features a different main dish for $2.75 and a soup for either 60 or 80 cents. Soups offered include vegetable bean, lentil, mushroom barley and others, all freshly made. California vegetable quiche, eggplant Parmesan, stir-fried vegetables with brown rice, vegetables mornay are among regular main course items. Desserts, like the other food, are made from all-natural ingredients. The Bread Shop Kitchen also serves dinner portion salads.

BREAD SHOP KITCHEN, 3411 North Halsted Street, Chicago. Telephone: 871-3831. Hours: noon-10 pm, Tuesday-Saturday. No cards. No bar service; you may bring your own. Parking on street.

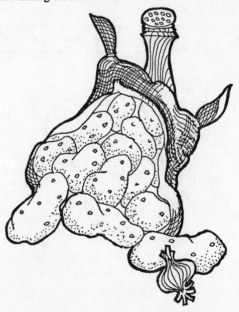

Chicago
BUSGHETTI
Italian $$

The emphasis here is on value and lots of food for your money. The spaghetti dinners begin as low as $3.95 and you can build your selection the way you might choose a pizza, adding ingredients as you please. Busghetti does not limit your choice to merely one all-purpose tomato sauce; there is a selection of several, although Mama's Original is the house specialty. The restaurant goes a little far afield in its offering of some rather far-out creations including a Busghetti Indienne which is curried, or a Busghetti Cuban with fried egg and black beans on top of the pasta. Dinners are all inclusive from salad to dessert.

BUSGHETTI, 2520 North Lincoln Avenue, Chicago. Telephone: 525-2599. Hours: 11:30 am-11 pm, Sunday-Thursday; until midnight, Friday-Saturday. Cards: MC, VISA. Reservations only taken for groups. Full bar service. Casual dress acceptable. Parking nearby.

K/Rating 16/20 • Food 5/7 • Service 5/6 • Decor 3/4 • Value 3/3

Chicago
CAFE AZTECA
Mexican

$$

This fairly small restaurant has charm not bounded by four walls and a ceiling. A dozen or so tables take up most of the main floor area. Whitewashed stucco walls, rough wooden beams, a skylight, stained glass and hanging plants create the south-of-the-border ambiance. And if that were not enough to create a pleasant evening's atmosphere, delightful music is played on a Spanish harp by a roving musician each evening except Monday and Thursday. When weather is warm, a garden is opened for dining under the stars. Lunch and dinner menus are the same, except at lunch prices are lower by as much as $1.50. You might want to begin with a cocktail; a snappy Margarita is a good opener. Then try an appetizer or two such as guacamole or hamoosh, often called Mexican pizza, which has a topping of cheese and tomato sauce baked on a taco chip. All main course selections include rice, refried beans and hot tortillas. Steak ranchero is served with a fairly mild tomato and chili sauce. Chicken *mole* is excellent, with a sauce of chocolate, pepper and slightly sweet seasonings. The enchiladas stuffed with chicken, mushrooms and sherry cream sauce are just short of elegant. For dessert do not pass up flan, a wonderfully creamy baked custard with caramel.

CAFE AZTECA, 215 West North Avenue, Chicago. Telephone: 944-9854. Hours: noon-midnight, daily; until 1 am, during the summer. Cards: AE, CB, DC. Reservations taken. Full bar service. Casual dress acceptable. Private party facilities for up to 75 people. Parking nearby.

K/Rating 18/20 • Food 6/7 • Service 5/6 • Decor 4/4 • Value 3/3

Chicago
CAFÉ DE PARIS
French   **$$$**

I am happy to note that maître d' Alex Abraham is back
working at Café de Paris after a nearly two-year hiatus
elsewhere. With his return and good taste there is no doubt
that the Café is returning to its position of excellence.
Tucked away inside a Near North Side apartment-hotel,
Café de Paris displays a cozy sophistication lacking in many
larger and more pretentious establishments. A newly de-
signed menu still retains some of the house specialties: the
classic duckling à la Belasco with its crackling crisp skin and
caramelized orange sauce; duckling à l'orange, flamed with
Grand Marnier; duckling à la Montmorency with black
cherries and Cointreau. À la carte entrées include a house
salad. The table d'hôte dinners for $13.25 offer a full
choice from appetizers, salad, vegetables, luscious desserts
and coffee or tea. In sheer value, this one is hard to beat.
Café de Paris, by the way, is owned by a TWA subsidiary
but this is anything but airline food. Some management
changes and accompanying corporate domination have
caused problems since the restaurant's first listing in *Best
Restaurants Chicago,* but happily, all is in good hands again.

CAFÉ DE PARIS, 1260 North Dearborn Parkway, Chicago.
Telephone: 943-6080. Hours: 5 pm-11 pm, Monday-Satur-
day; from 4 pm, Sunday. Cards: AE, CB, DC, MC, VISA.
Full bar service. Jackets required for men. Validated park-
ing lot nearby.

K/Rating 18/20 • Food 5.5/7 • Service 6/6 • Decor 3.5/4 • Value 3/3

Table d'Hote Dinners

13.25 per person

Pâté de Provence	Steamed Mussels Cafe de Paris	
Blue Points	Onion Soup Gratinee	
Hearts of Artichoke Vinaigrette	Oysters Rockefeller	1.75
Melon in Season	Shrimp Cocktail Supreme	1.50
Half Grapefruit	Mushrooms Stuffed with Seafood Morany	1.50
Herring in Sour Cream	Escargots Bourguignonne	1.75

CHEF's PLAT DU JOUR
Chef Joseph's special creation, prepared especially for tonight's menu

DUCKLING A LA BELASCO
Our specialty since 1941

TENDERLOIN STEAK DIANE A LA CAFE DE PARIS
Sauteed with shallots, fresh mushrooms and delicate red wine sauce

FILET OF DOVER SOLE, BALMORAL
Gently sauteed in sweet butter, with tender shrimp, topped with
delicate smoked salmon and butter lemon sauce

TOURNEDOS CAFE DE PARIS
Twin tenderloin medallions, perfectly broiled, served with Bordelaise Sauce

ALASKA KING CRAB SUPREME
Sauteed with shallots and white wine, laced with light cream sauce

POACHED SALMON
Fresh salmon, gently poached and enhanced with Hollandaise Sauce

SOFT SHELL CRABS SAUTE
Sauteed till light and very crisp, sprinkled with toasted almond slices

ENTRECOTE, SAUTE
The delectable cut taken from between the ribs of beef, sauteed
with mushrooms

BEEF TENDERLOIN TIPS AU VIN
Generous cuts of beef tenderloin, sauteed with wine sauce, served on a
bed of wild rice

BROOK TROUT, SAUTE VERONIQUE
Simply prepared with butter and crowned with sweet seedless grapes

INDIVIDUAL FILET OF BEEF WELLINGTON
Prime filet, wrapped in light flaky pastry, served with Sauce Perigourdine

All of Cafe de Paris' entrees are served with appropriate garnish

Steak Tomato, Caesar Salad or Mixed Green Salad
Garlic, Clear French or Thousand Island Dressing

Creme de Menthe Parfait	Vanilla or Chocolate Ice Cream
Mocha Rum Layer Cake	Pot au Creme
Chocolate Sundae	Fresh Fruit in Season
Mousse au Chocolate	Raspberry Sherbet — Lemon Sherbet

Coffee, Tea, Sanka

Chicago
THE CAJUN HOUSE
Creole

$$

Cajun food is not just catfish and red beans with rice. This is a sophisticated, often spicy cuisine that combines elements of French, African, Spanish and ante-bellum plantation kitchens. The Cajun House features some of the traditional recipes for classic New Orleans preparations. Jambalaya will make you think that you are back on the bayou. Chicken Pontalba is a masterpiece. And the bayou seafood bake is a buttery casserole of mixed soft- and shellfish. Great appetizers include the shrimp pâté served with all dinners and such soups as peanut, seafood gumbo or turtle. For an adventurous dining experience allot two and a half wonderful hours to "Dine with Walter" and let

SHRIMP CREOLE 11.75

Fresh Gulf shrimp are simmered to perfection in a rich Creole sauce. Served with a bed of fluffy white rice.

CAJUN HOUSE BARBECUED PRAWNS... 12.75
The House Specialty

The word barbecue is mis-leading — for in fact the shrimps are baked in almost every known spice and herb found in the kitchen. Pure vegetable oil, dry white wine, garlic and onion complete the array of ingredients — served with natural brown rice and grilled tomato. This is a finger food!

CREOLE RED SNAPPER 9.75

Baked to perfection in lemon-butter, covered with Creole sauce and engulf by fluffy white rice.

BAYOU SEAFOOD BAKE 11.50

Filet pieces of red snapper, catfish, shrimp and oysters (when available) are blessed by an array of fine herbs, spices, garlic, onion and white wine. Served with natural brown rice — the chef's answer to a seafood platter!

CAJUN CATFISH with Hush Puppies   9.75

Catfish is truly favored by the Cajun appetite — caught in fresh water streams, breaded lightly and deep fried. The finest catfish in the Midwest.

CAJUN FRIED OYSTERS 11.50
when available

Lightly breaded in a seasoned breading, deep fried to perfection. Served with bataille potatoes with selection of sauces and garnished with wedge of lemon.

proprietor Walter Mazur plan your meal from start to finish. He will also recommend appropriate wines, some choices not on the regular wine list. The restaurant itself is in a cozy townhouse with just the right decor to take you gustatorially to the Crescent City. Upstairs is a cocktail lounge and parlor that might be the envy of any "sportin' house" this side of the Vieux Carré.

THE CAJUN HOUSE, 3048 West Diversey Avenue, Chicago. Telephone: 772-1230. Hours: 5 pm-10 pm, Tuesday-Thursday; until 11 pm, Friday-Saturday. Cards: AE, MC, VISA. Reservations required. Full bar service. Casual dress acceptable; no jeans. Private party facilities for 10 to 50 people. Parking on street.

K/Rating 19/20 • Food 6.5/7 • Service 6/6 • Decor 3.5/4 • Value 3/3

CREOLE STUFFED EGGPLANT *11.50*
when available

The eggplant is stuffed with a mixture of Titi shrimp, crab meat, onion, fine herbs, spices and bread crumbs — all of which is covered by a rich Creole sauce.

CAJUN KITCHEN JAMBALAYA *9.75*

You take "a little of this and that" as a Cajun would say. We take rice as the staple ingredient and to it we add chicken, shrimp, ham, sausage and what ever else the chef sees fit — served En Casserole — a delight!

CHICKEN PONTALBA *10.50*

Deboned chicken — pan fried and served on a bed of diced potatoes, ham, scallions and mushrooms with Bearnaise sauce. One of the most unique chicken dishes ever to be created!

CHICKEN ROYALE *11.50*

The filet of chicken is touched with a special garlic butter, wrapped around a large Gulf shrimp, and cooked in white wine. Sauce Bearnaise places the final touch to this unique creation, and is served on a bed of natural brown rice. A true gourmand's delight.

TOURNEDOS BURGUNDY *17.00*

This dish favors the French influence in New Orleans cookery — tender pieces of marinated filet are blessed with a rich Burgundy sauce over Holland rusk — served with chef's special rice and grilled tomato.

Yes! *We do have crawfish when they are in season!*

Chicago
CAPE COD ROOM
Seafood

$$

When people think of seafood in Chicago, the first place that comes to mind is the Cape Cod Room. There was a period a few years back when the restaurant's success seemed to interfere with the pleasures of fine dining. It was as if the place had been taken over by former U-boat captains who treated customers as if they were so much bilge. But that scourge has been lifted and the Cape Cod Room is right back up there among Chicago's topnotch restaurants. There is some splendid eating here, from the selection of fresh blue points at the oyster bar to the pastries from the Drake Hotel's kitchen. Begin with a soup, perhaps the seafood gumbo, the creamy New England clam clowder or the famous Bookbinder's snapper soup with an accent of sherry. The selection of whole fish is excellent. In addition to menu choices, there are always daily specials. Among shellfish choices, I like the shrimp à l'Indienne with its special curry accent. Crab meat Maryland will attract diners with a taste for buttery richness. The restaurant is a nautical vision, practically awash with artifacts from Davy Jones's locker. You will think that you are dining in a New England whaling village a century or more ago, when in fact you are just steps from Michigan Avenue and stylish Oak Street on Chicago's Magnificent Mile.

CAPE COD ROOM, 140 East Walton Street (in the Drake Hotel), Chicago. Telephone: 787-2200. Hours: noon-midnight, daily. Cards: AE, MC, VISA. Reservations required. Full bar service. Coats and ties required for men. Valet parking.

K/Rating 19.5/20 • Food 7/7 • Service 6/6 • Decor 4/4 • Value 2.5/3

Soups

The Cape Cod's Famous

Bookbinder Red Snapper Soup with Sherry..Cup.. 1.75	Bowl.. 3.50
Seafood Gumbo......Cup.. 2.00	Bowl.. 4.00
New England Clam Chowder......Cup.. 1.75	Bowl.. 3.50
Clam Broth ....Cup... 1.50	

Bouillabaisse Marseillaise

Variety of fresh and salt-water fishes and seafoods with fresh vegetable garniture;
seasoned with garlic, parsley, thyme, saffron and Chablis wine,
served with garlic French bread........ 11.25

Approximately 45 minutes to prepare.

Oysters

Baked: Ancienne, Baltimore, Casino, Fitzpatrick,
   Florentine, Nantucket, Rockefeller........................ 6.25
Fried, with Rémoulade Sauce...................... 6.25
En Brochette, with Bacon and Mushrooms on Rice Bed............ 6.25

Seafood Stews

Oysters with milk.......... 4.75	Clams with milk.... 4.50
with cream.......... 5.00	with cream...... 4.75
Lobster with milk.......... 7.50	Scallops with milk.. 5.25
with cream.......... 7.75	with cream...... 5.50

Seafood à la Drake........ 8.50

From the Ocean

Pompano, Papillote—Filet enclosed in Parchment with Lobster and
   Mushrooms in Red Wine Sauce.............. 12.75
Pompano Sauté, Amandine...................... 11.50
Whole Dover Sole, Sauté Meuniere—(for Two)............. 19.50
Filet of Dover Sole, Broiled or Sauté................. 10.25
Filet of Lemon Sole Sauté Amandine.................. 8.75
Broiled New England Scrod................. 8.50
Broiled Red Snapper, Lemon Butter.............. 10.50

From the Great Lakes and Canada

Lake Trout, Broiled or Sauté 8.50
Filet of Pike, Saute Amandine 7.75
Filet of Whitefish, Broiled or Saute 9.25

From Mountain Streams

   Rainbow Trout—Saute Amandine or Bleu.......... 8.75

*All entrées served with au gratin potatoes, choice of mixed green salad or
Cape Cod cole slaw.*

29

Chicago
CAPTAIN NEMO'S
Sandwiches $

This is the ultimate submarine sandwich shop. A large board behind the counter lists several sandwiches, most in the $2.70 to $3.40 range and all available in half-loaf form for about half the price. By the time you finish with a soft drink, cup of soup and dessert, you will be hard pressed to spend much more than $5 per person. Sandwiches are built before your eyes on foot-long French loaves. They start with a dressing, your choice of a mild mustard or mayonnaise. Then comes your selection of meats such as turkey, ham, bologna, hot meat loaf, plus cheeses, seasoned oil and vinegar dressing, onion, eggs, radishes, tomatoes, pickles, shredded lettuce ... a veritable garden of sandwich delights. If you really have an ambitious appetite, you can order the soup of the day for about half a buck. Often served is thick and steamy split pea in a broth that would make Julia Child take notice. What more can you say about a sandwich shop? A great deal in this case because there is a moral to be learned here. No matter what you do in life, do it well and your effort will be appreciated. I have never been in a restaurant where customers are greeted with such genuine friendliness and regard and where more pride is taken in what is being prepared. And yes, there is a real Captain Nemo who makes sure that all comers are well fed and satisfied.

CAPTAIN NEMO'S, 7367 North Clark Street, Chicago. Telephone: 973-0570. Hours: 11 am-9 pm, Monday-Saturday. No cards. No reservations. Parking on street.

Chicago
CASBAH
Armenian

$$

The hospitality of owner Juliette Vartanian and her staff is by now nearly legendary on Chicago's North Side. Despite the North African name, Casbah serves Armenian-style foods and drink. Exotic preparations such as maglubéh (spiced rice with lamb, cauliflower and pignolias) and sarma-kashlama (stuffed grape leaves with lamb) are among traditional favorites. These and other preparations are explained on the menu; any other questions about preparation or ingredients are deftly answered by waiters. The combination dinner for $9.50 is always appealing because of the variety of taste and texture it offers. All dinners include soup, salad and appropriate vegetable or rice pilaf. New to the Casbah is the introduction of three additional dinner choices not on the regular menu. They will change from time to time, but a recent selection included trout Leila, baked brook trout stuffed with puréed eggplant and topped with a yogurt sauce for $8.95. Another of the special dinners might be veal sautéed with olives and onions in a creamed brandy sauce for $10.95. While preparations and ingredients may seem exotic, in fact, fish, veal and beef as well as the seasonings used here are not that uncommon. Casbah is a fine introduction to ethnic dining.

CASBAH, 514 West Diversey Avenue, Chicago. Telephone: 935-7570. Hours: 5 pm-11 pm, daily. Cards: DC, MC, VISA. Reservations suggested. Full bar service. Casual dress acceptable. Parking in Hamden Court Garage.

K/Rating 19/20 • Food 6.5/7 • Service 6/6 • Decor 3.5/4 • Value 3/3

Chicago
CHEF ALBERTO'S
Continental

$$

Chef Alberto is a hunter of some renown in Chicago and the walls of his beautiful restaurant boast some of the trophies he has taken. But don't expect braised lion or buffalo steak. Chef Alberto's specializes in excellent French and Italian cuisines. From among the dinner entrées, don't miss the duckling in orange sauce. The sauce carries a flavorful accent of Cognac that marries beautifully with the other ingredients. Veal Parmigiana is good, not exceptional. The veal picante is served in a rich lemon-butter sauce. Pepper steak is prepared with green peppercorns rather than sharply pungent black peppercorns. Pastas offer particular distinction. Canneloni Alfredo, stuffed with ground chicken and beef, is served in a creamy wine sauce garnished with sliced mushrooms. And don't miss the fettuccini Alfredo, which, as custom demands, is prepared tableside with fresh, sweet cream blended into the pasta. The wine list is small and not overpriced.

CHEF ALBERTO'S, 3200 North Lake Shore Drive, Chicago. Telephone: 549-2515. Hours: 4:30 pm-midnight, Tuesday-Sunday. Cards: AE, DC, MC, VISA. Reservations recommended. Full bar service. Casual, neat dress acceptable. Private party facilities for up to 135 people. Indoor parking.

K/Rating 18/20 • Food 6/7 • Service 5/6 • Decor 4/4 • Value 3/3

Appetizers

Oysters Rockefeller 2.95	Italian Prosciutto 2.25
Escargots a la Francaise 3.50	Eggplant Parmigiana 2.75
Baked Clams 2.95	Blue Points or Clams (in season) 2.75
	Jumbo Shrimp Cocktail 2.95

Chef Alberto's Gourmet Dinners
ALL DINNERS INCLUDE APPETIZERS SOUP, SALAD AND PASTA

Melon and Prosciutto in Season   Chopped Chicken Livers Paté   Italian Antipasto

Tomato Juice   Iced Fresh Hawaiian Pineapple   Marinated Herring

Italian Minestrone Soup or French Onion Soup

Caesar Salad (Tossed at Table), Green Goddess or Chef's Salad Bowl

Fettuccini, Alfredo or Spaghettini, Bolognese with All Entrees

Coq Au Vin a la Bourguignonne, Wild Rice **8.95**
Breast of Capon in Red Wine, Pearl Onions, Mushrooms, Wild Rice Dressing

Roast Long Island Duck, Flambeau (Half),   **9.50**
Wild Rice Dressing, Cognac Orange Sauce, Sweet Potato

Boneless Double Breast of Chicken a la Kiev (Our Own) . **8.95**
Chicken a la Kiev, Handed Down from the Czar

Peppered Steak Burgundy **9.75**
Filet Mignon Split, Fresh Green Peppers, Onions, Mushrooms, Tomatoes

Chicken Vesuvio (for garlic lovers) **8.50**
Disjointed Chicken and Potatoes Sauteed in Olive Oil with Garlic, Dry Wine

Veal Cutlet a la Parmigiana **8.50**
Cutlet Baked with Tomato Sauce, Mozzarella Cheese, Fried Egg Plant

Scallopine of Veal en Casserole **8.50**
Fresh Mushrooms Sauce, Marsala Wine

Milk Fed Veal Medallions a la Picante . . . **9.25**
Seasoned Veal, Mushrooms, Lemon Butter Sauce

Chicken a la Cacciatore, Hunter Style **8.50**
Disjointed Chicken, Onions, Mushrooms, Tomatoes, Italian Black Olives

Shrimp de Jonghe en Casserole **9.25**
Sauteed in Dry Wine with Garlic Toasted Bread Crumbs

Fried Calamari (Squid), Butter and Lemon Sauce . . **8.95**

Canneloni, Alfredo en Casserole Au Gratin . . . **7.50**
Crepes Stuffed with Chicken and Beef, Mornay Sauce

Manicotti, en Casserole Salsa Pomidori . . . **7.50**
Crepes Stuffed with Ricotta Cheese, Tomato Sauce

Coffee .50	Tea .50	Sanka .50	Grade "A" Milk

$$$

There is a suburban edition of Chez Paul in Rolling Meadows, but I am not ready to give it a recommendation at this time. Instead, to experience all that the Chez Paul reputation means, visit the downtown location. The food and service are on a par with the lovely old-mansion decor. Among appetizers on the à la carte menu enjoy a seafood crêpe and its luscious balance of firm little shrimp and other edibles in a butter-rich sauce. Escargots are delicious little morsels tucked in their curved shells waiting to be dunked in melted butter. The hot and cold appetizers number about a dozen other choices, including beluga caviar ($14.25). Among main course selections, seafood is always exquisite. Rack of lamb for two is expensive, carved tableside and perfectly garnished. Roast duck offers splendid dining with its tart-sweet fruit sauce. Pepper steak flamed with Armagnac is one of the more potent samples of beef I can recall. The fillet is studded with peppercorns and the bold sauce makes a stunning accompaniment to the meat. Veal kidneys, sweetbreads, tripe and less esoteric cuts of meat help complete the menu. A revised wine list includes a phenomenal collection of great drinking.

CHEZ PAUL, 660 North Rush Street, Chicago. Telephone: 944-6680. Hours: Lunch: 11:30 am-2:30 pm, Monday-Friday; Dinner: 6 pm-11 pm, daily. Cards: AE, CB, DC, MC, VISA. Reservations required. Coats and ties required for men. Private party facilities for 10 to 70 people.

K/Rating 17/20 • Food 6/7 • Service 5/6 • Decor 4/4 • Value 2/3

Froids:

Stuffed Avocado Parisienne 4.75   Blue Points on Half Shell 3.95
Alaskan King Crab Remoulade 5.25   Hearts of Palm Vinaigrette 3.50
Shrimp Cocktail 4.25
Pâté de Foie Gras de Strasbourg 13.75   Terrine de Canard Truffé 4.25
Beluga Caviar 14.25

Chauds:

Baked Shrimps à la Papa Paul 5.00   Baked Alaskan King Crabe 5.25
Quiche Lorraine 3.00   Escargots Chablisienne 4.95   Baked Oysters Bercy 4.50
Crêpes aux Fruits de mer Dieppoise 3.25

Les Potages

Potage du Jour 1.75   Visque de Homard 2.95   Vichyssoise Glacée 2.25
Soupe à L'Oignon Gratinée 2.50

Les Grillades

Filet de Boeuf Bordelaise or Bearnaise 11.50   Lamb Chops à la Papa Paul
Minute Sirloin Maitre d'Hotel 10.75   Le New York Sirloin 11.75
Chateaubriand Bouquetière 25.75   Double Lamb Chops

Les Entreés

Escalopes de Veau Normande 10.25   Filet au Poivre Flambé Armagnac 12.25
Escalopes de Veau Citron 9.95   Canard Rôti a L'Orange 9.75
Canard Rôti Tutti Fruiti 10.25   Roast Back of Lamb (for two)
Filet de Boeuf à la Colbert 11.95   Rognons de Veau Sautés Napoléon 9.50
French Market Mickel 9.95   Tripes à la Mode de Caen 8.75
Ris de Veau Financiere 10.25   Foie de Veau Lyonnaise 9.25

Les Poissons et Crustacés

French Turbot Sauté Armononville 12.75   Dover Sole Menière or Amandine 13.25
Dover Sole en Goujons 11.25   Cuisses de Grenouilles Provençales 10.25
Homard Cardinal 12.50   French Turbot Poché Hollandaise 12.75
Whitefish Amandine 8.95   Red Snapper Broiled Duglèrè 10.50
Langoustines Grillées Nantua 12.25

Salade Maison Included

Les Desserts

Profiteroles au Chocolat 2.50   Crème Caramel 2.00   Mousse au Chocolat 2.50
Tarte aux Fruits Maison 2.50   La Pêche Melba 3.75   Fruits de Saison
Sundae à la Paul 2.25   Crêpes Suzette (for two) 6.75   Les Fromages
Les Fraises Romanoff 3.75   Cerises Jubilee 4.25

35

Chicago
CHICAGO PIZZA AND
OVEN GRINDER COMPANY
Italian/American $

This is the only place I know of where pizza is served by the pound rather than by the diameter. The pizza is Chicago-style, deep dish with a puffy dough that rises up over the side of the baking pan. You get your pizza in either of two ways, sausage or vegetarian. The meat pizza is the better of the two, as the vegetarian can be a bit over-sauced with not enough cheese. On the plus side, the sauce is made fresh from tomatoes which have been crushed, simmered and spiced. Don't forget the grinders, which include an Italian combination and an incredibly gargantuan meatball sandwich loaded with garlic on a toasty long loaf. Man does not live by grinders and pizza alone, so splurge and get a salad. They are justly called "salad dinners" because one will feed a whole tableful of hungries. Mixed drinks, wines and beer are available. Finally, a bit of history. The Chicago Pizza and Oven Grinder Company is just across the street from a vacant lot on which once stood the garage made famous by the St. Valentine's Day Massacre.

CHICAGO PIZZA AND OVEN GRINDER COMPANY, 2121 North Clark Street, Chicago. Telephone: 248-2570. Hours: noon-midnight; Sunday-Thursday; until 1 am, Friday-Saturday. No cards. No reservations. Full bar service. Garage nearby.

K/Rating 16/20 • Food 5/7 • Service 5/6 • Decor 3/4 • Value 3/3

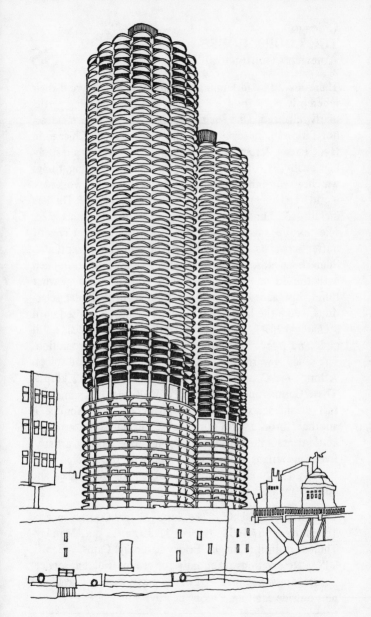

Marina Towers

Chicago
THE COURT HOUSE
American/Continental　　　　　　　　　　**$$**

There are a few restaurants which above and beyond their inherently good food and service, strike me as being particularly civilized. One such restaurant is The Court House, not far from the campus of the University of Chicago in Hyde Park's Harper Court Shopping Mall. There is a refreshing quality to The Court House's way of doing things which, in my mind at least, sets it apart from the workaday world. The menu presents an interesting mélange. Dinners include an abundance of hot bread with a delicious cake-like texture, made even better by spreading sweet creamy butter across its grained surface. The soups are exceptional. Spinach cheddar has a marvelous cheesy taste combined with the distinct flavor of spinach. Gazpacho is somewhat timid, but acceptable. Among the excellent dinner selections, I like the lamb shish kebab. The meat is braised until a charcoal black crust forms, leaving the meat inside still pink and juicy. Beef stroganoff is a luscious preparation. The sauce is warm and pungent with seasonings and spices. A long-time Court House specialty is Königsberger klopse. These German meatballs are served with rice in a somewhat tart cream sauce of vinegar and capers. Beef fondue is another favorite of Court House regulars. An array of condiments will help enhance your own cooking artistry. Even vegetarians can make out well with the sautéed vegetables au naturel or spinach lasagne. All side dishes and courses are à la carte.

THE COURT HOUSE, 5211 South Harper Court, Chicago. Telephone: 667-4008. Hours: 11:30 am-11 pm, Monday-Thursday; until midnight, Friday-Saturday. Cards: AE, MC, VISA. Reservations taken only for groups. Full bar service. Casual dress acceptable. Private party facilities available plus outside catering. Parking nearby.

K/Rating 17.5/20 • Food 6/7 • Service 6/6 • Decor 3.5/4 • Value 2/3

Appetizers

creamy chicken liver pâté	1.85	shrimp bisque	2.75
mushrooms ou vinaigrette	1.00	creamed herring	1.60

Soups

spinach cheddar	1.25	baked french onion	1.50
gazpacho	1.00	vichyssoise	1.00

Salads

Court House tossed salad	1.00
cucumbers in sour cream	1.00
tomatoes au vinaigrette	1.00

Entrees

Boeuf Fondue Bourguignonne – bite sized sirloin   for one   8.50
   served au natural with herbs, spices and sauces   for two   16.00
Chicken Teriyaki – half chicken, marinated and broiled, served with rice   5.85
Mushrooms sauteed in wine – side order 1.00   entree.   2.25
New York Strip Sirloin Steak – 13-14 oz. boneless center cut,
   sauce Bearnaise, choice of baked or ch. potatoes   9.25
Court Steak – one half pound butt, sauce Bearnaise, choice of baked
   or ch. potatoes   7.00
Moussaka – delicate ground lamb and eggplant casserole   4.85
Chicken Livers – sauteed in wine with mushrooms and onions, rice   4.65
Crabmeat Casserole, rice   6.85
Beef Stroganoff, buttered noodles or rice   6.85
Vegetables au Natural – sauteed fresh vegetables   4.25
Spinach Lasagne – layers of spinach, cheese and pasta in a
   piquant – tomato sauce   5.00
Braised Peppersteaks – sirloin, green pepper and onion in a
   spicy tomato sauce   6.15
Fresh Whitefish, poached in lemon butter, parsley potatoes
   (with hollandaise, 1.00 extra) served only when fresh whitefish
   is available   6.85
Broiled Trout – with tartar sauce and parsley potatoes, sauteed
   almonds on request   8.25
Lamb Shish kabob, with onion, green pepper and tomato, rice   8.25
Hamburger – half pound pure ground sirloin on bavarian
   black bread, ch. potatoes   3.85

Daily Specials

Monday – königsberger klopse – German meatballs in pungent cream
   caper sauce – rice   5.00
Tuesday – Coq au Vin – chicken in wine sauce, served with mushrooms,
   onions and rice   6.50
Wednesday – Lula kabob – a blend of spiced ground lamb and beef,
   rolled and broiled, rice, tomato provencal   5.25
Thursday – Poached breast of chicken in cream tarragon sauce   6.25
Friday – Fresh Whitefish in dill sauce   7.25

Open Wines	glass	carafe	Beers	
domestic burgundy	1.00	2.50	heineken on draft	1.25
domestic chablis	1.00	2.50	Berliner Weisse	
imported Mosel	1.25	3.25	(raspberry beer)	1.50

Chicago
THE CREOLE HOUSE
Creole

$$

Creole cuisine is that remarkable blend of influences that centered around New Orleans about 150 years ago. It brings together the influences of black Africa via the West Indies, southern plantation cooking, classical French cuisine and the culinary ingenuity of the Acadians, those refugees from Canada who became known as Cajuns and inspired Longfellow's poem *Evangeline*. With such antecedents, there is much for the eager diner to savor. The Creole House brings a goodly mixture of seasonings and flavors to the dining table. The gumbos and jambalayas are not to be missed. Similar, yet dissimilar dishes, gumbo is more like a thick soup or stew, while jambalaya resembles a casserole. A bit of filé, powdered dried sassafras leaves, serves as a thickening agent for the gumbo, to be used as little or as much as you like. Peppery flavors are characteristic of the gumbo and jambalaya. If you have a taste for fried chicken, you will be well satisfied at The Creole House: served with corn fritters, it is real Southern eatin', made even better by a

ℓℓ

CHEF'S APPETIZER

Peanut Soup
Creole Seafood Gumbo
Bayou Chili

MIXED GREEN SALAD
clear garlic, 1,000 island, roquefort or remoulade dressing
or
SEVEN-VEGETABLE COLE SLAW

SHRIMP JAMBALAYA A LA LOUISIANE—*a true creole dish of shrimp, rice, vegetables, spices, and herbs blended together and serve en casserole, topped with shredded cheddar cheese.* **14.00**

CREOLE SEAFOOD GUMBO—*the creole, it has been said, puts everything into his gumbo except the creole. Our gumbo is made up of vegetables, ham, shrimp, oystesr, crab and lobster meat—delicately seasoned with herbs and spices. served over rice.* **10.00**

CHICKEN JAMBALAYA—*full of deboned chicken, rice, vegetables, spices, herbs and flavored with white wine, served en casserole, topped with shredded cheddar cheese.* **12.00**

CREOLE BEEF ROLLS—*rolled slices of beef stuffed with salami, green onion, cheese, hard-cooked egg and spices, simmered in a rich creole red wine sauce, served with our own savory rice.* **13.00**

liberal flow of honey. Catfish is farm bred and popular among devotees of Creole cooking. Bayou chili is served over rice. Among the appetizers, I like the peanut soup with its chickeny-rich broth. Gumbo may be ordered as an appetizer if you want just a small taste and prefer something else for your main course. Often a chef's appetizer course is also served. Desserts are extraordinary and will change from night to night. They might include various kinds of pies, cakes and tarts. A historical note: The Creole House is owned by the same people who previously owned a restaurant under this same name on West Diversey Avenue. The Diversey Avenue restaurant now has no connection with The Creole House. Chicago restaurants can sometimes be confusing that way.

THE CREOLE HOUSE, 5343 West Devon Avenue, Chicago. Telephone: 631-9755. Hours: 5:30 pm-9:30 pm, Wednesday-Sunday. No cards. Bring your own wine; no hard liquor. Reservations required. Casual dress acceptable; no jeans. Ample parking.

K/Rating 16.5/20 • Food 6/7 • Service 5/6 • Decor 2.5/4 • Value 3/3

CREOLE HOUSE FRIED CHICKEN with CORN FRITTERS—*thinly breaded chicken cooked to a golden brown, then splashed with our own special clear sauce.* / 0.00

CAJUN CATFISH with HUSH PUPPIES—*fish caught in the channels of fresh-water streams. Lightly breaded, and deep fried. try eating the tail and fins, too!* / 2.00

CREOLE HOUSE JAMBALAYA—*this special dish is a mixture of chicken, sausage and ham with rice, spices, herbs and vegetables. served en casserole and topped with shredded cheddar cheese.* 13.00

CRABMEAT IMPERIAL EN COQUILLE—*a lucious combination of backfin lump crabmeat, mixed with pimientos, green pepper and mayonnaise. Baked to a golden brown, served with brabant potatoes.* / 4.00

DESSERT

COFFEE   TEA
chickory or regular

CREOLE HOUSE GARLIC BREAD
thick slices of crusty bread, spread with our own garlic butter, sprinkled with fresh grated parmesan cheese, served bubbling hot. $1.00 per order
CORN FRITTERS $1.00 per order
HUSH PUPPIES $1.00 per order

Chicago
CRICKET'S
French/American $$$

To the diner expecting plush surroundings, thick-pile carpeting and dim romantic lighting, Cricket's will come as a surprise. The atmosphere is decidedly masculine, almost "clubby." The place reminds me of taverns that used to be called "tack rooms," with their horseracing memorabilia—except at Cricket's the memorabilia includes baseball, football, newspapers and even earth-moving toys suspended from beams or attached to walls. Food and service are exceptional. Waiters and captains seem to anticipate every need, from replenishing an exhausted supply of hot rolls to topping up a glass of wine. The à la carte menu includes some beautifully prepared selections. Braised sweetbreads are served in an elaborate financière sauce of wine, bacon and green olives. The English sole is perfectly complemented by a cream sauce with delicate white seedless grapes. Other sauces, such as bigarade or Madeira, stand up well with their respective meats—duckling for the orange-based bigarade and beef in pastry for the more pungent Madeira. Soups, such as the cold crème Senegalaise or the delicate consommé, are perfect preparations. Among appetizers, I like the seafood crêpe with just a hint of curry. Sometimes featured among daily selections is a hot chicken pâté which is coarsely ground and baked in pastry. Desserts, not listed on the menu, include crêpes suzette, fresh fruits in season and a creamy, sweet chocolate pudding. A good selection of wines complements the menu.

CRICKET'S, 100 East Chestnut (in the Tremont Hotel), Chicago. Telephone: 280-2100. Hours: 7 am-11 pm, daily for breakfast, lunch, and dinner. Cards: AE, CB, DC, MC, VISA. Reservations required for lunch and dinner. Full bar service. Coats and ties required for men. Private party facilities for up to 150 people. Valet parking.

K/Rating 17/20 • Food 6/7 • Service 6/6 • Decor 3/4 • Value 2/3

APPETIZERS

Imperial Beluga Caviar	Market Price
Smoked Sturgeon	4.50
Imported Scottish Salmon, Fumé	5.75
Smoked Brook Trout, Raifort	4.50
Oysters of the Season	4.00
Cherrystone Clams	3.50
Cracked Dungeness Crab, Mustard Mayonnaise	5.75
Shrimp Sauté, Vin Blanc	6.50
Snails Bourguignonne	4.75
Proscuitto Ham with Melon	3.75
Baked Clams, Provencale	4.00
Artichoke	
Vinaigrette, Hollandaise or Mayonnaise	3.75
Mushrooms à la Daum	3.00
Terrine de Pâté, Maison	3.00
Melon in Season	1.75
Baked Oysters in Pernod	4.75
Assorted Seafood Platter	7.75

SPECIALTIES

Tournedos Sauté, au Madére	11.50	
Sweetbreads Braisé, Financière	9.50	
Escalopine of Veal, "Cricket"	10.25	
Chicken Hash Mornay, with Wild Rice	7.75	
Fettucine, à la Francaise	8.50	
Roasts for Two, Bouquetière		
Rack of Lamb	16.50	per person
Chicken	9.25	per person
Roast Baby Squab, Grandmère	12.25	
Long Island Duckling, Bigarade	10.25	

FISH

Filet of Lemon Sole Sauté, Amandine	9.50
Red Snapper Sauté, Fine Herbes	10.00
Whitefish Grillé, Choron	9.00
Brook Trout Poche, au Porto	9.25
English Sole Sauté, Veronique	12.75
Salmon Poche, a L'Oseille	9.75
Swordfish Steak Sauté, Beurre Noir	10.50

STEAKS AND CHOPS

Steak au Poivre, Vert	12.75	
Filet Mignon, Béarnaise	11.50	
Double Sirloin Grillé, Tyrolienne	14.00	per person
Steak Diane	12.25	
Steak Tartare	10.50	
Calf's Liver Grillé, Bacon	9.25	
Double Lamb Chops, French-Cut	14.50	

Chicago
D. B. KAPLAN'S
Delicatessen

$

Where is it written that delicatessens always have to be dark, crowded and smell of pickles? That is not the case with D. B. Kaplan's, a rather glitzy establishment with bright enameled walls and bold graphic designs. For the hungry Water Tower Place shopper who wants to refresh on Jewish K-rations, this is the place. But it is also more than corned beef, pastrami and pepper beef: some 150 things more. The menu may be the *War and Peace* of restaurant menus with its scores of sandwiches, omelettes, fish platters and ice cream desserts. It is also a compendium of puns. For instance there are the obvious ones like "Standout from the Kraut" (hot dog and sauerkraut), "Ike and Tina Tuna" or "Goldie Lox and the Three Eggs." If you crave pepper beef, Swiss cheese, chopped liver and all the trimmings on egg challah, try "Live and Let Liver." "Studs Turkey" is not only the bird, but lots of tongue and Canadian bacon plus shredded lettuce and cranberry sauce. Despite the cutsie names, the sandwiches are all that you could expect between two slices of bread, bagels or rolls. There is lots more, including a six-foot triple-decker with Danish ham, salami, bologna, summer sausage and all the trimmings, just the thing for a party of 40 or so sandwich-starved friends. For $85 and three days notice it's yours. If you are an ice cream freak you will find all you could ever want, including more outrageous puns like the "Yalta Malta" and the "Starship Enterprise."

D. B. KAPLAN'S, 845 North Michigan Avenue, 7th Level Water Tower Place, Chicago. Telephone: 280-2700. Hours: 10 am-11 pm, Monday-Thursday; until 1 am, Friday-Saturday; 11 am-11 pm, Sunday. No cards or checks. No reservations. Full bar service. Private party facilities for up to 50 people with a minimum of 20.

K/Rating 17.5/20 • Food 6.5/7 • Service 5/6 • Decor 3/4 • Value 3/3

REUBEN, RUBIN!—Vienna corned beef or N.Y. style pastrami, swiss cheese, sauerkraut and russian dressing served HOT on bavarian black bread. _____ **$3.95**

THE HUGH HEFFER—Our famous rare roast beef topped with N.Y. herkimer cheddar, onions, DBQ sauce served sizzling HOT on a kaiser roll.____**$3.85**

HOLED YOUR TONGUE—Beef tongue, swiss cheese, polish baked ham, and bavarian mustard served HOT on a kaiser roll._____**$3.85**

ALL HENS ON DECK—Breast of turkey, polish baked ham, swiss cheese and stone ground mustard served HOT on an onion roll._____**$3.85**

THE OUTER SPICE—Proscuitto ham, provolone cheese, onions, horseradish, and spicy brown mustard served HOT on french bread._____**$3.85**

ANY PORK IN A STORM—Hickory smoked bacon, vienna corned beef, swiss cheese, cole slaw and dusseldorf mustard served HOT on french bread.__**$3.85**

LORD NOSE—Beef tongue, Norwegian brisling sardines, N.Y. herkimer cheddar, shredded lettuce, tomato slices and mayo served on an onion roll.____**$3.85**

LAKE SHORE CHIVE—Rare roast beef, cream cheese with chives served on bavarian black bread. _____**$3.85**

SORRY, CHOLLY—White meat tuna salad, herkimer cheese, shredded lettuce and tomato slices served HOT on Rosen's toasted cholly._____**$3.85**

LANA TUNA—White meat tuna salad and american cheese, shredded lettuce served HOT on a kaiser roll. _____**$3.85**

PERKY HERK—Genoa salami, N.Y. herkimer cheese, shredded lettuce, tomato slices and russian dressing on bavarian black bread._____**$3.50**

THERE OUGHTTA BE A SLAW—Vienna corned beef, cole slaw and light mustard served HOT on rye toast._____**$3.50**

A BIRD TO THE WISE—Breast of turkey set on a bed of shredded lettuce and whole cranberry sauce served HOT on french bread._____**$3.50**

THERE IS NOTHING LIKE A DANE—Danish ham, cream cheese with chives served on french bread. _____**$3.50**

BIBER'S SPECIAL—Our rare roast beef, shredded lettuce, bermuda onion and russian dressing on rye. _____**$3.50**

THE SPICE WHO CAME IN FROM THE COLD—Vienna pepperbeef, N.Y. herkimer cheddar, spicy brown mustard served HOT on bavarian black bread. _____**$3.50**

Chicago
DAE HO
Korean

$

Dae Ho (meaning "great lake") has become my favorite Korean restaurant. The foods are fresh and plentiful, and while the menu offers Mandarin selections on its menu, I usually stay with the Korean choices. Lest the idea of something as foreign as Korean cuisine alarm you, rest assured it is an easy style of food to enjoy. Tasty finger foods, such as the Korean version of egg rolls called mandu are a good way to start. They look like stuffed three-cornered hats and each order is ample for two or three people. The real heart of Korean dining lies in the preparation of barbecued beef dishes. Among favorites you are certain to enjoy is bulkogi, charbroiled sirloin steak marinated for a full day in a slightly sweet soy sauce. Rib lovers will enjoy digging into gal-be. Senjuk is a Korean version of shish kebab, flavored by a marinade of soy sauce, sugar, ginger, garlic and onion, then sizzled over open coals. A more unusual selection is beem-beem-bop, a beef and vegetable broth topped with a fried egg. It is a most interesting preparation and I urge you to include it among your choices. A variety of pork, chicken and seafood specialties, as well as meat and noodle broths, substantial as meals in themselves, are part of the menu.

DAE HO, 2741 West Devon Avenue, Chicago. Telephone: 274-8499. Hours: 11 am-11 pm, Wednesday-Friday and Sunday; until 1 am, Saturday. Cards: AE, CB, DC, MC, VISA. Reservations suggested for weekends. Full bar service. Casual dress acceptable. Parking on street.

K/Rating 17.5/20 • Food 7/7 • Service 5/6 • Decor 2.5/4 • Value 3/3

Chicago
DIANNA'S OPPA
Greek

$

Petros Kogeonos is probably the most flamboyant character in Chicago's Halsted Street/South Greektown neighborhood. Everyone is "cousin" to Petros. But aside from the character of its proprietor, Dianna's Oppa creates one of the cheeriest settings in Chicago for good Greek food. The restaurant looks like a Greek town square brought indoors. Waiters bustle back and forth between tables and kitchen calling out "Oppa!" (Olé!) with each flaming of the popular appetizer saganaki (kaseri cheese flamed with brandy). The best deal in the house is the combination platter. Or if there are several in your group, order family style and get avgolemono soup, Greek salad with tomatoes, lettuce and feta cheese, saganaki, gyros, pastitsio, moussaka, dolmades, rice, vegetables plus braised lamb or beef.

DIANNA'S OPPA, 212 South Halsted Street, Chicago. Telephone: 332-1225/332-1349. Hours: 11 am-2 am, daily. Cards: AE. Reservations taken. Full bar service. Free parking.

K/Rating 18/20 • Food 6/7 • Service 6/6 • Decor 3/4 • Value 4/4

$$$

The first thing you will notice upon entering Dr. Shen's is that it is like no other Chinese restaurant you have ever seen. The second thing you will discover is that it is the most expensive Chinese restaurant to which you have ever been. Suffice it to say that dinners are likely to cost $15 to $20 per person including tax and tips, but excluding cocktails and wine. One reason Dr. Shen's is so costly is the extravagant decor. Designed at a cost of over $1,000,000, the restaurant is done up in Oriental plum, cinnabar and shades of red. Artifacts from Hong Kong collections were gathered to grace Dr. Shen's. Unlike so many Chinese restaurants which offer page after page of choices, Dr. Shen's menu is fairly limited, but it is not without diversity. The menu is à la carte and I suggest you go with a small group to expand your tastes. Consider Dr. Shen's Sweet Meat Box of hors d'oeuvre ($4.50) with its selection of quail eggs with mushrooms, spicy cabbage, marinated chicken, won ton and Shanghai fried beef. Minced crab meat in lettuce roll ($3.50) is a delicious adventure in subtle tastes. Mushrooms moo shu ($2.95) are wrapped in small crêpes to contain their goodness. The adventurous diner will even find thousand year old eggs ($2.25), which while ad-

mittedly a culinary overstatement, are rather well preserved (and taste it). Main course choices run a gamut of meats, poultry and seafood plus some imaginative vegetarian choices. Among selections I like are the steamed whole fish (priced at market availability), Mongolian beef with green onions and crispy bean threads ($7.50) and Shantung roast duckling ($8.95). If you have reason for celebration, put together at least a party of six people and order the special ten-course gourmet feast ($25 per person). You should order that one or two days in advance when you make your reservation. There is also a selection of wines to complement the Oriental cuisine. Dr. Shen's is unquestionably a unique contribution to the Chicago restaurant scene. As owner Phil Shen explains, he is interested not so much in traditional preparation as in creating a new and lighter Chinese cuisine, akin to the French nouvelle cuisine.

DR. SHEN'S, 1050 North State Street (in the Newberry Plaza Mezzanine), Chicago. Telephone: 440-2322. Hours: Lunch: 11:30 am-2:30 pm, Monday-Saturday; Dinner: 5 pm-midnight, every evening; Brunch: 11:30 am-2:30 pm, Sunday. Cards: AE, DC, MC, VISA. Reservations taken. Full bar service. Jackets required for men. Private party facilities. Parking in Newberry Plaza Garage.

K/Rating 15.5/20 • Food 6/7 • Service 4/6 • Decor 4/4 • Value 1.5/3

Chicago
DORO'S
Northern Italian

$$$

Doro's has proven itself to be one of the city's most important restaurants. I am still somewhat put off by the overly bright and garish ambiance, but there is no question that food here is of the highest caliber. Fresh pastas are made in one of the most elaborate restaurant kitchens I have ever toured. Ravioli al burro e salvia (pillows of ravioli in butter and sage sauce) are so light and delicate they practically float off their platter. Seafood gets special attention at Doro's, from its storage in uniquely designed coolers to its individual preparation. While poached turbot with hollandaise or trout meunière seem more indicative of a French restaurant, Doro's is a wonderful reminder that French cuisine began south of the Alps in Renaissance Tuscany. Still, most preparations retain their Italian individuality, regardless of approbation by the Francs. Zuppa di pesce is as indigenous to Italy as is bouillabaise to Mar-

Farinaceous
PASTA

Tagliatelle Verdi Bolognese	7.00	**Fettuccine Alfredo**	7.00
Green Noodles With Meat Sauce.		Egg Noodles With Heavy Cream, Butter And Parmesan Cheese.	
Ravioli Al Burro E Salvia	7.00	**Spaghetti**	7.00
Ravioli With Butter And Sage.		Tomato, Bolognese or Marinara Sauce.	
		Linguine Vongole	7.50
Risotto Milanese	7.00	Linguine, White or Red Clam Sauce.	
Rice Made With Imported Saffron.			
Cannelloni Doro's	7.50	**Linguine Shrimp Marinara**	8.50
Homemade Meat Stuffed Macaroni.		Linguine With Shrimp, Marinara Sauce.	
Tortellini Panna	7.25	**Lasagna Verde**	7.50
Tortellini, Prosciutto Ham, Cream Sauce.		Green Lasagna With Red And White Sauce.	

seilles. Fettuccine Alfredo is redolent with heavy cream, butter and rich freshly grated Parmesan cheese, just as it is served in Rome. Veal, sweetbreads, chicken and beef preparations all receive sinfully extravagant treatment, whether piccata Lombarda in classic lemon butter with vino bianco or spezzatino de pollo from the Piedmont region, in wine and peppers. Desserts are as incredibly expensive as are other courses, perhaps even more so considering zabaglione or crêpes Suzette will cost $7 for two. But when money and caution can be thrown to the wind Doro's offers Lucullan self indulgence.

DORO'S, 871 North Rush Street, Chicago. Telephone: 266-1414. Hours: Lunch: 11:30 am-2:30 pm, Monday-Friday; Dinner: 6 pm-11:30 pm, Monday-Saturday. Cards: AE, CB, DC, MC, VISA. Reservations recommended. Full bar service. Valet parking in evenings.

K/Rating 16/20 • Food 7/7 • Service 5/6 • Decor 2/4 • Value 2/3

Vitello
VEAL

Piccata Lombarda 8.75
Scaloppine Sauted With White Wine, Lemon And Butter.

Scaloppine Saute Florio 9.25
Scaloppine Sauted With Mushrooms And Marsala.

Bracioline Di Vitello 9.25
Veal Birds Stuffed With Cheese And Prosciutto.

Saltimbocca Alla Romana 9.25
Scaloppine Sauted With Prosciutto, Sage And White Wine.

Fegato Alla Veneta 9.00
Calf's Liver Sauted With Onions And White Wine.

Costoletta Di Vitello Alla Milanese 9.25
Breaded Veal Chop Sauted.

Scaloppini Alla Sorrentina 9.50
Scaloppine Sauted With Eggplant, Prosciutto And Cheese.

Costoletta Parmigiana 9.75
Veal Chop With Tomato Sauce And Mozzerella Cheese.

Costoletta Al Madeira 9.75
Veal Chop With Sauce Madeira.

Costoletta Valtostana
Stuffed Veal Chop With Prosciutto And Cheese.

Animelle Saute 10.25
Sweetbreads, Saute Meuniere.

Cervella Al Burro Nero 9.50
Calf's Brains With Black Butter And Capers.

51

Chicago
EL CRIOLLO
Argentinian/Mexican $$

El Criollo is a unique restaurant. Besides being the only restaurant in Chicago to serve the specialties of Argentina, it also manages to radiate its own comfortable hospitality, in spite of its location in a rather shabby industrial neighborhood. The decor reflects the Latin heritage of its owners and while nothing is fancy, there exists the kind of comfort and welcome that you usually find only at a friend's well-worn kitchen table. In addition to the specialties of Argentina there are several typical Mexican dishes. Beef steak Tamipquena is typical of the better fare. The platter includes a mild cheese enchilada, rice, refried beans and guacamole, along with a large cut of skirt steak. Other Mexican dishes include filling chiles rellenos, tacos and enchilada platters. But since Mexicän food is available everywhere these days, why not try the Argentinian foods? Argentina is a great cattle raising nation and so as you might expect, the cuisine uses a lot of beef. Try churrasco, a large and thick strip steak served with thick-cut fried potatoes and a salad. If you have a small appetite, you can get a half order for under $5. Perhaps the most outstanding beef dinner is the steak Milanesa. If you are from south of the Mason-Dixon line, you might mistake this for chicken-fried steak. In fact, it is batter-fried meat, two large chunks of beef steak that practically spill over the sides of the serving platter, topped with fried eggs. You get a side of potatoes and salad which makes this dinner a real gaucho-sized bargain. Another Argentinian specialty is parrillada, a dish of sausages, ribs and sweetbreads. And, by the way, do not pass up an intense, delicious garlic sauce made from garlic juice, olive oil, vinegar, crushed parsley and a dash of oregano. It really hits the spot on grilled meats. For appetizers try an excellent guacamole and empanadas, small meat-filled pastries that will leave you crying for more, they are so good. Desserts include flan and a sweet potato tart served with a slice of mild brick cheese which offsets the intense sweetness of the filling.

EL CRIOLLO, 1706 West Fullerton Avenue, Chicago. Telephone: 549-3373. Hours: noon-11 pm, daily. Cards: AE, DC, MC, VISA. Reservations taken. Full bar service. Casual dress acceptable. Parking on street.

K/Rating 17.5/20 • Food 6.5/7 • Service 5/6 • Decor 3/4 • Value 3/3

Chicago
ELI'S THE PLACE FOR STEAK
Steak $$

Eli's remains a fixture for great beef-eating in Chicago, although at least one prominent restaurateur I know likes Eli's primarily for the calves' liver. It is a rare treat, sautéed chunks of tender liver with pieces of green pepper, slivers of grilled onion and mushrooms. Boneless breast of chicken Parmesan has its partisans, too. Among the steaks, of course you will find all the cuts including T-bone, sirloin and butt (my favorite). Proprietor Eli Schulman seems to know just about everybody in town; his restaurant and lounge have become a regular stop on the celebrity circuit. So if you want a glimpse of Shecky, Henny or Don when they come to town, Eli's is the place for steaks and staring.

ELI'S, 215 East Chicago Avenue, Chicago. Telephone: 642-1393. Hours: Lunch: 11 am-2:30 pm, Monday-Friday; Dinner: 4 pm-midnight, daily; piano bar until 1:30 am. Cards: AE. Reservations recommended. Jackets required for men. Parking in Carriage House Garage.

K/Rating 17/20 • Food 5.5/7 • Service 6/6 • Decor 3/4 • Value 2.5/3

Chicago
EUGENE'S
American

$$

Gene Sage has made a rousing success of this restaurant cum entertainment lounge. It is a rather romantic kind of a place with dim lighting, comfortable seating and whatnot. But Eugene (I don't know anybody who would call him that to his face) has a sense of humor about as large as his menu. It is studded with little bon mots, as a quick glance will reveal. Taking a cue from Chicago's gangster heritage, Eugene's menu tips its hat to the kind of characters who might be more at home with Damon Runyon than as theme figures for chops, fish and even chili. The food, however, is uniformly good and even though Eugene's is in a rather posh neighborhood, you won't lose your bankroll here. Chances are you will like Eugene's . . . or else, see?

EUGENE'S, 1255 North State Parkway, Chicago. Telephone: 944-1445. Hours: 5 pm-2 am, daily. Cards: AE, CB, DC, MC, VISA. Reservations recommended. Full bar service. Jackets required for men. Valet parking.

K/Rating 18/20 • Food 6/7 • Service 5/6 • Decor 4/4 • Value 3/3

fishes and Shellfishes

RED SNAPPER ARLESIENNE baked iwth White Wine,
some tomato, and green pepper and pernod which is served in
honor of Big Joe the Dealer 8.95
DOVER SOLE which is fixed with a special sauce of Shrimp and
Mushrooms named Norman Across the Hall 11.50
DOVER SOLE saute with an unusual sauce of
melted down butter 11.50
BROILED ALASKAN KING CRAB LEGS, with a butter sauce or perhaps
it is your choice of a mustard sauce- the personal choice of
Tommy the Gunsel 8.95
SOFT SELL SOLLIE'S SHRIMP DE JOHNGHE OR JOHN, if you
are of the mind 8.95
SAM THE GONOPH'S MAINE LOBSTER, boiled in beer or
broiled (at prevailing prices)
COLD MAINE LOBSTER, Finicky Phil's, personal selection is
served with Lobster Mayonnaise - at market

It is a sure think that the dishes up-front
are brought with things that are called for in such a situation,
like potatoes, mostly fresh vegetables, unusual garnishes and every
citizen's choice of what is a permissible salad under the circumstances,
like Mushroom or **EUGENE'S**

The Big Beef

BEEF BONES, BAR B QUED, Lenny the Lifer 6.95
LITTLE ISIDORE'S CHOPPED SIRLOIN STEAK, Sauce Large 6.50
STEAK TARTAR, Big Bob the Safe Opener, with Toast Points and
a small bit of caviar 7.95
THE STAND-UP PERSONS BEEF FILETS which is served up in pieces and is
in a splendid indeed sauce with Salsify and Wild Rice   8.95
STEAK! Which is prepared somewhat as if for Miss Hortense the Hoofer
with onions, mushrooms, just a pinch of garlic,
flamed in cognac
that is from across the drink 9.50

Entrées. Which means
the Main Event

ROAST DUCKLING with Wild Cherry Sauce, as ordered by Miss Sarah
the Thrush on the occasion of the release of The Delicate Dane 8.95
SLOW McCOOL'S MARINATED BABY BACK RIBS, with an Ethical and
Legal Sauce 8.95
MR. G's TIPS OF TENDERLOIN, A LA JUDGE MURPHY with Truffle sauce
and Chantrelle Mushrooms, hot house Charlotte's very wild rice 9.50
VEAL, BLACK MIKE FROM MILAN, which is made from very young
calves of whom it is said only drink milk and do not eat very much
else, and is fixed with lemon butter, some Capers
and perhaps a tiny bit of Caviar, which is
not from across 9 95
BRANDY AL'S VEAL which is also from Baby Calves who imbibe only on Milk,
served with an up-front Brandy Sauce laced with a plentitude of
Mushrooms and Cream. Truly high class groceries   9.95
IRISH HYMIE'S RACK of SPRING LAMB, Bouquetiere, Mint Apple 13.50 – 26.00

Chicago
FAMILY CORNER
Northern India $

Where else but in Chicago are you likely to find an Indian restaurant across the street from a Hebrew bookstore? That is where you will find the Family Corner. And would you believe an Indian restaurant where the specialty is pizza? This is not your basic Italian pizza of course, but a spicier, more exotic food. The pizza crust is moderately thin. The sauce has hints of coriander and cardamom among its various seasonings. The toppings, if you choose, can be all vegetarian. For instance, a combination of water chestnuts and green beans or peas, potatoes and perhaps cauliflower might be to your taste. Family Corner has a limited menu of other more familiar Indian foods. Because the cuisine is Kashmiri, from the north at the foot of the Himalayas, you won't find any tropical curries. But that does not mean bland seasonings by any means. Try jammu lamb shorva, chunks of the meat in a dark yogurt-based gravy with a complexity of flavors as tightly wound together as the Gordian knot. Other stew-like dishes include sweet peas and minced meat in a thick gravy, shrimp in garlic and spices plus a handful of vegetarian choices. Somewhat milder are the several kebab selections. Murgh kebab is a large portion of cut-up chicken pieces that have been marinated in a yogurt-based sauce and then broiled. The idea is to squeeze some lemon juice on the chicken, dip it into mint chutney, then into a spicier fruit chutney, add a slice of tomato and shreds of onion and finally eat and savor the wonderful flavors. You might want to begin dinner with an appetizer or soup. I like samosa, the well known Indian pastries stuffed with peas and potato, best eaten with a hot pepper sauce. The fresh desserts are traditional Indian sweets. Gulab jamun is a blend of little wheat and cheese balls, deep-fried and served in rosewater syrup. My favorite is kulfi, a rich Indian ice cream.

FAMILY CORNER INDIA RESTAURANT, 2901 West Devon Avenue, Chicago. Telephone: 262-2854. Hours: Lunch: 11:30 am-2 pm, Monday-Friday: 5 pm-11 pm, Monday-Thursday; until midnight, Friday; noon-midnight, Saturday; until 10 pm, Sunday. No cards. Reservations taken. Full bar service; you may bring your own wine for a $2 per bottle corkage fee. Casual, neat dress acceptable. Restaurant may be taken over for private parties. Parking on street.

K/Rating 17/20 • Food 6.5/7 • Service 5/6 • Decor 2.5/4 • Value 3/3

kashmiri shorvas ... meat

kofta shorva -- $4.40
Meat cutlets in tomato-masala gravy.

mutter keema shorva -- $3.50
Sweet peas and minced meat in Sirinagar-style thick gravy.

gobhi keema shorva -- $3.75
Cauliflower and minced meat in Sirinagar-style thick gravy.

jammu lamb shorva -- $4.25
Special cut of lamb chunks in garlic-onion-yogurt gravy.

saag lamb -- $4.50
Special cut of lamb chunks in creamed spinach-garlic gravy.

jhinga shorva -- $5.50
Shrimps and green peppers in masala-garlic gravy.

kashmiri shorvas ... vegetarian

mutter panir -- $3.25
Indian cheese and sweet peas in onion-garlic gravy.

mutter khumb -- $3.25
Mushrooms and sweet peas in onion-masala gravy.

saag panir -- $3.25
Chunks of Indian cheese in creamed spinach-garlic gravy.

Chicago
FAMILY HOUSE
Greek

$$

If you have a gargantuan appetite, Family House is the restaurant for you. Chef/owner Louis Katsaros is about as effusive a fellow as you are likely to find along Greektown North's restaurant row. Chances are as soon as you step inside someone will thrust a glass of wine into your grasp. Then it is off to the first available table for so much food that you may walk away gasping for breath. Begin with a house appetizer platter that gives you myriad tastes of delicacies like loukaniko, spiced Greek sausage, or taramasalata, delicious creamy fish roe salad. Even if you don't see your favorite Greek specialty on the menu, ask— they probably have enormous quantities of it in the kitchen. Fresh fish is a specialty of the house, either snapper, seabass or turbot, depending upon what is being shipped in. Combination platters make up the best value; a combo also gives you a chance to dine family style and taste several things. The combination dinner for $6.95 may be the best bargain in this entire book. As a matter of fact, if you take the time to tell Louis how good everything is, he will probably think of something else to bring out to serve to you.

FAMILY HOUSE, 2421 West Lawrence Avenue, Chicago. Telephone: 334-7411/334-0552. Hours: 11 am-2 am, daily. Cards: CB, MC. Reservations taken. Full bar service. Casual dress acceptable. Private party facilities for 30 to 300 people. Parking lot nearby.

K/Rating 19/20 • Food 7/7 • Service 6/6 • Decor 3/4 • Value 3/3

**TRY
OUR FAMOUS
COMPLETE FAMILY DINNER**

NATIONAL GREEK DISHES

PASTITSIO **3.95**
Grecian Delight, Served with Special Sauce,
Parmigiana Cheese

MOUSAKA with Eggplant **3.95**

ATHENIAN SPINACH-CHEESE PIE .. **3.25**

DOLMADES AVGOLEMONO **3.95**
Stuffed Vine Leaves with
Selected Ground Beef, Lamb and Rice.
Served with Egg Lemon Sauce

ENTREES

BABY SPRING LAMB, Giouvetsi **3.95**
With Rosa Marina

BRAISED SPRING LAMB **3.95**
With Our Special Sauce, Rice Pilaf,
or Fresh Vegetable and Potato

ROAST SPRING LEG OF LAMB **4.50**
With Rice Pilaf, or Fresh Vegetable and Potatoes

**½ BROILED or BAKED ORIENTAL
STYLE SPRING CHICKEN** **3.95**
Rice Pilaf and Potatoes

**SPECIAL COMBINATION PLATE
With 6 Different Samplings
of Grecian Delights** **5.25**
Pastitsio, Breast of Lamb, Stuffed Vine Leaves,
Rice, Vegetable and Potatoes

STUFFED BREAST OF SPRING LAMB **3.50**
Rice and Potato

Chicago
FRENCH PORT
Country French Seafood

$$

What visions the words "French port" create in the mind's eye! Fishermen of Brittany hauling in their nets; a steamy waterfront dive in Marseilles. This French Port offers cozy dining in surroundings of polished plank-topped tables or booths and lath and plaster wall decor. The dinner menu consists almost entirely of fresh fish, in most cases prepared simply over a charcoal broiler with nothing added to detract from their natural goodness. There is also the obligatory steak for confirmed carnivores, plus duck à l'orange, chicken and veal Madeira. On Thursdays only, French Port serves couscous, the Moroccan staple of millet, vegetables and seasonings. Couscous is served either vegetarian-style or with lamb. The luncheon menu is quite reasonable and includes various crêpes, omelettes, fried fish and burgers.

FRENCH PORT, 2585 North Clark Street, Chicago. Telephone: 528-6644. Hours: 4 pm-11 pm, Monday-Thursday; until midnight, Friday-Saturday; 3 pm-11 pm, Sunday. Cards: MC, VISA. Full bar service. Casual dress acceptable. Free parking in New Town Garage.

K/Rating 16.5/20 • Food 5.5/7 • Service 5/6 • Decor 3/4 • Value 3/3

Stuffed Fish - whole fresh fish stuffed with fresh vegetables & shrimp.

STUFFED SEA BASS	8.25
STUFFED FLOUNDER	8.75
STUFFED BLUEFISH	9.00
STUFFED SEA TROUT	9.00
STUFFED RED SNAPPER	9.75

Broiled Fish - whole fresh fish broiled with special herbed butter.

BROILED FLOUNDER	7.25
BROILED SEA BASS	7.25
BROILED MONKFISH	7.75
BROILED BLUEFISH	8.00
BROILED SEA TROUT	8.00
BROILED RED SNAPPER	9.00

Cuisine provençale - fresh fish fillets sautéed, glazed with tomato sauce & fresh vegetables

RED SNAPPER PROVENÇAL	8.00	SEA TROUT PROVENÇAL	8.00
BLUEFISH PROVENÇAL	8.50	GROUPER PROVENÇAL	9.00

Chicago
GARDEN OF HAPPINESS
Korean/Chinese

$$

When I first started visiting the Garden of Happiness, it was primarily a Korean restaurant with a sprinkling of Chinese preparations. Since its listing in the first *Best Restaurants Chicago* a larger emphasis has been placed on the Chinese menu. Thus you will find competent preparations of Mandarin favorites ranging from soups, such as sweet and sour or abalone, to princess chicken to snow peas with prawns among the several dozen Mandarin selections. I still enjoy choosing from the Korean foods. Relegated to the back page of the restaurant's four-page menu, these exotic creations still excite my tastebuds. Fire meat, marinated in a tangy sauce and charcoal grilled is mouthwatering. San juk offers a more complex array of seasonings and ingredients. Poultry is well represented by dahk boken, which is chicken sautéed in a semi-sweet preparation of vegetables, a fried egg and rice. And although it is not on the menu as a separate choice, you may order kim chee, the peppery-hot Korean cabbage appetizer. Best value is the special dinner, all inclusive for $6 per person; you can take your choice from two listings.

GARDEN OF HAPPINESS, 3450 North Lincoln Avenue, Chicago. Telephone: 348-2120. Hours: 11:30 am-2 am, Wednesday-Monday. Cards: AE, CB, DC, MC, VISA. Reservations taken. Full bar service. Casual dress acceptable. Private party facilities for up to 40 people; there is also a small private tea house. Ample parking.

K/Rating 17/20 • Food 6/7 • Service 5/6 • Decor 3/4 • Value 3/3

Chicago
GAYLORD INDIA RESTAURANT
Indian

$$

Gaylord India Restaurant offers the best Indian cooking available in Chicago. Though far from what we usually think of as a chain restaurant, it is part of an international chain with branches in India, London, New York and San Francisco. There are scores of cooking styles in the large and populous subcontinent of India. At Gaylord we get a taste of the northern cuisine, characterized by tandoori cooking. The tandoors are deep clay-lined pits embedded in a tile-covered counter. Each holds a bed of white-hot charcoal over which long-marinated meats are quickly cooked to seal in flavor and juices. When roasted in the tandoor, chicken or lamb, covered with a red-colored, yogurt-based marinade, take on a complex charcoal taste that you just can't capture in your backyard barbecue. No beef is served because of the Hindu taboo, but delicious chicken, lamb, prawns and vegetarian dishes are regular menu items. Naturally, vegetables are handled in an outstanding way, some spicy, others mild. Combination platters offer beginners a good assortment of textures and tastes. At the end of your meal take hot tea and any of the refreshingly sweet desserts. Wines are available, but beer is preferable with curries.

GAYLORD INDIA RESTAURANT, 678 North Clark Street, Chicago. Telephone: 664-1700. Hours: Lunch: 11:30 am-2:30 pm, Monday-Thursday; Dinner: 5:30 pm-10:30 pm, Monday-Thursday and Sunday; until 11 pm, Friday-Saturday; Brunch: 12:30 pm-3 pm, Sunday. Cards: AE, DC, MC, VISA. Reservations recommended. Full bar service. Neat, casual dress acceptable. Private party facilities. Free parking.

K/Rating 19/20 • Food 7/7 • Service 6/6 • Decor 3/4 • Value 3/3

Chicken 3.95

Chicken Jaipuri — (Tender chicken cooked in yoghurt, mildly spiced, and served with boiled egg)
Murg Mussalam — (Chicken marinated in cream, mildly spiced, cooked and flavoured with herbs)
Tandoori Chicken Masala — (Tandoori baked chicken, cooked in oriental spices with chopped tomatoes and butter)
Chicken Do-Piaza — (Gravy chicken cooked with onions)
Chicken Chilli Masala — (Chunks of chicken cooked with green peppers and tomatoes)
Chicken Bhuna Masala — (Chicken cooked in spices and flavoured with green herbs)
Sagwala Chicken — (Chicken cooked with creamed spinach, cooked in spices)

Lamb 4.25

Roghan Josh — (Cubes of lamb cooked in mildly spiced gravy)
Lamb Pasanda — (Lamb marinated in yoghurt and cooked in cream and spices will melt in the mouth)
Kofta Masala — (Mince meat balls with gravy)
Keema Matter — (Minced lamb and peas)
Gobi Meat — (Lamb cooked in spices with cauliflower)
Sag Meat — (Lamb cooked in spices with spinach)
Dal Meat — (Lamb cooked in spices with lentils)

Fish 4.75

Prawn Curry — (Fresh shrimps cooked in Oriental style gravy)

Rice

Shahjahani Baryani — (Rice cooked with off the bone chicken, nuts, saffron, a dish fit for kings) 4.50
Chicken Baryani — (Rice cooked with chicken and saffron) 4.25
Lamb Baryani — (Rice cooked with lamb and saffron) 4.50
Peas Pullau 1.50

Vegetarian 2.95

Mattar Paneer — (Green peas cooked in home made cheese)
Chana Masaladar — (Chic peas cooked in spices)
Kofta Paneer — (Home made cheese chunks spiced and fried and cooked in a delicious gravy)
Alu Gobbi Masala — (Potatoes and cauliflower, cooked with herbs and spices)
Dal Special — (Creamed lentils)
Bhindi — (Fried okra)
Sag Paneer — (Creamed spinach and home made cheese cooked in spices)
Alu Bengan — (Egg plant and potato)
Alu Raita — (Old fashioned yoghurt and potatoes and cucumber flavoured with mint leaves)
Sukhi Dal — (Lentils delicately spiced)
Vegetables mixed

Salads

Chicken Chaat (Tender cold chicken with spices, lemon juice) 2.50
Alu Chaat (Potatoes with hot spices and lemon juice 1.50   Katchumer (Indian Style Salad) 1.25

Pakoras

Mixed Vegetable (Fritters made of Gram Flour) 1.50   Veg Samosa 0.65
Special Indian Pickles 0.75   Popadum 0.40

Tandoori Specialities

Chicken — (Chicken marinated in spices and cooked on charcoal in a clay oven) Full 5.50 Half 2.75
Boti Kabab — (Cubed leg of lamb roasted on a skewer) 3.95
Seikh Kabab — (Minced lamb mixed with onions and herbs and roasted on skewers) 3.95
Chicken Tikka Kabab — (Boneless chicken pieces roasted Tandoori style) 3.95
Chapati — (Unleavened Indian bread) 0.65
Nan — (Tandoori style Indian bread) 0.75
Keema Nan (Tandoori Style) — (Leavened bread stuffed with cooked minced lamb) 1.25
Special Paratha — (Buttered layered whole wheat bread) 1.00
Alu Paratha — (Baked whole wheat bread stuffed with potatoes) 1.25
Egg Paratha — (Baked whole wheat bread stuffed with eggs) 1.25
Puree — (Fried whole wheat bread, served puffy) 0.75

Chicago
GEJA'S CAFE
Fondue

$$$

Tables are covered with muted Tartan cloths, bottles of wine line shelves in almost every nook and cranny, lights are kept low as conversation murmurs and laughter ripples from a table here or there. The atmosphere at Geja's is conducive to fondue, for this type of cooking is as much a social activity as anything else; it seems to stimulate good conversation. There is a camaraderie that seems to grow in the simple act of preparing and eating foods together, and that of course, is what civilized dining is all about. Fondue cooking here is sometimes done in a pot of hot peanut oil. The various ingredients are speared with a slender small-tined fork and cooked in the bubbling oil to individual preference. The method works well with meat, firm-fleshed fish and vegetables. Another branch of fondue cooking is cheese fondue. In this, melted cheeses are blended with kirsch, wine and seasonings. The satisfaction comes in dip-

GEJA'S FONDUES
MINIMUM 2 PERSONS

Beef and Lobster Fondue — **11.75** per person
Baby lobster tails and choice aged beef tenderloin with fresh vegetables.

Seafood Fondue — **11.50** per person
Lobster tails, shrimp, whitefish, scallops with fresh vegetables.

Beef Fondue — **9.75** per person
½ lb. choice aged beef tenderloin with fresh vegetables.

Beef and Shrimp Fondue — **11.75** per person
Jumbo Gulf shrimp and choice aged beef tenderloin with fresh vegetables.

INTERNATIONAL FONDUE — **10.50** per person
Combination of beef, chicken, shrimp with fresh vegetables.

Beef and Chicken Fondue — **8.75** per person
Combination of aged beef tenderloin and boneless breast of chicken with fresh vegetables.

Chicken Fondue — **7.50** per person
½ lb. of boneless breast of chicken with fresh vegetables.

Fresh Vegetable Fondue — **6.75** per person
Mushrooms • Green Peppers • Onions • Cauliflower
Zucchini • Egg Plant • Broccoli • Irish Potatoes

Above fondues include sliced green peppers, onions, mushrooms, broccoli spears, Irish potatoes and Geja's salad.

ping chunks of crusty bread and tart apple wedges into the caldron of smoothly melted cheese, covering your food with the warm bubbly sauce and enjoying the complexity of taste and texture sensations. By dinner's end, if you are up to dessert, the traditional way to go is chocolate fondue. Thick melted chocolate and kirsch are blended together and served with a selection of fruits and poundcake. Geja's has a definite following among wine lovers. Owner John Davis is a dedicated purveyor of better wines at reasonable cost; wine goes hand-in-hand with the fondue experience at Geja's.

GEJA'S CAFE, 340 West Armitage Avenue, Chicago. Telephone: 281-9101. Hours: 5 pm-11:30 pm, Monday-Thursday; until midnight, Friday; until 1 am, Saturday; 4:30 pm-11 pm, Sunday. Cards: AE, MC, VISA. Reservations taken Sunday-Thursday. Full bar service. Casual dress acceptable. Private party facilities for up to 50 people.

K/Rating 16/20 • Food 6/7 • Service 4.5/6 • Decor 4/4 • Value 1.5/3

SPECIALTIES

PREMIER FONDUE DINNER

14.50 per person

Cheese Fondue Appetizer

Salad

Your choice of Beef & Lobster, Beef, Beef & Shrimp, Seafood, or International Fondue.

Chocolate Dessert Fondue

Coffee

MINIMUM 2 PERSONS

Cheese Fondue*

Cheeses blended with white wine, Kirsch, and spices. Served with apple wedges and crusty chunks of French bread for dipping (Salad included)

5.50 per person

MINIMUM 2 PERSONS

*Side order of fresh mushrooms, green peppers, broccoli and onion rings.

1.50 per person

Chicago
GENE & GEORGETTI
Steaks/Italian

$$

Ask some folks where the best steak is served in Chicago and they will tell you at Gene & Georgetti. I am not quite ready to bestow that much of an accolade, but there is no question that this is one of the best of its kind. Served without embellishment, steaks come straight from broiler to table. Ask for a garlic rub or salt and pepper to taste, at your table, and you will get perfect satisfaction. Gene & Georgetti does a commendable job with Italian specialties. I particularly like linguini in white clam sauce. Meat sauces are thick, with any tomato harshness cooked away in the Tuscan manner. Gene & Georgetti has always been popular not only with local Chicago types, but with out-of-towners doing business at the nearby Merchandise Mart and the New Wolf Point Apparel Center. At a time when the London House, Stockyard Inn and Mr. Kelly's are nothing but memories, Gene & Georgetti is showing them all how to stick around.

GENE & GEORGETTI, 500 North Franklin Street, Chicago. Telephone: 527-3718. Hours: 11:30 am-midnight, Monday-Saturday. Cards: AE, DC, VISA. Reservations recommended. Full bar service. Casual dress acceptable. Private party facilities for up to 20 people. Free parking.

K/Rating 17/20 • Food 6/7 • Service 6/6 • Decor 3/4 • Value 2/3

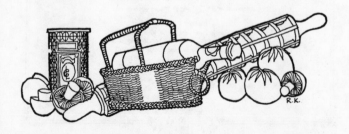

Entrees

Calf's Liver and Bacon	$8.25
Chopped Sirloin Steak	7.25
Half Spring Chicken (Broiled or Fried)	7.25
Beef En Brochette	10.75

Italian Specialties

Chicken Cacciatora	$7.95
Chicken Vesuvio	7.95
Chicken Florentine Style	7.95
Veal Scaloppine	8.25
Veal Florentine	8.25
Veal Cutlet Parmigiana	8.25
Breaded Veal Cutlet	7.95

Sea Foods

Lobster Tail	$13.50
Lobster Tail De Jonge	13.50
Lobster a La Diavolo	14.50
Whitefish	9.25
Shrimps De Jonge	8.25
French Fried Shrimps	8.25

COTTAGE FRIED POTATOES, HEAD LETTUCE AND TOMATO SALAD WITH OIL AND VINEGAR OR FRENCH DRESSING INCLUDED WITH ABOVE.

Spaghetti and Ravioli

Canelloni	$7.50
Ravioli With Meat Sauce	7.25
Spaghetti With Meat Sauce	6.50
Spaghetti a La Marinara	6.25
Spaghetti L' Acciughe	6.25
Spaghetti Al Burro	6.25
Spaghetti With Mushroom Sauce	6.95
Spaghetti With Meat Balls	6.95
Mostaccioli With Meat Sauce	6.75
Linguini White Clam Sauce	7.95
Spaghetti White Clam Sauce	7.95

Salads

Limestone Lettuce Salad	$1.50
Cole Slaw	1.50
Sliced Tomatoes	2.00
Sliced Tomatoes, Onions	2.25
Sliced Tomatoes, Onions, Anchovies	3.00
Garbage Salad	3.25
Thousand Island or Blue Cheese Dressing	.50 extra

Chicago
GENNARO'S
Italian

$

Gennaro's remains a lasting tribute to the old Taylor Street Italian neighborhood. Like so many neighborhood restaurants, there is a certain clubiness that permeates the place, although as an outsider, I have always found my welcome and service congenial. Still, the locked front door and buzzer entry sets an almost seige-like atmosphere in a neighborhood undergoing great social change. Gennaro's menu does not appear extraordinary at first glance. But everything served is fresh, hot and homemade. Seasonings are mellowed, well married in the sauces. Something as commonplace as veal Parmigiana is exceptionally delicious. The cheese topping is perfectly enhanced by a deep red tomato sauce that tastes as if it were cooked for hours at slow simmer. The veal itself is tender, well textured and ample. To really experience the excellence of Gennaro's, you must order an à la carte specialty. Homemade gnocchi is not to be missed. These little potato dumplings are rich and chewy, and I am sure sinfully fattening, but as pleasurable a way to put on weight as I can think of. The gnocchi are bathed in that wonderful, full-bodied tomato sauce, the backbone of Gennarro's kitchen creations. Other homemade pastas are ravioli, stuffed manicotti and broad, homemade noodles. Spumone and tortoni are offered for desserts, but cannoli is the homemade standout.

GENNARO'S, 1352 West Taylor Street, Chicago. Telephone: 243-1035/733-8790. Hours: 5 pm-9 pm, Thursday; until 10 pm, Friday-Saturday; 4 pm-9 pm, Sunday. No cards. Reservations recommended. Full bar service. Casual dress acceptable. Parking on street.

K/Rating 19/20 • Food 7/7 • Service 6/6 • Decor 3/4 • Value 3/3

Specialties

Made Fresh Daily by Mrs. Gennaro for Your Eating Enjoyment

HOMEMADE GNOCCHI *3.20*
    (Cavatelli)

HOMEMADE EGG NOODLES *3.20*

HOMEMADE RAVIOLI *3.20*
    (Cheese only)

HOMEMADE MANICOTTI *3.30*
    (Cheese and Meat)

HOMEMADE EGG NOODLES *3.30*
(Butter & Cheese)

Meat Ball or Sausage *80* extra

BRACIOULE DINNER (Spaghetti and Salad) *6.25*

CHICKEN MARSALA (Salad and Potatoes) *5.50*

CHICKEN VESUVIO (Salad and Potatoes) *5.25*

PORK CHOPS & PEPPERS (Salad and Potatoes) *6.00*

VEAL PARMESIAN (Spaghetti and Salad) *6.50*

VEAL & PEPPERS (Spaghetti and Salad)............. *6.50*

VEAL SCALLOPINI (Egg Noodles and Salad)............... *6.50*

EGG PLANT PARMESIAN (Spaghetti and Salad) *5.25*

SPAGHETTI *2.45*

SPAGHETTI (Meat Ball or Sausage) *3.25*

SPAGHETTI (Mushrooms) *3.45*

SPAGHETTI (Oil and Garlic) *3.10*

SPAGHETTI (Oil, Garlic, and Anchovies) *3.35*

LINGUINE *2.45*

LINGUINE (Meat Ball or Sausage) *3.25*

LINGUINE (Mushrooms) *3.45*

LINGUINE (Oil and Garlic) *3.10*

LINGUINE (Oil, Garlic, and Anchovies)....................... *3.30*

MOSTACCIOLI *2.65*

MOSTACCIOLI (Meat Ball or Sausage)........................... *3.45*

MEAT BALL PLATE (2 Meat Balls) *1.85*

ESCAROLE *1.90*

ESCAROLE (with Meat Balls or Sausage) *3.25*

While inflation has pushed Genesee Depot out of the bare-bones budget category, you still will find a bounty of good dining at bargain prices. Dinners include soup or salad, homemade bread, fresh vegetable plus an appropriate starch such as dumplings, potato or rice. Desserts are extra. Genessee Depot is like visiting a country kitchen of half a century or more ago. This tidy storefront restaurant has only nine tables. Bare brick, wood and quaint floral wallpaper create the atmosphere. Fresh flowers add a splash of color to each table. There is no printed menu; entrées are listed on a board near the entrance. While diners' selections may be limited on any given evening, this does insure freshness of all foodstuffs, a characteristic sorely missed at many of the more expensive establishments. Each evening one of the entrées on the printed board will be beef, one fish and the third sometimes chicken, sometimes pork. Stuffed turbot ($6.50) is served with a mushroom and herb stuffing and cream sauce. Red snapper Creole ($6.25) or fillet of sole ($6.25) are among other seafood choices. Pepper steak ($5.75) is served over a bed of egg noodles. Boiled brisket of beef ($5.75) is ample and hearty. Should chicken be your choice, chicken pêche ($6.75) offers a boneless breast stuffed with a peach half and served with a brandied peach sauce. Perhaps a bit more elegant is chicken Florentine ($7.00) cooked in butter, set on a bed of spinach, capped with mornay sauce and served au gratin. Desserts are all homemade.

GENESEE DEPOT, 3736 North Broadway, Chicago. Telephone: 528-6990. Hours: 5 pm-10 pm, Wednesday-Saturday; until 9 pm, Sunday. No cards. No reservations. No bar service; you may bring your own. Casual, neat dress acceptable. Parking on street.

K/Rating 17/20 • Food 5/7 • Service 5/6 • Decor 4/4 • Value 3/3

GINO'S EAST
Italian/Pizza

$$

A place popular with college kids, hospital technicians and secretaries, Gino's East just happens to have some of the best pizza around. It is Chicago-style pizza, deep dish with a thick, almost cake-crumb crust, rich pizza sauce and gobs of toppings over cheese. If something other than pizza is your choice, pasta dishes are most satisfying; I particularly enjoy green noodles with meatballs. There are two dining rooms served by the same kitchen. One is downstairs, a grotto-like affair with wooded tables and bench seating. The upstairs dining room has a gracious white-tablecloth setting. Take your pick, depending on how you are dressed and what mood suits you. By the way, you can stick with the house wines by C-K Mondavi and not go wrong.

GINO'S EAST, 160 East Superior Street, Chicago. Telephone: 943-1124. Hours: 11 am-2 am, Monday-Saturday; 4 pm-2 am, Sunday. Cards: AE. Reservations suggested. Full bar service. Parking nearby.

K/Rating 18/20 • Food 7/7 • Service 5/6 • Decor 3.5/4 • Value 3/3

SPAGHETTI
WITH GINO'S EAST DELICIOUS MEAT
SAUCE, BREAD AND BUTTER 3.10
WITH MEAT BALLS. 3.95
WITH ITALIAN SAUSAGE 4.30

MOSTACCIOLI
WITH GINO'S EAST MEAT SAUCE,
BREAD AND BUTTER. 3.10
WITH MEAT BALLS. 3.95
WITH ITALIAN SAUSAGE . . . 4.30

LASAGNA
BAKED WIDE RIBBONS OF MACARONI
LAYERED WITH RICOTTA CHEESE,
MEAT, EGGS & SAUCE, BREAD
AND BUTTER 3.95
WITH MEAT BALLS. 4.95
WITH ITALIAN SAUSAGE 5.30

RAVIOLI SQUARES
DOUGH FILLED WITH RICOTTA
CHEESE OR MEAT IN OUR MEAT
SAUCE, BREAD AND BUTTER . . 2.95
WITH MEAT BALLS. 3.95
WITH ITALIAN SAUSAGE 4.30

GREEN NOODLES
SERVED WITH OUR HOMEMADE MEAT
SAUCE, BREAD AND BUTTER 3.10
WITH MEAT BALLS. 3.95
WITH ITALIAN SAUSAGE 4.30

EGG NOODLES
SERVED WITH OUR MEAT SAUCE,
BREAD AND BUTTER. 3.10
WITH MEAT BALLS. 3.95
WITH ITALIAN SAUSAGE 4.30

BROILED ITALIAN SAUSAGE
DINNER WITH GINO'S EAST SPECIAL
SAUCE, MILD GREEN PEPPERS,
FRENCH FRIES OR SIDE ORDER OF
SPAGHETTI, BREAD AND BUTTER . . 5.35

ITALIAN BEEF
DINNER WITH NATURAL GRAVY,
FRENCH FRIES OR SIDE ORDER OF
SPAGHETTI, BREAD AND BUTTER . . 5.35

EGG PLANT PARMIGIANA
WITH GINO'S EAST DELICIOUS MEAT
SAUCE, BREAD AND BUTTER 3.95

Chicago
THE GOLDEN OX
German

$$

The Golden Ox is all you think a German restaurant ought to be. For more than a half century, the kitchen has been dishing up everything from hasenpfeffer to zwiebelfleisch, warming the hearts and filling the stomachs of thousands of patrons. An ornate bar sets the tavern theme in the cocktail lounge just off the main entryway. Among the dining areas, I like the Seigfried room with its glowing murals which bring back imagery from the "Ring of the Nibelungen." As a cuisine, German generally tends toward heaviness. But some dishes, particularly veal at the Golden Ox shows a masterfully light touch in its preparation. For instance, veal Frederick is sautéed in butter and served in fresh lemon and parsley sauce. White asparagus and golden spätzle accompany the delicately flavored, tender meat. Still, the general conception of German food is more hearty stokings and the Golden Ox has that, too. Such tastes are easily satisfied with excellent sauerbraten. The marinade has a mild brine aftertaste, obviously the tender beef has been soaked for several days. Pot roast, Bavarian style, is another of the dinners I enjoy. The gravy has a definite mushroom flavor. Potato pancakes and chunky, warm applesauce add to the dining pleasure. The zwiebelfleisch, a traditional roast beef in wine sauce is accompanied by Cheddar cheese and noodles. Roast German-style duckling is served with red cabbage or sauerkraut in a traditional recipe.

THE GOLDEN OX, 1578 North Clayborn Avenue, Chicago. Telephone: 664-0780. Hours: 11 am-10:30 pm, Monday-Saturday; 3 pm-9 pm, Sunday. Cards: AE, MC, VISA. Reservations suggested. Full bar service. Casual dress acceptable. Private party facilities for up to 80 people, including rathskeller with private bar. Valet parking.

K/Rating 17/20 • Food 7/7 • Service 4/6 • Decor 4/4 • Value 2/3

German Specialties

PAPRIKA RAHM SCHNITZEL
*Veal Steak
Cooked in Creamy Wine Sauce,
Fresh Mushrooms, Onions
with Spätzle*
8.95

WIENER ROAST BRATEN
*Prime Beef Tenderloin
Sauted with Mushrooms,
Onions, Red Wine
Butter Noodles*
9.50

ZWIEBELFLEISCH
*Roast Beef – Simmered in
Sherry Wine Sauce with Onions,
Topped with Cheddar Cheese
Noodles*
7.95

WIENER SCHNITZEL
*A Tender Veal Steak
dipped in Egg Batter,
Flaked with Special Breading
Pan Fried in Butter.
Mushroom Sauce,
Home Made Spätzle*
8.95

SAUERBRATEN
*Prime Beef Marinated
in Wine and Vinegar
with it's Own Flavorful Gravy.
Potato Dumpling,
Red Cabbage*
8.50

KASSLER RIPPCHEN
*Lean, Tender Cured and
Smoked Pork Loin
Cooked to Perfection
Burgundy Red Cabbage,
Salz Kartoffel*
7.95

HASENPFEFFER (in season)
*Imported Rabbit
Marinated in Tangy Herbs,
Stewed in Our Own Cream Sauce
Potato Dumpling,
Red Cabbage*
8.50

*Compliment your meal
with a bottle of fine wine.
We have one of the most extensive
wine selections in the country.*

FREDERICK VEAL
*Sauted in Butter, Natural Sauce
with Fresh Lemon and Parsley
Home Made Spätzle,
White Asparagus*
8.95

BAVARIAN VEAL
*The Finest in Veal
Dipped in Flour and Egg only
Sauted in Butter.
Home Made Spätzle,
White Asparagus*
8.95

SCHWEINE KOTTELETEN PANIERT
*Old Fashioned
Breaded Pork Chops
Served with Hot Potato Salad,
Apple Sauce*
7.95

PORK TENDERLOIN
*Sauted with fresh
Mushrooms and Pfifferlings
in Wine Sauce. Wild Rice*
9.50

BAVARIAN POT ROAST
*Fresh Potato Pancakes,
Hot Apple Sauce*
8.50

BRAISED OX TAILS
*Fresh Vegetables
Boiled Potato*
7.50

PORK SHANK
*baked or simmered
Sauerkraut, Boiled Potato*
6.95

BAVARIAN BRATWURST *
*Hot German Potato Salad
Red Cabbage*
6.50

**CRISP ROASTED
YOUNG DUCKLING (half)**
*Red Cabbage or Sauerkraut,
Potato Dumpling*
8.95

BRAISED LAMB-SHANK
Fresh Vegetables, Boiled Potato
7.95

BAKED VEAL-SHANK
*Fresh mixed Vegetables
Spätzle*
8.50

PEPPER STEAK
*Prime Beef Tenderloin
Sauted with Green Peppers,
Mushrooms and Onions,
Butter Noodles*
9.50

**GENUINE VEAL
SWEETBREADS**
*Sauted in Butter
Mushrooms and Slivered Green Onions*
9.50

CALVES LIVER
*Sauted – Bacon or Onions
(from pen fed calves)*
8.50

**BARBEQUED CANADIAN
BABY BACK RIBS**
Golden Ox Sauce
7.95

———•———

*Side Orders:
Two fresh grated Potato Pancakes
Apple Sauce or Sour Cream*
1.50

*Cottage Fries, Lyonnaise,
German Fries*
1.00

Wild Rice 1.50

Chicago
GORDON
Continental

$$$

Add to your basic categories of restaurants—French, Oriental, Trendy, etc.—the new category Skidrow Chic. Gordon occupies what for some 70 years had been a bar and grill in a neighborhood of cheap hotels and transient walkups. The neighborhood is still that way but Gordon is something else again. Rosewood paneling sweeps halfway up the walls toward a nearly 20-foot high ceiling. The rest of the walls and the floor are tiled with an overall effect of steambath-Gothic. Next to a far wall, sitting on its pedestal, is a terra cotta sheepshead with attached moose antlers and a gold crown that is so tastelessly ugly you have to love it at first sight. Gordon's menu is handwritten and changes with the seasons. Appetizers are a standout: Perhaps you will be fortunate enough to visit when steamed mussels in clear sauce ($2.95), artichoke fritters with béarnaise ($2.75) or vegetable terrine with lobster mousse ($3.25) are offered. Each shows a delicacy that captures their perfectly balanced flavors and textures. Soups usually include a fresh vegetable selection such as cream of asparagus ($1.50) or oyster bisque ($2.25). The eclectic menu can offer some unusual surprises. Breast of duckling en croûte ($9.95) is served with prunes, pistachio nuts and port wine sauce. Beef fillet with green pepper maître d'hôtel butter ($11.95) is excellent.

GORDON, 512 North Clark Street, Chicago. Telephone: 467-9780. Hours: 11:30 am-2:30 pm, Tuesday-Friday; Dinner: 5:30 pm-10:30 pm, Tuesday-Thursday; until 11:30 pm, Friday-Saturday; 5:30 pm-9:30 pm, Sunday; Brunch: 11:30 am-3 pm, Sunday. Cards: AE, MC, VISA. Reservations taken. Full bar service. Casual, neat dress acceptable. Private party facilities. Parking lot nearby.

K/Rating 17/20 • Food 6.5/7 • Service 5/6 • Decor 3/4 • Value 2.5/3

Chicago
GREAT GRITZBE'S FLYING FOOD SHOW
American/Eclectic
$$

Gritzbe's is a perfect spot in the general Rush Street and Near North nightclub scene for some casual dining at moderate prices. While waiting for your table, the cocktail lounge offers a unique cheese and cracker bar for your nibbling pleasure. The lounge by the way, has what appears to be a random stair-step design of giant blocks which offer plenty of seating space à la indoor bleachers. Gritzbe's dinner menu ranges widely from omelettes and salads to sandwiches plus more ambitious specialties. For instance, chicken teriyaki ($5.50) is half the bird baked, then broiled to a plump and sweet goodness in teriyaki sauce. Carnivores should be satisfied with either the sirloin or tenderloin of beef ($8.95), served *à la bouquetière* on a plank with an accompanying garden of vegetables. Duck in cherry sauce ($6.50) remains a favorite. Nowhere but at Gritzbe's will you find the French Toast Connection ($2.95), the best thing to happen to bread since it was first sliced. The egg-rich toast is stuffed with chicken salad and cheese, dipped in batter and deep-fried. Pineapple jam and potatoes on the side complete the platter. And who could visit GGFFS without taking a pass or two at the dessert bar? It is $1.75 with dinner, a bit more with sandwiches or à la carte and includes a panoply of fruits, gooey cakes and pastries displayed on an ornate Italian sideboard.

GREAT GRITZBE'S FLYING FOOD SHOW, 21 East Chestnut Street, Chicago. Telephone: 642-3460. Hours: 11:30 am-11:30 pm, Monday-Thursday; until 1 pm, Friday-Saturday; 10:30 am-11:30 pm, Sunday. Cards: AE, MC, VISA. No reservations. Full bar service. Casual dress acceptable. Parking in nearby garages.

K/Rating 17.5/20 • Food 5/7 • Service 6/6 • Decor 4/4 • Value 2.5/3

Chicago
GREEK ISLANDS
Greek

$$

There is no abatement of the partisan rivalry which exists among Chicago's Greek restaurants; it may be even more intense than the rivalry between the Cubs and the Sox. The restaurants proudly advertise their support, plastering windows with letters, photographs and endorsements. There is probably no Greek restaurant in Chicago with as vocal a following as the Greek Islands. The restaurant foreswears most of the gimmicks such as bazoukis and belly dancers; they do have baklava. As with its competitors in the Halsted Street South Greektown area, the food here is abundant and reasonably priced. My lack of enthusiasm displayed in the first edition of *Best Restaurants Chicago* for the fish at Greek Islands has been washed away by subsequent experiences with broiled seabass, served with lots of oregano and lemon and beautifully boned at tableside by a waiter with the dexterity of a cardiac surgeon. In addition to the seafood, you will find the ubiquitous array of Greek foods —braised lamb, loin and leg of lamb, souvlaki, pastitsio, moussaka and all the rest. The combination platters are the best buys; they give you several different foods and lots of it.

GREEK ISLANDS, 766 West Jackson Boulevard, Chicago. Telephone: 782-9855. Hours: 11 am-midnight, Sunday-Thursday; until 1 am, Friday-Saturday. Cards: AE, CB, VISA. Full bar service. No reservations. Free valet parking.

K/Rating 17/20 • Food 5/7 • Service 6/6 • Decor 3/4 • Value 3/3

Soups

Avgolemono (Chicken,
Rice, Egg, Lemon) ..... .60 - .90   Soup du Jour .... .60 - .90

Salads

Horiatiki (Greek HillBilly Salad) ......per person 1.50
Greek Salad (Bowl) ....1.30   Taramosalata 1.35
Greek Salad Platter ....2.40   Boiled Greens 1.60

ENTREES

All Dinners are $2.65 Extra

Dinner includes: Soup, Salad, Dessert and Coffee

Nogatina or Greek Coffee Extra

A La Carte

Braised Lamb Rice 3.95
Braised Lamb Potatoes 3.95
Braised Lamb with Vegetables 3.95

GREEK ISLANDS SPECIALS

Family Style Taramosalata, Saganaki, Salad, Gyros, Roast Lamb, Dolmathes,
Mousaka or Pastichio, Dessert & Coffee (Two or More) ....per person 6.95
Gyros Plate 3.65
Combination Plate (Leg Lamb, Mousaka, Shrimp, V. Leaves, Veg. Pot.) 4.75
Stuffed Vine Leaves (Dolmades) 3.50
Mousaka (Stuffed Egg Plant) 3.50
Pastichio (Stuffed Macaroni) 3.25
Rice Pilaf with Yogurt 2.75
Spanakotiropita (Spinach-Cheese Pie) 3.50
Baked Lima Beans 1.50

Roasts

Special Loin of Lamb 4.95
Roast Leg of Lamb 4.50
Roast Leg of Lamb (Children's Portion) 3.50

From The Broiler

Broiled Lamb Chops ....(2), 6.75; (3) 8.95
Broiled Greek Sausage 3.50
Broiled Pork Chops (2) 4.15
Broiled Steak - N.Y. Sirloin 7.95
Souvlaki - Shishkebab 4.75
Fried Lamb Liver and Sausage 3.50
Fried Lamb Livers 3.50

Beverages

Coffee .... .45   Greek Coffee .... .60
Sanka .... .45   Milk .... .45
Tea .... .45   Soft Drinks .... .45

Home-Made Desserts

All Fruits in Season

Baklava .... .75   Famous Nogatina Special 1.00
Creme Caramele .... .75   Galaktobouriko .... .75
Rice Pudding .... .75

Chicago
HALF SHELL
Seafood   **$**

While other restaurants may have opted for trendy decor, the Half Shell continues to go about like a free spirit. Tucked in a basement without a sign visible out front, you really have to search this one out. But the quarry is worth the quest. The Half Shell is above all else a neighborhood place, but among those who know, it seems to include the entire Chicago area as its neighborhood. Big spenders will find two ounces of caviar for $9 which can be washed down with Heidsieck champagne for another $12. But the Half Shell is noteworthy for its budget dinners and sandwiches. Two people can still eat for about $10 to $12. The Mulligan stew is a standard of the species. Served in a cast-metal cooking platter, it is chockfull of clams, whole shrimp, perch and vegetables—all mulled together in a delicious and filling broth. Six dollars will get you batter-fried or steamed jumbo shrimp; $5.70 brings frogs' legs seemingly right out of Calaveras county. A combination platter brings a goodly mix of shrimp, frogs' legs, oysters, clams plus smelts and perch when in season. Confirmed carnivores will relish the Turkish shish kebab for $4.80. Service can be annoyingly slow at times, but the Half Shell is a good place to linger with a friend or lover.

HALF SHELL, 576 West Diversey Avenue, Chicago. Telephone: 549-1773. Hours: 11:30 am-1 am, daily. No cards. No reservations. Full bar service. Casual dress acceptable. Parking garage nearby.

K/Rating 16.5/20 • Food 6.5/7 • Service 4/6 • Decor 3/4 • Value 3/3

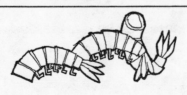

Chicago
HAMBURGER HAMLET
American $

It is amazing how many people are willing to pay nearly $5
for a hamburger. Now, I am not willing to say that Marilyn
and Harry Lewis' West Coast hamburger chain has done the
best thing for burgers since the invention of mustard, cat-
sup and relish, but there is a certain panache about the
place. Sure, Hamburger Hamlet caught the fancy of Chicago's "beautiful people," but let's not shortchange the
Hamlet merely because it is "ground-round-chic." Some of
the creations are really very good with touches of original-
ity. And there is no question that service and surroundings
take you and your burger buns beyond the realm of the
ordinary. What we essentially have here is a multi-million
dollar practical joke. The restaurant is a high ceilinged, large
room reminiscent of a well kept turn-of-the-century men's
bar and grill. There is fashionable use of dark woods, gas
lamp period fixtures, white mosaic tile floors and similar
accoutrements. Waiters, who seem to have a keen sense of
how to perform their functions (yet, with a sense that all
we really are talking about are hamburgers and booze, plus
a few side dishes) are attired in tuxedo trousers, white shirt,
galluses and black tie. There is grand overstatement in the
entire presentation, from decor to menu. The joke of
course, is that beneath it all lies the preparation and con-
sumption of America's number one short-order food–the
hamburger. Burgers come in regular and larger sizes and
include either French fries or a rather nice salad when you
order the biggie. Some pretty good soups serve as a neat
prelude. Or order a platter of tidbits that includes four large
fried chicken wings, four crisply fried zucchini circles and
four fried oysters which hold plenty of succulence inside
their crispy coatings. Hot dog fanatics will find some foot-
long choices and there is a whole page of the elaborate
menu turned over to egg dishes, steaks and other specialties.
I don't always go wild over dessert but the delicious hot

apple pie with thick rum butterscotch sauce and a scoop of cinnamon ice cream really hits the spot. The Hamburger Hamlet also has an elaborate New Orleans-style Sunday brunch that has become tremendously popular with Chicagoans and their guests.

HAMBURGER HAMLET, 44 East Walton Street, Chicago. Telephone: 649-6601. Hours: 11:30 am-11 pm, Monday-Thursday; until midnight, Friday-Saturday; noon-11 pm, Sunday. Cards: AE, DC, MC, VISA. No reservations. Full bar service. Casual dress acceptable. Parking in nearby garages.

K/Rating 17.5/20 • Food 5.5/7 • Service 6/6 • Decor 4/4 • Value 2/3

Chicago
HOUSE OF BERTINI
Steaks/American/Italian $$

This trim little restaurant continues to do what it has done well since the 1930s—serve good dinners at reasonable prices. The present proprietor, John Rossi, is a grandson of the original Mr. Bertini. In fact, the Rossis live above the restaurant in its stylish two-floor Italianesque building. My favorite selections here are the steaks, choice rather than prime in most cases, but excellent values. Should you prefer one of the tasty Italian specialties, try subtle veal à la lemon, chicken cacciatore in its full-flavored tomato sauce or hearty veal Parmigiana. For a convenient and pleasant dinner spot, House of Bertini is the place.

HOUSE OF BERTINI, 535 North Wells Street, Chicago. Telephone: 644-1397. Hours: Lunch: 11:30 am-2:30 pm, Monday-Saturday; Dinner: 5 pm-11:30 pm, Monday-Saturday. Cards: AE, MC. Full bar service. Casual dress acceptable. Parking nearby.

K/Rating 17/20 • Food 5/7 • Service 6/6 • Decor 3/4 • Value 3/3

Complete Dinner Menu

Appetizers (Choice of One)

Soup — Tomato Juice — Spaghetti

Extra Cut T-Bone (24 oz.)	10.25
Large T-Bone (18 oz.)	9.25
Extra Cut Sirloin (16 oz.)	9.00
Sirloin (12 oz.)	8.25
Filet Mignon (9 oz.)	9.00
Junior Filet Mignon (6 oz.)	7.75
Loin Pork Chops (2)	6.75
Loin Lamb Chops (2)	7.50
Pan Fried Chicken (½)	5.75
Chicken a la Cacciatora	6.25
Calf's Liver & Bacon	6.00
Chicken Parmigiana	6.25
Veal Parmigiana	7.75
Broiled Fresh White Fish	7.25
Veal ala Lemon	7.75

Tossed Salad — *French, Thousand Island, Oil & Vinegar
or Garlic (French or Bleu Cheese 50¢ extra)*

Vegetable and Cottage Fried Potatoes

Desserts

Spumoni
Vanilla Ice Cream
Bisque Tortoni
Chocolate Sundae
Homemade Cheese Cake - $1.25

Chicago
HOUSE OF HUNAN
Regional Chinese

$$

Chinese cuisine may be the world's oldest and most diversified: it can be dark and subtle, hot and fiery, light and almost playful. Drawing from the cooking of all the major regions of China, the food at the House of Hunan on Michigan Avenue can be all this and perhaps more. Shrimp toast practically bursts with succulence. Among other appetizers, barbecued beef is a delicious blend of seasoning that leaves a semi-sweet aftertaste on the tongue. The Chinese do not ignore cold appetizers, nor should you. Marinated beef is tantalizing with the complex flavor of five-spice. Bean curd, almost like cold chicken, tendrils of jellyfish much like transparent starch noodles, drunken chicken chilled in wine sauce, all give display to the Chinese penchant for pleasurable tastes and textures. With 19 separate appetizer selections, the temptation is to stay with the tidbits, but leaf through the detailed menu and savor more.

CHA LIU TZU CHEE – Empress Chicken *(Szechwan)* **6.95**
Chicken pieces dipped in egg batter and lightly fried, then sauteed with vegetables in secret sauce with dash of hot oil

CH'EN P'I CHEE – Orange Chicken *(Hunan)* **6.95**
HOT! Diced chicken breast, sauteed with orange peel in spicy sauce

SUNG TZU YÜ CHÜAN – Yellow Pike with Pine Nuts *(Shanghai)* . **7.25**
*Fillets of yellow pike, deep fried with pine nuts
Served in sweet and sour sauce*

SUNG TZU HSIA JEN – Shrimp with Pine Nuts *(Shanghai)*. **7.25**
Stir-fried shrimp with pine nuts and hot peppers

You may rave about sliced leg of lamb Hunan. The tender meat is served in a sauce that teases with Oriental peppers and scallions. Yet seasonings are held in check without destroying a complex balance. Shrimp Hunan is another recommended choice. Milder is Shanghai pike, bits of fish fillets prepared with egg whites for a silken texture, then served with vegetables in a delicate white wine sauce. Beef with broccoli is a pleasure, too. Vegetarians should enjoy any of several mixed vegetable preparations.

Note: House of Hunan on Michigan Avenue has no connection with the House of Hunan on Lincoln Avenue, q.v.

HOUSE OF HUNAN, 535 North Michigan Avenue, Chicago. Telephone: 329-9494. Hours: 11:30 am-10:30 pm, daily. Cards: AE, DC, MC, VISA. Reservations recommended. Full bar service. Casual, neat dress acceptable. Private party facilities for up to 60 people.

K/Rating 19/20 • Food 7/7 • Service 6/6 • Decor 3/4 • Value 3/3

HU NAN LA JOU – Smoked Pork *(Hunan)* 6.50
HOT! Preserved pork, typical of western regional cooking, sauteed with scallions and red peppers

HUA JOU PIEN – Pork with Cucumbers *(Szechwan)* 6.50
Slices of pork tenderloin, sauteed with cucumbers

TS'UNG PAO YANG JOU – Mandarin Lamb *(Peking)* 7.25
Stir-fried lamb with scallions in mild brown sauce

HU NAN YANG JOU – Leg of Lamb Hunan *(Hunan)* 7.25
HOT! Marinated leg of lamb, sliced and cooked with scallions in spicy hot pepper sauce

HUNG YAN NIU LI'O – Willow Beef *(Hunan)* 7.95
HOT! Slices of beef, sauteed in hot sauce, garnished with water cress

Chicago
HOUSE OF HUNAN
Chinese

$$

Under new ownership since the first edition of *Best Restaurants Chicago,* House of Hunan has still kept up its quality and value. The restaurant is in no way connected with the House of Hunan on Michigan Avenue, q.v., although they do share many similarities in the approach to Mandarin and Hunan cuisines. The original House of Hunan is in the same location, up a flight of stairs on the second floor of a commercial building just south of the intersections of Lincoln, Belmont, and Ashland. The restaurant is a good one to visit for both those diners new to exotic Chinese foods as well as the seasoned veterans of the subject. Classic preparations include shark's fin soup and Peking duck. The Peking duck is one of the best preparations in the city; the presentation is as visually exciting as is the complexity of flavors and textures. Remember to telephone ahead at least a day in advance if you plan to order the Peking duck. Less expensive, yet still delicious are the various appetizers, including steamed and fried dumplings. Another outstanding selection is beef with jade nan, chunks of fresh broccoli stir-fried with the meat in a sugar, soy and ginger-based sauce. Ask your waiter to provide specific suggestions for mild to highly seasoned choices. For the most fun, go with a group of hungry people and order from a wider selection. As the menu notes, no MSG is used in the preparation of food at this House of Hunan.

HOUSE OF HUNAN, 3150 North Lincoln Avenue, Chicago. Telephone: 327-0427. Hours: 11:30 am-10 pm, Sunday-Thursday; until 11 pm, Friday-Saturday. Reservations recommended. Cards: AE, DC, MC, VISA. Full bar service. Casual dress acceptable. Private party facilities for up to 60 people. Ample parking.

K/Rating 17.5/20 • Food 7/7 • Service 6/6 • Decor 2.5/4 • Value 2/3

Chicago
HUNGARIAN RESTAURANT
Hungarian
$

The atmosphere at Hungarian Restaurant has changed from the old days when it was like walking into a friend's kitchen where soup bubbled on the stove, meat simmered in the oven and the smell of rich seasonings hung in the air. Now there are Hungarian travel posters, a plastic grape trellis and red walls. But the food is as good as ever in this homey storefront restaurant with its 13 tables and a style sometimes less than polished. You won't spend a lot of money here and the Hungarian fare is splendid. The combination platter, as in other ethnic restaurants, is always a good choice for the novice. Of the entrées, the chicken paprikash is one of my favorites. The house salad is rather timid, but the desserts are excellent. Don't miss the palacsintas, the Hungarian version of French crêpes, wrapped around a filling of apricot preserves and sprinkled lightly on top with confectioners' sugar.

HUNGARIAN RESTAURANT, 4146 North Lincoln Avenue, Chicago. Telephone: 248-1003. Hours: 5 pm-10 pm, daily. No cards. Reservations taken. Full bar service. Casual dress acceptable. Parking on street.

K/Rating 16.5/20 • Food 5.5/7 • Service 5/6 • Decor 3/4 • Value 3/3

Chicago
JASANDS
American

$

The common practice among the big money restaurant developers who take over large, old mansions is to convert them into elaborate settings for the service of French or Continental foods. It is rather refreshing to see an alternative approach at Jasands. The architectural integrity of this old McCormick family mansion inside and out has, by and large, been preserved. There is highly polished wood molding and trim amidst dim lighting, but not everything is old. In fact, the cocktail lounge and dining rooms have a decidedly "hip" feel. And while there always seems to be room for one more good French restaurant in an old mansion, what we have at Jasands instead is a contemporary menu including omelettes, seafood, beef, chicken and a celebrated hamburger known as the Motherlode. The Motherlode is served virtually any way you want it, including your selection of cheese and any of several toppings, on black bread, bun or onion roll. And, as with all the dinners, the Motherlode may be ordered accompanied by unlimited trips to the salad bar. I know it has become fashionable among some to sniff at salad bars, but when properly set up, such as at Jasands, they can be a pleasurable part of the dining experience. Among other dinner choices you can find excellent barbecued beef ribs for $6.25, equally succulent sirloin teriyaki for $8.25 and assorted other cuts of beef, poultry and occasional fresh fish selections.

JASANDS, 720 North Rush Street, Chicago. Telephone: 787-2701. Hours: Lunch: 11:30 am-3 pm, Monday-Saturday; Dinner: 5 pm-10:30 pm, Monday-Thursday; until 12:30 pm, Friday-Saturday; 4:30 pm-9:30 pm, Sunday. Cards: AE, MC, VISA. No reservations. Full bar service. Casual dress acceptable. Parking nearby.

K/Rating 18/20 • Food 6/7 • Service 5/6 • Decor 4/4 • Value 3/3

CHICKEN FLORENTINE $6.95
Breast of chicken stuffed with cream spinach and
topped with crab meat and sauce hollandaise

CHICKEN TERIYAKI $5.95
Marinated breast of chicken broiled with vegetables and
served over specially prepared rice

CHICKEN AND SHRIMP TEMPURA $7.95
Dipped in our light tempura batter deep fried and served
with sweet and sour sauce and cocktail sauce

Crab Legs .... Market Price
Alaskan King Crab Legs steamed and served with rice
and drawn butter — serving approximately a pound —
salad bar, vegetable or potato, bread and butter included

TROUT TERIYAKI $7.25
Fresh lake trout marinated in a special teriyaki sauce and
char-broiled—served with rice pilaf—in season.

BOSTON SCROD $7.25
Fresh scrod lightly breaded and baked with butter

Sea and Lake Fish Specials .... Market Price
We will serve two to three fish specials nightly —
serving fresh fish unless not available — to insure the
fresh quality you would expect, specials will be served on
a limited basis — includes salad bar, loaf of bread
and butter

FILET NEPTUNE $9.75
Filet char-broiled to your taste topped with artichoke heart, crab
meat and finally hollandaise sauce.

SIRLOIN TERIYAKI $8.95
10 oz. (approx.) sirloin marinated in our teriyaki sauce and charcoal
broiled to your specifications.

FILET $8.75
7 oz. (approx.) filet — charcoal broiled.

Chicago
JOVAN
French

$$$

Jovan Trboyevic sold his namesake restaurant a couple of years ago to his maître d' Dieter Ahrens; but rest easily, all is as it should be. The food and service are impeccable although I have always been bothered by a feeling that tables are a little too close together. An à la carte luncheon menu has been initiated by the new management. At dinner the menu is verbal. The cuisine is classic French with such regular specialties as duck in green peppercorn sauce, veal scallopini in Dijon mustard sauce, baby lamb chops with fresh dill sauce and other meats such as beef Perigord. Beautiful seafood selections are highlighted by red snapper in a white wine and sorrel cream sauce, trout Veronique and salmon en croûte with lobster sauce. The complete dinner is $16.50 and includes a choice of four soups, ten appetizers, salad, coffee and dessert. The Grand Marnier soufflé has been a house specialty for years.

JOVAN, 16 East Huron Street, Chicago. Telephone: 944-7766. Hours: Lunch: noon-2:30 pm, Monday-Friday; Dinner: 5:30 pm-midnight, Monday-Saturday. Cards: AE, DC. Reservations required. Full bar service. Coats and ties required for men. Private party facilities for lunch only. Valet parking.

K/Rating 18.5/20 • Food 7/7 • Service 5.5/6 • Decor 3/4 • Value 3/3

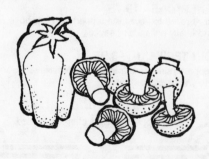

Chicago
KAMEHACHI
Japanese

$$

Those who know say Kamehachi has the best sushi bar in or around Chicago, without exception. I know of one person who went in for lunch one afternoon and consumed 36 seaweed-and-rice rolls, which may be a bit extreme, but it demonstrates something beyond gluttony, I suppose. Seated around the sushi bar at Kamehachi you can watch the sushi master at work, wielding his precision cutlery with samuri-sword precision, dicing up bits of fish, working the rice balls together, wrapping them in seaweed. Even the neophyte will find the initiation to sushi an appetizing experience. If pickled eel sounds like a bit more than you are ready for, try sashimi, the delicious belly of fresh tuna, eaten in a semi-sweet soy sauce or perhaps with a bit of horseradish. In any case, over the centuries, the Japanese have made an art of raw fish preparation and consumption. Sushi is just part of the Kamehachi story—also present are tempura, yakitori, teriyaki, sukiyaki—all traditional Japanese dishes prepared here with no compromise. With more and more Japanese businessmen traveling to Chicago, you can bet there is a pretty good reason why so many of them seek out the pleasures of Kamehachi again and again.

KAMEHACHI, 1617 North Wells Street, Chicago. Telephone: 664-3663. Hours: Lunch: noon-2 pm, Tuesday-Saturday; Dinner: 5 pm-11 pm, Tuesday-Thursday; until midnight, Friday-Saturday; 4 pm-10 pm, Sunday. Cards: AE, MC, VISA. Reservations required. Full bar service. Discount parking in American Towers Garage.

K/Rating 18.5/20 • Food 6.5/7 • Service 6/6 • Decor 3.5/4 • Value 2.5/3

Chicago
KASZTELANKA
Polish

$

Visiting Kasztelanka is like dropping in on a European café.
The barroom is a gathering place for students, workers and
others who enjoy each other's company and conversation.
The lingua franca is Polish in this solid ethnic neighborhood
of Northwest Side Chicago. An extensive menu features
such Polish specialties as pierogis filled with meat, cheese,
even fruit. The soups are excellent, highlighted by a superb
mushroom and the classic czarnina made from fresh duck's
blood, sweetened with plums, and served with raisins and
noodles in the broth. The Polish combination platter offers
a wide taste of sausages, dumplings, blintzes, meat and even
pastry. Among the more than two dozen dinner entrées
offered each evening, veal gets hearty treatment in several
fashions. Roast duck in wine is a traditional favorite. Chick-
en Kiev is a product of Kasztelanka's spotless kitchen, not
some outside purveyor who flash freezes and sells them by
the box.

KASZTELANKA, 3129 North Milwaukee Avenue, Chicago.
Telephone: 588-6662. Hours: 11 am-11 pm, daily. No
cards. No reservations. Full bar service. Casual dress acceptable. Limited street parking.

K/Rating 18/20 • Food 6/7 • Service 5/6 • Decor 4/4 • Value 3/3

DANIA OBIADOWE (DINNERS)

	ALA CARTE	DINNERS
POLEDWICA WOLOWA Z PIECZARKAMI I CEBULA Beef Steak with Mushrooms and Onions	$ 5⁵⁰	$ 6⁵⁰
BRYZOL CIELECY-WIEPRZOWY-WOLOWY Z PIECZARKAMI Bryzol – Veal Pork or Beef with Mushrooms	5³⁰	6³⁰
SZNYCEL PO "WIEDENSKU" Vienna Schnitzel	5³⁰	6³⁰
KOTLET CIELECY Z PIECZARKAMI Veal Cutlet with Mushrooms	5²⁰	6²⁰
KOTLET SCHABOWY SAUTÉ Z PIECZARKAMI I CEBULA Pork Cutlet with Mushrooms and Onions	4⁵⁰	5⁵⁰
KOTLET SCHABOWY Z KAPUSTA Pork Cutlet with Sauerkraut	3⁹⁰	4⁹⁰
SZTUKA MIESA W SOSIE CHRZANOWYM – KOPERKOWYM Beef in Horseradish or Dill Sauce	4⁰⁰	5⁰⁰
WOLOWINA W SOSIE WLASNYM Roast Beef in Gravy	4²⁰	5²⁰
RYBA SMAZONA LUB SAUTÉ Fried or Saute Fish	3⁶⁰	4⁶⁰
GOLONKA Z KAPUSTA Pork Shank with Sauerkraut	3⁸⁰	4⁸⁰
KURA GOTOWANA LUB PIECZONA Chicken – Boiled or Fried	3⁶⁰	4⁶⁰
KACZKA PIECZONA Roast Duck in Wine	5⁹⁵	6⁹⁵
ZEBERKA PIECZONE ZE SLIWKAMI Baked Ribs with Plums	3⁹⁰	4⁹⁰
KOTLET MIELONY Meat Loaf	3⁶⁰	4⁶⁰
KIELBASA Z KAPUSTA LUB CHRZANEM Sausage with Cabbage or Horseradish	3⁵⁰	4⁵⁰
POLSKI TALERZ Polish Platter (Food Assortment)	5⁹⁰	6⁹⁰
GOLABKI Stuffed Cabbage	3⁹⁰	4⁹⁰
PAPRYKARZ CIELECY Z KOPYTKAMI Veal in Red Pepper Gravy with Dumplings	4⁶⁰	5⁶⁰
RUMSZTYK WOLOWY Beef Cutlet with Onions and Mushrooms	5⁵⁰	6⁵⁰
KOTLET DEVOLAILE Breaded Chicken Kiev	4²⁰	5²⁰
SZTUFADA WOLOWA Roast Beef and Gravy	4⁴⁰	5⁴⁰
ESKALOPKI CIELECE Special Breaded Veal Cutlet	5²⁰	6²⁰
ANTRYKOT Z KURY Breaded Chicken Cutlet	4²⁰	5²⁰
KOTLET SCHABOWY PO PARYSKU Breaded Pork Cutlet a'la Paris	4²⁰	5²⁰
KLOPSIKI W SOSIE PIECZARKOWYM Polish Meatloaf with Mushroom Gravy (Veal & Chicken)	4⁰⁰	5⁰⁰
WATROBKA WIEPRZOWA DUSZONA Beef Chicken or Pork Liver – Stewed	4¹⁰	5¹⁰
OZORKI W SOSIE CHRZANOWYM Beef Tongue with Horseradish Gravy	4⁰⁰	5⁰⁰

KENESSEY'S
Hungarian/Continental

\$\$

When was the last time you dined in a wine cellar? I don't mean anything cold, clammy and cobwebbed, but rather, a warm and inviting room lined with fine bottles of the vintner's art. That rather describes Kenessey's. Food service is fairly new to Ivan and Kathy Kenessey's establishment which started out as a wine, pastry and gourmet specialty shop. But now reasonably priced and imaginative meals are served with vigor. The emphasis is on Hungarian and Middle European food, although you will find a seafood crêpe called the Cozumel, named after the Kenessey's favorite vacation spot. Beef gulyas is an excellent example of Hungarian cooking. Here it is served as a lusty entrée with sour cream. Technically, gulyas is a soup, not a stew, but there is little point in quibbling in semantics when the final results turn out so well. Whatever you decide to order, do not miss kerotzit for an appetizer. This is the traditional Hungarian cheese spread accented with paprika and eaten on a hard

SALADS

CHICKEN FESTIVAL, Curried Chicken Salad made with a
special Dressing, Mayonnaise, Apples and Celery,
accompanied with Freshly Cut Fruits of the season
on a bed of Lettuce $3.95

KENESSEY SALAD, Fresh Vegetables with Ham, Cheese,
Roast Beef, Mushrooms, Eggs and Caviar. $3.95

QUICHE LORAINE, A wonderfully light Ham and Cheese
combination baked in a delicious pie crust surrounded
with the Fruits of the season $3.95

A QUICHE LORAINE VEGETARIAN. $5.50

CREPES

THE ORIGINAL HAM & CHEESE CREPE, Imported Hungarian Ham, cheese,
green peppers, combined with sour cream, spices and then
rolled in a delicate crepe $3.95

THE GREEN MISTRESS, Spinach kissed by the garlic clove, bedded
in a cream sauce and blanketed in the most delicate of crepes
and covered with a fluffy coverlet of delicate smoked swiss. $3.50

THE GYPSY CREPE! "Cigány Palacsinta" Sirloin, chopped as only
Gypsies can, with mushrooms, peppers and onions embraced
by the bouquet of a fine burgundy. $4.50

CHICKEN VIENNESE CREPE, A very unique mixture of chicken, green
peppers, onions, pimentos, mushrooms and celery smothered
in a thick chicken gravy, cooked with dillweed and other
spices and wrapped into two crepes. A Specialty!. $3.95

COZUMEL SEAFOOD CREPE, Shrimp, crabmeat and scallops is steamed
to perfection, folded into a sherry mushroom sauce, then
rolled in two delicate crepes. $5.95

APPLE PALACSINTA, An old favorite. Traditional apple, cinnamon
and walnut filling folded in a thin crepe topped with
whipped cream (one crepe). $2.25

cracker. Nor should you pass by the pastry and strudel selection for desserts. Kenessey's has not ignored its role as a wine shop. As such, they have a unique policy: you may order any of their retail stock with dinner for the regular shelf price plus a one-dollar corkage fee, which means that you can drink some of the finest wines in the world at well under the double or triple mark-up that restaurants usually charge. By the way, on Thursday evenings the restaurant holds a seven-course wine tasting dinner (by reservation only). At a recent price of $14.95 per person it is an astounding value and a marvelous way to learn about good foods and wine together.

KENESSEY'S, 403 West Belmont Avenue (in the Hotel Belmont), Chicago. Telephone: 929-7500. Hours: 11 am-11 pm, Monday-Thursday; until midnight, Friday-Saturday; noon-9 pm, Sunday. Cards: MC, VISA. Reservations taken. Full bar service. Casual dress acceptable. Valet parking at Sheridan Road entrance.

K/Rating 16/20 • Food 5.5/7 • Service 5/6 • Decor 2.5/4 • Value 3/3

ENTREES

HUNGARIAN BEEF GULYASH, Here the Kenessey Family shares with you their own special family recipe for their native land's Gulyash. Choice Beef Cubes marinated and cooked with Onions, Tomatoes, Green Peppers and Mushrooms, then simmered with a special Burgundy and Sour Cream served with Spatzels or rice (Jo Etvagyat). $6.95

CHICKEN ALA VIENNESE, A very unique mixture of chicken, green peppers, onions, pimentos, mushrooms and celery smothered in a thick chicken gravy, cooked with dillweed and other spices, served over a bed of rice. $4.95

"GOMBA LETCHO" A MEDLEY OF DELIGHTS, The meeting of sweet green peppers with onions, mushrooms and tomatoes starring the ubiquitous Hungarian sausage in a paprika sauce, (served over rice), that only can be created by a native Magyar. $4.95

(FOR OUR VEGETARIAN FRIENDS) $3.95

THE "COZUMEL", From the romantic island of Cozumel comes this special seafood recipe. Crabmeat, scallops and shrimp is steamed to perfection then folded into a Sherry Mushroom Cream Sauce, served with rice and vegetable of the day $7.95

BEEF STROGANOFF, Tender slices of choice beef cooked in an authentic Russian sour cream sauce with fresh mushrooms, and simmered in Burgundy, served with buttered noodles and vegetable of the day $7.95

SZÉKELY GULYÁS, "The Transylvanian version of a Hungarian Gulyás". A culinary secret from Transylvania, tender morsels of choice pork lean smoked ham and smoked Hungarian sausage (kolbász). Simmered during the daylit hours to be served after nightfall on a bed of champagne soaked sauerkraut and seasoned with our famous Hungarian paprika. $5.95

Chicago
KHYBER INDIA RESTAURANT
Indian

$$

Khyber offers authentic Indian dining just off busy Rush Street. From the subtropical regions of India come highly seasoned curry dishes. From the north comes the tandoori style of roasting yogurt-marinated meats and poultry in large clay urns over charcoal. The three combination dinners ($6.95 or $7.95) offer the best values and widest taste selections. Begin with a chicken-stock-based mulligatawny soup and continue through with tastes of curried boned chicken, tandoori-roasted lamb or chicken, perhaps some fish and lamb in a mild gravy, called rogan josh. Gosht pasanda, lamb marinated in spiced yogurt is my favorite. Khyber also reflects India's ancient vegetarian tradition. Unusual and tasty breads may be flat, unleavened or puffy. Desserts tend to be very sweet. Particularly good is rasmalai, made from cottage cheese and sweetened condensed milk.

Note: Khyber also has a suburban branch at 954 West Lake Street in Oak Park (848-1710).

KHYBER INDIA RESTAURANT, 50 East Walton Street, Chicago. Telephone: 649-9060. Hours: Lunch: 11:30 am-2:30 pm, Monday-Friday; noon-3 pm, Saturday-Sunday; Dinner: from 5:30 pm, daily. Cards: AE, CB, DC, VISA. Reservations requested. Full bar service. Private party facilities for 50 to 100 people. Discount parking in Huguellette Garage.

K/Rating 16.5/20 • Food 7/7 • Service 4.5/6 • Decor 2.5/4 • Value 2.5/3

TANDOOR
CLAY OVEN PREPARATIONS

TANDOORI MURGH . . . . HALF — three fifty
Chicken marinated in yogurt and spices, cooked on charcoal FULL — six twenty five
in clay ovens

MURGH TIKKA . . . . four seventy five
Boneless chicken pieces cooked in clay oven

BOTI KABAB . . . . four seventy five
Cubed leg of lamb roasted in clay oven

SEIKH KABAB . . . . four seventy five
Minced lamb mixed with onions, herbs, spices, hand rolled on
skewers and cooked in clay ovens

TANDOORI MACHHLI . . . . seven dollars
Wholepomfret mildly spiced and baked in clay oven

MACHHLI TIKKA . . . . four seventy five
Boneless fish pieces roasted in clay oven

TANDOORI MIXED GRILL . . . . six ninety five
An assortment of Tandoori Chicken, and various other Tikkas
and Kababs

SIFARISHE MURG
CHICKEN SUGGESTIONS

MURGH KHYBER . . . . four seventy five
Chicken cooked with diced potatoes, mushrooms, sweet pepper,
and a secret blend of spices and herbs

MURGH MUSSALAM . . . . four seventy five
Tender chicken cooked in cream, served with boild egg and
mushrooms

MURGH MAKHANI . . . . four seventy five
Boneless Tandoori Chicken cooked with Indian spices, chopped
tomatoes and butter —*highly recommended*

MURGH SHAHI . . . . four seventy five
Chunks of chicken cooked with green pepper, onions and
tomatoes

KHASTA GOSHT
LAMB SPECIALTIES

ROGAN JOSH . . . . four seventy five
Cubes of lamb cooked in mild gravy

GOSHT PASANDA . . . . four seventy five
Lamb marinated in yogurt and cooked with tangy muglai spices

NARGISI KOFTA . . . . four seventy five
Minced lamb balls stuffed with eggs in a succulent gravy

PALAK GOSHT . . . . four seventy five
Spicy lamb cooked with creamed spinach

LAMB VINDALLU . . . . four ninety five
Lamb cooked hot with coconut. A South Indian Delight.

SUMANDRI KHAASIYAT
SEAFOOD DELICACIES

JHINGA PATIA . . . . five thirty five
Jumbo shrimp cooked, fried in herbs

JHINGA MASALA . . . . five thirty five
Shrimps cooked with green peppers, onions, in a curry sauce

FISH CURRY ala GOANESE . . . . five thirty five
Fish cooked as in a famous Goanese recipe, coconut based,
with herbs and spices

LA CHEMINÉE
French

$$$

La Cheminée must be one of the most romantic spots in town for your special rendezvous. The restaurant oozes coziness, although it remains true that on busy evenings that special intimacy can be lost. The restaurant adopted a new menu some months ago, discarding its prix fixe policy for à la carte dining. You will discover some fine treatment of familiar standards such as quiche Lorraine or baked clams among appetizers. Stuffed avocado is not to be missed; similarly, crab-stuffed artichoke bottoms do not lack succulent goodness. Selections of fish and main courses leave nothing to be desired. The poached turbot is as fine as turbot can be; choron sauce adds a bit of color to the béarnaise née Hollandaise. Stuffed Cornish hen will appeal to smaller, delicate appetites; beef Wellington attracts the lustier diner. The magnificent wine list and the well managed kitchen are two of the reasons that La Cheminée has come to the forefront of better dining establishments in Chicago. This is a restaurant that serious diners dare not overlook.

LA CHEMINÉE, 1161 North Dearborn Street, Chicago. Telephone: 642-6654. Hours: 5:30 pm-11:30 pm, Monday-Saturday. Cards: AE, CB, DC, MC, VISA. Reservations suggested. Full bar service. Private party facilities for up to 45 people. Discount parking in Elm Plaza Garage.

K/Rating 18/20 • Food 6.5/7 • Service 6/6 • Decor 3.5/4 • Value 2/3

La Cheminée
The Charm of Countryside France

Poissons

Sole Amandine (Dover Sole with Almonds, Sauted) $12.00
Turbot Poché (Poached Turbot, Sauce Hollandaise or Choron) $13.75
Homard à l'Américaine (Lobster in Brandy Sauce) $14.50
Cuisses de Grenouilles Provençale
(Frog Legs, Sauted, Tomato-Garlic Sauce) $8.50
Mousse de Saumon (Salmon Mousse with Two Sauces) $10.00
Coquille St. Jacques, Beurre Nantaise
(Poached Scallops in Butter Sauce) $9.25

Volaille

Coq au Vin A L'Ancienne (Chicken in Red Wine) $7.50
Canard à l'Orange Flambé
(Roast Duck in Orange Sauce Flamed in Brandy) $8.50
Pigeonneaux Farci
(Cornish Hen Stuffed with Fois Gras and Wild Rice) $9.50

Viande

Boeuf Wellington
(Tenderloin in Pastry Crust, Sauce Périgueux) $10.75
Steak au Poivre (French Pepper Steak,
Madagascar Sauce, Flamed in Brandy) $9.75
Veau Piccata
(Veal Medaillons Sauted with Lemon and Capers) $8.50
Veau Florentine (Veal with Spinach in Cream Sauce, Glazed) $8.75
Côtes d'Agneau (Broiled Lamb Chops) $10.50
Entrecôte Grillée (Broiled Sirloin Steak) $9.25
Tournedos Béarnaise (Filet Mignon with Béarnaise Sauce) $9.50
Châteaubriand Bouquetière de Légumes
(Double Filet Mignon with Garden Vegetables) for two $21.00
Carré d'Agneau (Rack of Lamb) $11.75
La Brochette de Filet Maison
(Beef Tenderloin Broiled on Skewer) $8.75

Desserts

Crème Caramel $1.50
Mousse au Chocolat $1.50
Pêche Melba $2.00
Fraises Melba $2.25
Glaces $1.25
Fraises au Kirsch $2.25

Cheminée Sundae $1.75
Gâteau au Fromage $1.50
Crêpes Suzettes Grand Marnier
for two $6.00
Patisseries du Jour $1.50
Fraises Romanoff for two $6.50

Chicago
LA CHOZA
Mexican

$

In a down-at-the-heels neighborhood, La Choza is yet another proof of that Chicago axiom: Location means little to a restaurant's success. La Choza just happens to be "the" Mexican restaurant for taco and tortilla buffs. This place is so authentic I am almost tempted to bring my own water. Fortunately, the water's fine, so eat with gusto, but be prepared for some spicy seasonings. For appetizers, Mexican pizzas called kamoosh are real favorites; the garlic soup is also a winner, and guaranteed to keep away vampires. Mole de pollo with its bittersweet chocolate aftertaste, is a good choice among the main courses. Among the desserts, the flan for one dollar is numero uno.

LA CHOZA, 7630 North Paulina Street, Chicago. Telephone: 761-8020/465-9401. Hours: 11:30 am-11 pm, Tuesday-Thursday; until 11:30 pm, Friday; until midnight, Saturday; noon-10 pm, Sunday. No cards. No bar; you may bring your own. Reservations taken for groups of six or more. Free parking at 1145 West Howard, across from the bowling alley.

K/Rating 18/20 • Food 7/7 • Service 5/6 • Decor 3/4 • Value 3/3

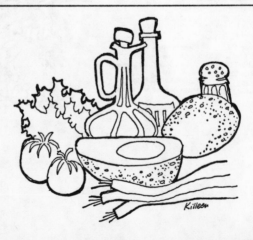

Appetizers

KAMOOSH, for two .... $1.75   for four $2.25
Mexico's threat to the pizza

GUACAMOLE $1.65
Avocado dip served with corn chips

CHORIZELA $2.15
A tasteful melted cheese garnished with our fresh
CHORIZO (Mexican Sausage)

CHOZALOTE $1.95
Grilled Mexican hard roll, spread with beans and
topped with delicious cheese.

CHILE CON QUESO $1.05
Melted cheese and hot sauce spread over a crisp fried tortilla

GARLIC SOUP .... Bowl $ .75

Antojitos Mexicanos

TACOS, ENCHILADAS AND TOSTADAS ARE THE SANDWICHES OF
MEXICO. THEIR BASE IS THE TORTILLA USED AS AN
ENVELOPE FOR THE FILLING.

CHILES RELLENOS $4.20
a favorite in Mexico City, 2 stuffed Chiles, one with meat and one
cheese and prepared in the Mexican tradition

TACOS DE PICADILLO $2.30
THE MEXICO'S OWN ROLLED TACOS, generously filled with
Mexico City style beef, sour cream, lettuce and mexican cheese

TACOS DE POLLO $2.30
A breast of chicken fills our tacos de pollo

TACOS DE AGUACATE $3.00
Avocado in a soft rolled tortilla

ENCHILADAS "CHOZA" $3.50
An Choza creation, cheese and chopped onions,
seasoning covered with mole and cheese

ENCHILADAS DE POLLO (SUECAS) $3.50
Chicken filled and broiled with a topping of
tomato sauce, cream and cheese

ENCHILADAS "MESTIZAS" POLLO
(Green Enchiladas) $3.50
Chicken filled and broiled with topping of Green Sauce, a melting
delicious cheese and cream.

ENCHILADAS DE PICADILLO $3.50
Beef Enchiladas smothered in mole and garnished with
sour cream and grated cheese

Chicago
LA FONTAINE
French

$$$

La Fontaine does not attract as much publicity as do other French restaurants in and around Chicago, but those who know it return again and again, as time and opportunity permit. Despite its location on a busy stretch of North Clark Street, diners are wrapped in a country French ambiance of brick, flowered wallpapers and fireplaces with their golden warmth. Chef Serge Roger Alfroy creates a host of nouvelle cuisine attractions. In addition to the wide menu array, evening specialties might include medallion de veau, salmon with a beurre Nantais, fillet of sole, turbot in mustard sauce and such pastry-wrapped specialties as le feuilleté de ris de veau or le feuilleté de crabe. Other specialties not on the printed menu will also make seasonal appearances. Among recommendations for a perfect dinner, I suggest the fresh mushrooms in mornay sauce for an appetizer or perhaps the lusciously flavored onion soup. Roast duckling is served as a main course with sliced peach halves and orange sauce. Grilled or poached salmon comes to the table with two sauces. The sauces, which are reduced rather than thickened with a roux, are so light and airy that they make the complementary flavors wonderful accompaniments rather than gluttonous superfluity. Veal Normande remains another of my favorites with its sublime combination of apples, cream and veal flavors. Pastries, tarts and mousse highlight the selection of desserts.

LA FONTAINE, 2442 North Clark Street, Chicago. Telephone: 525-1800. Hours: Lunch: 11:30 am-2:30 pm, Tuesday-Thursday; Dinner: 5:30 pm-10:30 pm, Monday-Saturday. Cards: AE, CB, DC, MC, VISA. Reservations required. Full bar service. Jackets requested for men. Private party facilities for up to 75 people. Parking at Avis garage.

K/Rating 19.5/20 • Food 7/7 • Service 6/6 • Decor 4/4 • Value 2.5/3

Les Amusettes.

La quiche Lorraine

La Coquille deauvilloise
Scollops . Shrimps . Fresh mushrooms

1.25 Les Escargots "Beaunoise"
Snails in butter Garlic Spices

Le délice de la fontaine
Fresh mushrooms . Ham morning Sauce

La Mousse de Saumon
Salmon mousse . Port wine

Le Melon au Pôrto

La Terrine de Canneton 1.25
House . Pâté of duck .

Le filet de Maquereau
Maquereau cooked in white wine .

Les Salades.
~ with your dinner ~

La Salade Verte (House dressing

1.75 Heart of palm

1.25 Tomatoes Salade

La Fontaine

Les Spécialités.

Le Veau Sauté Normande
Veal sauté . Fresh mushrooms Calvados .

Les Médaillons de boeuf aux Girolles
mignons of beef sauted specials mushrooms .

Le Suprême de Volaille "Belle France"
breast of chicken braised with ham and cheese .

La Côtte de boeuf à l'ivrogne
Baked : beef, fresh mushrooms, onion red wine sauce .

Le Canard Rôti "Façon du Chef"
Roast duck . Peaches Orange Sauce
~ With Pommes Soufflés . Served for two .

Les Grillades. 1.50

Le Coeur de Filet "grillé"
filet mignon Sauce bearnaise .

L'entrecote "grillée"
Sirloin broiled "Sauce bearnaise "

La Côte d'Agneau
Lamb chops, marinated "bouquet de
in herbs and broiled . Provence"

Les Rôtis
for two . 3.50

Le Carré d'Agneau Rôti
Roast Rack of Lamb

Le Chateaubriand Bouquetière
Chateaubriand . bouquetière Sauce béarnaise .

Le Double Sirloin au Poivre
double peper steack flamed with Cognac .

Les Poissons.

La Paupiette de Saumon
Salmon stuffed crab meat . fresh mushrooms

La Cassolette Provençale
Scollops . Shrimps tomatoes . Garlic .

La Truite braisée Champagne
Trout Stuffed with Pike Mousse

Le Saumon Grillé or Poché
Salmon Broiled or Pocked . two Sauces .

Le Filet de Lotte florentine
Filet of white munk fish fresh spinach .

La Sole de Douvre Meunière
Dover Sole Sauté . Butter Lemon .

Chicago
LA FONTANELLA
Italian

$$

There is a tidy little section in and around the 2400 block of South Oakley Boulevard that seems to defy change. The neighborhood is Italian. It is not uncommon on warm summer nights to see children at play on the sidewalks while their parents gather on front steps to while away the evening. Scattered among the row houses are a handful of excellent restaurants. One of them is La Fontanella. Here you will find the gentle cuisine of Tuscany. There is less reliance on tomatoes and garlic; sauces tend to be creamier, flavors more subtle. True, you will find a few Sicilian specialties such as arancino, marvelous fried rice-balls stuffed with meat and served with an antipasti selection. And there is frittata, as much a delight to consume as it is to say; La Fontanella's version is an egg and sausage omelette filled out with mushrooms, onions, green peppers and potatoes. House specialties include some standard fare such as veal scaloppini, saltimbocca and chicken Vesuvio. But lamb scaloppini, wine sautéed meat served with hearts of artichoke, remains a constant favorite of mine. Turkey picata is a lower priced version of this popular preparation usually done with veal. Fish entrées include calamari sautéed in tomato sauce and served over fettuccini. La Fontanella does a fine job in a fairly intimate setting. Add $2 to the price of an entrée and you will get the complete dinner from soup or pasta to dessert and coffee.

LA FONTANELLA, 2414 South Oakley Boulevard, Chicago. Telephone: 927-5249. Hours: 11 am-1 pm, Tuesday-Friday; 4:30 pm-11 pm, Saturday-Sunday. No cards. Reservations recommended. Full bar service. Parking on street.

K/Rating 17/20 • Food 6.5/7 • Service 5/6 • Decor 2.5/4 • Value 3/3

Pasta

Served with Meat Sauce (Tomato Sauce Upon Request)
Served with Meat Balls or Sausage ... $1.00

SPAGHETTI	2.50	RAVIOLI	3.25
MOSTACCIOLI	2.50	TORTELLINI	3.25
SPAGHETTI ALL'OLIO	2.75	LASAGNA	3.75
PASTA VERDE in Cream Sauce	3.50	MANICOTTI	3.75

House Specialties

VEAL SCALOPPINI 5.50
(thin slices of veal sauteed in wine with mushrooms)

SALTIMBOCCA ALLA ROMANA 5.75
(veal sauteed in wine with herbs and prosciutto)

VEAL PARMIGIANA 5.75
(veal cutlet with tomato sauce, mushrooms and
melted cheese)

LAMB SCALOPPINI 6.00
(lamb sauteed in wine with artichoke hearts)

FILET OF BEEF PIZZAIOLA 7.00
(slices of filet with zesty Tomato sauce)

BREAST OF TURKEY PICATA 5.00
(slices of turkey breast with a delicate lemon butter)

CHICKEN ALLA FRANCA 4.00
(chicken stuffed with garlic butter, lightly breaded,
fried, then baked)

CHICKEN VESUVIO 4.00
(chicken lightly browned and baked with garlic, olive
oil, herbs, and a hint of lemon)

Additional Charge of $2.00 for a Complete Dinner
Includes Soup or Mostaccioli, Salad, Pastry or Ice
Cream and Coffee.

Chicago
LA LLAMA
Peruvian

$$

Of the three Peruvian restaurants operated by the Asturrizaga family, this one is my favorite. Most dinners are $15 and include a taste of three appetizers, soup, main course, dessert, coffee and of course, bread and butter. Special occasions might call for paella, the classic Spanish rice casserole of lobster, crab, shrimp, ham, chicken and vegetables priced at $25 per person. I prefer the $15 dinners which are better values. On a given evening the main course might be a preparation of duck, rabbit, fish, veal or even baby goat when available. If beef is your main course selection, the dinner price drops to $12. Among excellent appetizers is turbot, fried and served in a wine-based marinade with a hint of chili peppers amidst its complex seasonings. Palate pleasing appetizers include a puréed potato, stuffed with ground beef, raisins and seasonings, fried until golden brown and finely chopped broccoli that is molded into patties and deep-fried. Peruvian food has a certain characteristic spiciness to it, but you will not confuse its delicate complexities with other Latin American styles such as Mexican or Cuban.

LA LLAMA, 2651 West Peterson Avenue, Chicago. Telephone: 728-1314. Hours: 5 pm-10:30 pm, Tuesday-Sunday. Cards: AE. Reservations suggested. No bar service: you may bring your own (customers are encouraged to bring Pisco, the Peruvian brandy, for preparations of native cocktails). Casual dress acceptable. Restaurant available for private parties of 45 to 50 people. Ample parking.

K/Rating 18.5/20 • Food 7/7 • Service 6/6 • Decor 3/4 • Value 2.5/3

Chicago
LAWRY'S
American

$$

This Los Angeles import (yes, they are the same people who make the seasoned salt) features prime rib in three basic cuts. The thinner slices of the English cut and the regular Lawry's single large slice from the standing rib roast are $11.75; the larger Chicago cut portion with the bone is $13.75. The roast beef dinners include a tossed salad, Yorkshire pudding, mashed potatoes and creamed horse-radish to accent the meat. The beef is carved from full-standing rib roasts prepared in a bank of eight electric ovens where they are roasted over rock salt. Then each roast is put into a temperature controlled silver serving cart for individual tableside service. In addition to the featured roast beef, Lawry's now has additional chef's selections which could be veal, lamb or steak on any given day as well as fresh fish, generally priced from $5.50 to $7.50. But the roast beef is king here and that is the thing to order. Desserts are sweet and grandiose. Lawry's wine list includes an excellent selection from California producers.

LAWRY'S THE PRIME RIB, 100 East Ontario Street, Chicago. Telephone: 787-5000. Hours: Lunch: 11:30 am-2:30 pm, Monday-Friday; Dinner: 5 pm-11 pm, Monday-Friday; 5 pm-midnight, Saturday; 3 pm-10 pm, Sunday. Cards: AE, MC, VISA. Reservations recommended. Full bar service. Jackets requested for men. Private party facilities for 40 to 150 people. Valet parking.

K/Rating 16/20 • Food 6/7 • Service 5/6 • Decor 3/4 • Value 2/3

Chicago
LAWRENCE OF OREGANO
Italian $$

Lawrence and the folks at Lettuce Entertain You, Inc. have
not lost either their sense of humor or their flair for some
pretty good food since the first edition of *Best Restaurants
Chicago.* If anything, the menu has become more ambitious
with such fish preparations as baked trout with mushrooms
and scallions, sole Florentine and scallops in garlic butter.
As any good Italian restaurant worth its checkered table-
cloths should, Lawrence of Oregano does not ignore veal.
You will find it in such classic preparations as saltimbocca
Romana, Milanese and Parmigiana, among others. Braciola
remains a favorite among beef selections. The place serves
up miles and miles of spaghetti, fettuccine and other pastas
in the $3.50 to $5 price arena. Family-style dinners for
tables of five or more people run $7.95 per person and
include the works from zuppa to dolces. Light eaters will
find a selection of sandwiches à la Italia, but not excluding
cheeseburgers, which are not exactly Florentine fare.

LAWRENCE OF OREGANO, 662 West Diversey Avenue,
Chicago. Telephone: 871-1916. Hours: 5 pm-11 pm, Mon-
day-Thursday; until midnight, Friday-Saturday; 4 pm-11 pm,
Sunday. Cards: AE, MC, VISA. Limited reservation policy:
on busy nights you wait. Full bar service. Casual, neat dress
acceptable. Parking in Century Garage on Clark Street.

K/Rating 17/20 • Food 5/7 • Service 5/6 • Decor 4/4 • Value 3/3

Cena Di Lawrence
(Dinner Specials)

All our Dinner specials include our bread and salad bar, vegetable, and sherbet intermezzo.

Vitello
(Veal)

Costoletto Milanese $6.95
Scaloppine double-dipped in parmesan cheese and bread-crumbs, then fried and served with lemon

Piccata Prezzemolo $6.95
Thin slices of tender veal sautéed a la Northern Italy in lemon and butter

Saltimbocca Romana $7.50
Folded scaloppine stuffed with paper-thin prosciutto, sautéed and served in a white wine sauce

Costoletto Parmigiana $7.50
Veal scaloppine first sauteed, then baked with tomato sauce and mozzarella cheese

Scaloppine Marsala $7.50
Veal sautéed in butter with a Marsala-laced mushroom sauce

Bistecca
(Beef)

Bistecca Della Nonne (Chopped Steak) $4.75
Chopped steak lightly seasoned with thyme, onion, garlic and char-broiled

Chopped Steak Parmigiana $4.95
Broiled chopped steak topped with tomato sauce and mozzarella cheese

Braciola Siciliana $6.75
Rolled sirloin stuffed with Italian cheeses, then sauteed in white wine and served with marinara sauce

Bistecca Florentina $8.95
Char-broiled sirloin steak

Pollo
(Chicken)

Pollo Parmigiana $5.95
Sautéed boneless chicken breasts baked in tomato sauce and mozzarella cheese

Petti Di Pollo al Limone $5.95
Thinly sliced breasts of chicken sautéed in a delicate Northern Italian lemon and butter sauce

Pollo Cacciatore $5.95
Half a chicken gently simmered in white wine with fresh green peppers, onions, tomatoes, and mushrooms

Pesces
(Fish)

Sole Florentine $5.95
Tender Filet of Sole placed atop a bed of fresh creamed spinach and covered with a delicate mornay sauce.

Trota Federico $6.75
Golden rainbow trout baked in the oven on a bed of fresh mushrooms and topped with seasoned bread crumbs and scullions

Conchiglie Botticelli $6.75
Scallops baked in a garlic sauce with toasted breadcrumbs

Scampi Al Vino Bianco $8.50
Juicy jumbo shrimp sautéed in a white wine sauce

Pasta

All of our Pasta is Homemade

Spaghetti Marinara $3.50
Spaghetti with our fresh tomato sauce

Spaghetti With Meat Sauce $3.95

Spaghetti Polpetti Di Mama Moauro $4.25
Spaghetti and meatballs with meat sauce

Linguine With Meat Sauce $3.95
Flat spaghetti with meat sauce

Tagliatelle Bolognese $3.95
Homemade white ribbon noodles in an authentic Northern Italian extra-thick meat sauce

Tagliatelle Verde Bolognese $3.95
Homemade green noodles with extra-thick meat sauce

Linguine Vongole Bianco $4.75
Homemade Linguine with a fresh white clam sauce

Baked Mostaccioli* $3.95
Mostaccioli baked in meat sauce with melted mozzarella cheese
*not homemade

Ravioli Alferno $4.95
Our homemade Italian Ravioli ladled with a rich butter & cream sauce, topped with imported Romano cheese then baked to a delicate crispness

Ravioli Nostrani $4.75
Homemade paper-thin ravioli stuffed with a tangy cheese and spinach filling, and topped with our meat sauce

Manicotti Verde $4.95
Our own "Cannelloni"—two giant homemade green noodles stuffed with parsley and cheese, topped with marinara sauce

Lasagna $4.95
Homemade noodles layered with cheese and topped with meat sauce and served with sausage and a meatball

Fettuccine Alfredo Di Roma $4.95
Made-to-order white ribbon noodles in a rich cream and-butter sauce, topped with freshly grated parmesan cheese

Fettuccine Verde Alfredo $4.95
Homemade green ribbon noodles in a rich cream and butter sauce, topped with freshly grated parmesan cheese

> **Eggplant Parmigiana $4.95**
> Our own interpretation of eggplant parmesan

All of the above include our bread, salad bar and sherbet intermezzo.

Chicago
LEE'S CANTON CAFE
Chinese (Cantonese)

$$

In the rush of some diners to explore the subtleties of the now fashionable cuisines of Szechwan and Northern China, the old standby, Cantonese, may be ignored. And that is a shame, because in the hands of artists, good Cantonese food can be unusual and delicious. Some evening, forget your neighborhood carry-out, put a group of eight or 10 people together and visit Lee's Canton Cafe. Here is a menu that is more than chow mein, chop suey and fried rice. For appetizers try crab Rangoon, a fried won ton noodle stuffed with crab meat—not to be missed. Sui mi are dumplings filled with fried meat and chicken. Shrimp toast, a spread of minced shrimp on a thick crustless dough, is deep fried and sprinkled with sesame seeds. Outstanding main course selections include incredibly delicious sweet and sour soft-shelled crab. Beef eaters should try the Tony special; similar to Hong Kong steak, the beef slices come in an oyster sauce with mushrooms and snow peas. Portions are large and the food is in a class by itself. This is one of the better restaurants in Chinatown and is a real favorite with those who know.

LEE'S CANTON CAFE, 2300 South Wentworth Avenue, Chicago. Telephone: 225-4838. Hours: 11 am-midnight, Sunday-Thursday; until 2 am, Friday-Saturday. Cards: AE, VISA. Reservations taken. No bar service; you may bring your own. Private party facilities for 10 to 100 people. Parking nearby.

K/Rating 19/20 • Food 7/7 • Service 6/6 • Decor 3/4 • Value 3/3

BEEF - CANTONESE STYLE

BITTER MELON WITH BEEF..................................3.25
BEEF (with Oyster Sauce)..................................3.95
CURRY BEEF..3.95
BEEF KEW (Beef with Chinese Vegetables)...........3.95
STEAK KEW (Sirloin with Chinese Vegetables)...............6.55
BEEF WITH STRING BEANS (Chopped or Regular)......2.95
SUT DOWL MAR TA GNOW (Beef with Snow Peas
and Water Chestnuts)....................................4.15
PEPPER BEEF WITH OR WITHOUT TOMATO...........3.15
BEEF BOCK CHOY (Beef with Chines Greens).............3.15
BEEF ALMOND DEN 4.25
SNOW PEAS WITH BEEF 3.95
HONG KONG STEAK.......................................8.55

SEAFOOD - CANTONESE STYLE

STEAMED WHITE FISH....................................3.55
SWEET AND SOUR SOFT SHEEL CRAB..............5.95
CHOW LONE HARR (Jumbo Live Lobster with Shell
Cantonese Style..9.95
CHOW LONE HARR KEW
(Lobster Meat with Vegetables)....................6.95
CHOW HARR KEW
(Fresh Shrimp with Chinese Vegetables)...................4.95
HONG SUI HARR
(Shrimp fritter with Chinese Vegetables................4.95
FRESH SHRIMP ALOND DEN..........................4.95
FRESH LOBSTER ALOMOND DEN.....................6.75
SWEET AND SOUR SHRIMP.............................4.95
FRESH SHRIMP WITH LOBSTER SAUCE
OR GARLIC SAUCE 4.55
STEAMED YELLOW PIKE...................7.50 and up
SLICED FISH (with Mixed Chinese Vegetables)......4.75
FRIED LOBSTER WITHOUT SHELL OR
WITH SHELL (Cantonese Style)......................9.95
SNAIL CHINESE STYLE...................................3.55

Chicago
LE FESTIVAL
French

$$$

For those times when the maddening crowd is more than you can bear, visit Le Festival. To begin with, the cocktail lounge, just off the entryway, is an oasis of sophistication. The dining rooms, small and intimate, are graced with Oriental carpeting over dark hardwood floors. Tapestries adorn the walls and lighting is soft. The prix fixe dinner ($14.50) includes such outstanding specialties as veal Normande, lobster thermidor ($1.50 extra) as well as fine fish, beef and poultry. Among appetizers try the pheasant pâté, a coarse grind bound with cognac and port. Onion soup is baked in the crock, topped with copious amounts of melted cheese.

LE FESTIVAL, 28 West Elm Street, Chicago. Telephone: 944-7090. Hours: Lunch: 11:30 am-2:30 pm, Monday-Friday; Dinner: from 5:30 pm, Monday-Saturday. Cards: AE, CB, MC, VISA. Reservations recommended. Full bar service. Jackets required for men. Private party facilities. Valet parking.

K/Rating 18/20 • Food 6/7 • Service 6/6 • Decor 4/4 • Value 2/3

DOVER SOLE SAUTÉE MEUNIÈRE OU AMANDINE

TRUITE FARCIE "FESTIVAL"
(trout stuffed with crab meat, champagne sauce)

CUISSES DE GRENOUILLES A LA PROVENCALE
(frog legs sauted, garlic & tomato)

FILETS DE SOLE BONNE-FEMME
(poached sole, mushrooms, cream sauce)

SCALLOPS AU GRATIN
(scallops, vermouth sauce)

SAUMON GRILLÉ BEARNAISE
(grilled salmon, bearnaise sauce)

TURBOT ALEX HUMBERT
(turbot, mushrooms, tomato, safran, cream sauce)

WHITE FISH AMANDINE
(fresh fish sauted amandine)

HOMARD THERMIDOR
(+ one fifty -- lobster thermidor)

ESCALOPE DE VEAU NORMANDE
(veal, apple jack, mushrooms & cream)

VEAU FLORENTINE
(veal, spinach, cream sauce gratinee)

TOURNEDOS BEARNAISE
(filet, bearnaise sauce)

STEAK AU POIVRE
(sirloin steak, ground pepper, cognac flamed)

TOURNEDOS ROSSINI
(beef tenderloin, goose liver, truffles & wine sauce)

CANARD A L'ORANGE
(roast duck, orange sauce)

COQ AU CHAMBERTIN
(chicken, bacon, mushrooms, onions, red wine sauce)

PIGEON POÉLE SAUCE SMITANE
(roast squab, cream sauce)

ROGNONS DE VEAU DIJONNAISE
(veal kidneys in mustard sauce)

BOEUF STOGANOFF

RIS DE VEAU AUX CÉPES
(sweetbread, imported mushrooms)

Chicago
LE PERROQUET
French

$$$

If there is such a thing as perfection in dining, Le Perroquet is it. Owner Jovan Trboyevic and his fine staff have made culinary waves in Chicago which have been felt from coast to coast. Prix fixe dinners are $25.75; the dining is sublime whether the main course be sweetbreads in tarragon butter, steak à la Dijonnaise or any of the several daily specialties not on the printed menu. Seating is in plush velvet-covered chairs or banquettes. Once the cocktail order is taken, a tray of canapés is presented. From the printed menu one can choose any of several appetizers (some at a surcharge). A beautiful presentation of vegetables accompanies the main course. Everything is understated; nothing is out of proportion. Even something as mundane as sherbet is special, made from fresh fruits and running over with sweet goodness. At the conclusion, after dessert and coffee, a platter of chocolate-dusted kisses is offered as a final reminder of an extraordinary dining experience. Le Perroquet is faultless and without equal, a "must experience" restaurant whether you are a visitor or Chicago resident.

LE PERROQUET, 70 East Walton Street, Chicago. Telephone: 944-7990. Hours: Lunch: noon-3 pm, Monday-Friday; Dinner: 6 pm-9:30 pm, Monday-Saturday. Cards: AE, DC. Reservations required. Full bar service. Coat and tie required for men. Parking at 100 East Walton Street.

K/Rating 20/20 • Food 7/7 • Service 6/6 • Decor 4/4 • Value 3/3

BLUE POINTS

LES SURPRISES

TOURTE AUX CHAMPIGNONS

POTAGE DU JOUR

PÂTÉS ASSORTIS

MOUSSE DE SAUMON

BISQUE DE HOMARD

SAUMON FUMÉ (IMPORTÉ)

CAVIAR MALOSSOL (18.00)

LA TRUFFE EN FEUILLETAGE (8.00)

LES ESCARGOTS

RIS DE VEAU AU BEURRE D'ESTRAGON

LES POISSONS FRAIS

CANETON RÔTI MAISON (2 PERS.)

NOS PLATS DU JOUR

DODINE DE PIGEON

CONFIT D'OIE, POMMES SARLADAISE

NOISETTES D'AGNEAU FARCIES

TOURNEDOS AUX ECHALOTES

STEAK À LA DIJONNAISE

PIÈCE DE BOEUF POELÉE (2 PERS.)

113

Chicago
L'ESCARGOT
French

$$$

Despite its location in a definitely non-Gallic neighborhood, L'Escargot is enjoying great popularity among those Chicago diners who take the trouble to seek out its charms. Under the stewardship of chef Lucian Verge, the kitchen regularly turns out some of the best Provençal-style French cooking around this part of the Midwest. The restaurant is decidedly unpretentious; one of its dining rooms, off the central foyer, has a certain bourgeois French feel to it; the bistro-like barroom is my favorite area with its long bar on one side of the room and wooden booths and banquettes on the other side for dining and drinking. Although the menu changes seasonally, there are several selections served all year round. The cassoulet is a classic casserole of duck, pork, lamb and sausage baked with white beans. Veal kidneys with mustard sauce are invariably tender. Fresh fish including poached salmon and trout leave nothing to be desired. Table d'hôte dinners include a choice from the excellent hors d'oeuvre selection, soup, salad, dessert and coffee. French aperitifs, cocktails and of course, beer and wine are offered. Should you plan to see a play at the St. Nicholas Theatre just down Halsted, L'Escargot is a popular spot for pre- or post-evening dining. Reservations made for dinner by 6:15 pm qualify for the early supper plan and a special low-priced menu.

L'ESCARGOT, 2925 North Halsted Street, Chicago. Telephone: 525-5525. Hours: 5 pm-midnight, Monday-Saturday. Cards: AE, DC, MC, VISA. Reservations recommended. Full bar service. Casual, neat dress acceptable. Parking lot nearby.

K/Rating 17.5/20 • Food 6/7• Service 5/6 • Decor 4/4 • Value 2.5/3

Menu

Les Entrées

Saumon froid sauce verte   14.50
  (Cold, fresh poached salmon, cucumber salade
         herbs and home made mayonnaise)

Poulet froid glacé Favorite   11.50
  (two poached breast of chicken, served cold with a salade of
   fresh string beans, mushrooms and almonds)

Le poisson du Jour sauté Caprice   14.50
  (fresh fish of the day sauteed with lemon and banana)

Truite Duglèré   14.50
  (fresh trout poached in white wine and mushroom sauce with tomatoes)

Poulet au Whisky   13.25
  (Roast chicken with cream, mushrooms and whisky sauce)

Canard rôti aux pêches   14.50
  (Roast duckling with orange sauce wild rice and peach)

Rognons sautés à la moutarde   14.25
  (Veal kidneys sauteed with mustard and cream sauce)

Gigôt d'Agneau rôti Bretonne   14.75
  (roast leg of lamb served au jus with white beans)

Cassoulet Toulousain   15.50
  (duck, lamb, pork and sausage baked with white beans in casserole)

Filet de boeuf rôti Bordelaise   15.50
  (roast fillet of beef with Bordelaise sauce)

La Douzaine d'Escargots Bourguignonne   12.50
  (one dozen of snails baked in their shells with garlic butter)

+ Our Daily Specials

La Salade Verte   Les Desserts au choix   Le Café (espresso + 75 cts)

9/78

L'Épuisette is a little jewel box of a restaurant which continues year after year to present fine food in a fine atmosphere. Dim lighting and muraled walls of 18th century harbor fishing scenes set the ambience. Begin with soup, such as an always fine red snapper with a good deal of the snap still in it. Trout meunière stuffed with crab meat is a house specialty. When in season, soft shell crabs are a real delicacy, sautéed in butter and served with slivers of golden almond for a texture accent. Complete your dinner with coffee and dessert, perhaps a coconut snowball or cheesecake. A more than adequate wine list and service that fits the standard of the food have helped make L'Épuisette a favorite with knowledgeable Chicagoans and their guests.

L'ÉPUISETTE, 21 West Goethe Street, Chicago. Telephone: 944-2288. Hours: 5 pm-11 pm, Tuesday-Sunday. Cards: AE, CB, DC, MC, VISA. Reservations required. Full bar service. Parking in garage or lots.

K/Rating 18/20 • Food 6.5/7 • Service 6/6 • Decor 2.5/4 • Value 3/3

LES OEUFS
Omelettes

$

Just a few steps off the magnificent mile, tucked next to the lobby in the Playboy Towers, is one of the more intriguing restaurants in Chicago. Les Oeufs specializes in omelettes and other egg entrées. Humpty Dumpty never had it so good, whether your taste is for a fairly simple omelette Florentine or for the "customer's choice" omelette, where you decide what goes into the works. The omelette veronique is one of my favorites. Large bits of chicken and sautéed fresh mushroom slices are complemented by white seedless grapes in a wine sauce. The ratatouille omelette gives a new twist to the classic French vegetable preparation. Most selections include soup or salad from the salad bar. A limited choice of wines and a full range of cocktails are offered. The surroundings leave nothing to be desired, with lots of open space, comfortable seating and Mexican tile accents. Service is generally good.

LES OEUFS, 163 East Walton Street (in the Playboy Tower), Chicago. Telephone: 751-8100. Hours: 11 am-11 pm, Tuesday-Friday; 10 am-midnight, Saturday-Sunday; Cards: AE, CB, MC, VISA. No reservations. Full bar service. Valet parking.

K/Rating 18/20 • Food 6/7 • Service 5/6 • Decor 4/4 • Value 3/3

Chicago
MARTINI'S
Steaks/Italian/American

$$

If Chicago has one culinary stereotype, it is as a steak town. In fact, the town is teeming with restaurants which claim to serve the greatest steak anywhere. I cannot say it is the best of the lot, but Martini's is a pleasant enough way station for beef. No newcomer to the Chicago scene, Martini's has been a family operation since 1935. Many people think of Martini's as an Italian restaurant. That is true to the extent that half of the menu includes such specialties as chicken Vesuvio, veal Parmigiana or scallopine, plus Italian sausage and nearly a dozen different preparations of spaghetti and other pastas. Yet the house specialty, boneless breast of chicken sautéed in butter with mushrooms and served in a sherry sauce falls outside of that category. So do the steaks. The best the house has to offer are the top fillet or top sirloin. At a recent price of $8.75, that is anywhere from $2 to $4 less than comparable dinners at other steak houses. The reason Martini's brings it home for so relatively little is because they use choice graded beef, not prime. Before you turn up your bib and tucker, believe it or not, the steaks turn out juicy, tender and tasty. True, you may not find that special succulence that sets prime beef on its own pedestal. But a choice steak in the right hands will turn out without a touch of gristle or toughness. Steaks may be better elsewhere, but not for the same money.

MARTINI'S, 232 West Grand Avenue, Chicago. Telephone: 337-2935. Hours: 11 am-11 pm, daily. Cards: AE, MC. Reservations recommended. Full bar service. Casual, neat dress acceptable. Private party facilities for up to 40 people. Parking in adjacent lot.

K/Rating 16/20 • Food 5/7 • Service 5/6 • Decor 3/4 • Value 3/3

Famous Italian Dishes

VEAL CUTLET A LA PARMIGIANA...................... 6.75

VEAL SCALLOPINE, simmered with sherry wine.............. 6.75

VEAL SCALLOPINE A LA CACCIATORA.................... 6.75

MARTINI'S SPECIAL ROLLED TENDERLOIN TIPS, with chicken
livers, mushrooms and bacon............................ 7.00

BONELESS CHICKEN A LA PARMIGIANA................... 6.00

BEEF TENDERLOIN A LA MARSALA.................... 7.00

HALF CHICKEN, Cacciatora style........................ 6.00

CHICKEN VESUVIO, "a real taste thrill".................. 6.00

BAKED ITALIAN SAUSAGE............................. 5.25

Pasta

Served with Imported Italian grated cheese.

HOME MADE RAVIOLI................................ 4.75

GREEN NOODLES (20 minutes)...................... 4.75

SPAGHETTI, mushroom sauce........................ 5.00

SPAGHETTI, meat sauce............................. 4.75

SPAGHETTI, meat balls............................. 5.25

SPAGHETTI AND CHICKEN LIVERS.................... 5.25

COMBINATION SPAGHETTI AND RAVIOLI, "what a meal".... 4.75

MOSTACCIOLI, meat sauce, "a true Italian delicacy"............ 4.75

LASAGNA EN CASSEROLE, salad included................ 5.25

Seafood Suggestions

SHRIMP DE JONGHE..................................... 5.50

LOUISIANA STUFFED SHRIMPS.......................... 5.25

JUMBO FROG LEGS, tartar sauce........................ 5.75

FRIED SOFT SHELL CRABS, tartar sauce.................. 5.75

BROILED FRESH WALL-EYED PIKE, lemon butter, in season...... 5.75

BROILED LOBSTER TAIL, drawn butter.....................

JUMBO FRENCH FRIED SHRIMPS, Figaro sauce.............. 5.25

Chicago
MATEGRANO'S
Italian

$

Anybody who knows anything about budget Italian dining, knows Mategrano's Thursday and Saturday night buffets. These $4.95, all-you-can-eat extravaganzas are as much a party as anything else with tables heaped high with dozens of house specialties, some familiar, some not always so. Annette Mategrano and her sister, Millie Miccucio keep things moving along, and even on other nights when the buffet is not offered, it is hard to spend much more than $8 to $10 a person; often you will spend much less. Mategrano's is one of the old timers in the old Taylor Street Italian community. Much of the area was taken away by the wrecker's ball for construction of the U of I, Chicago Circle Campus. But Mategrano's and a few other places still remain intact. The food is typical homemade Neapolitan. Seafood specialties such as calamari, polpi and when it is available, baccala are among favorites here. Pastas are homemade. Braciola is one of the house specialties I could eat 'til Judgment Day. Mategrano's is a fine place to take children; after all, what kid doesn't like spaghetti and meatballs?

MATEGRANO'S, 1321 West Taylor Street, Chicago. Telephone: 243-8441. Hours: 11 am-9 pm, Tuesday-Sunday. Cards: AE, VISA. Reservations required for Thursday and Saturday buffet. Full bar service. Casual, neat dress acceptable. Private party facilities for up to 125 people. Free parking.

K/Rating 18/20 • Food 6/7 • Service 6/6 • Decor 3/4 • Value 3/3

Italian Dishes

SPAGHETTI OR MOSTACCIOLI 3.25
SPAGHETTI OR MOSTACCIOLI WITH MEAT BALLS OR SAUSAGE 4.25
BAKED LASAGNA WITH MEAT BALL OR SAUSAGE 4.95
FETTUCCINE, Red Gravy 3.50
FETTUCCINE WITH MEAT BALL OR SAUSAGE 4.50
FETTUCCINE AL ALFREDO (Cheese and Butter) 3.95
HOME-MADE CHEESE RAVIOLI 3.50
HOME-MADE CHEESE RAVIOLI WITH MEAT BALL OR SAUSAGE 4.50
HOME-MADE MEAT RAVIOLI 4.00
HOME-MADE MEAT RAVIOLI WITH MEAT BALL OR SAUSAGE 4.95
HOME-MADE CAVATELLI 3.45
HOME-MADE CAVATELLI WITH MEAT BALL OR SAUSAGE 4.45
LINGUINI OR SPAGHETTI AL AGLIO OLIO (Oil and Garlic Sauce) 3.50
LINGUINI OR SPAGHETTI WITH CLAM SAUCE (Red or White) 4.50
HOME-MADE MANICOTTI 3.95
HOME-MADE MANICOTTI WITH MEAT BALL OR SAUSAGE 4.95
SPAGHETTI WITH MUSHROOM SAUCE 3.95
SPAGHETTI WITH ANCHOVIES 4.50
HALF MEAT AND HALF CHEESE RAVIOLI 4.50

Above Orders Include: Salad, Bread and Butter

Special Plates

PEPPERS AND EGGS ON PLATE 2.95
ONIONS AND EGGS ON PLATE 2.95

Above Includes: Salad, Bread and Butter

Specialties of the House

FRETTA: Combination of a Green Vegetable and Egg Pan Fried,
   with Meat Balls or Sausage 3.25
PASTA FAGIOLI 2.25
ESCAROLE AND BEANS 2.25
TRIPPA (Tripe with Tomato Sauce) 3.50
CALAMARA with Spaghetti (Squid) 3.75
POLPI with Spaghetti (Octopus) 3.95
BRACIOLE BREGILIANO, Mostaccioli and Salad
   (Flank Steak Rolled) 5.95
EGG PLANT PARMIGIANA AND MOSTACCIOLI
   (Egg Plant with Moscella Cheese), Salad 4.75

Steaks and Chops

NEW YORK STRIP STEAK with Onions 6.95
BROILED LAMB LOIN with Vegetable 6.95

Above Orders Include: Salad and Mostaccioli or Spaghetti

Veal Dishes

VEAL AL LEMONE 6.25
VEAL PARMIGIANA 6.25
VEAL SCALLOPINI 6.25
BREADED VEAL CUTLET 6.25

Above Orders Include: Mostaccioli and Salad

121

Chicago
MATSUYA
Japanese

$

This is one of the dozens of little finds that dot Clark Street. There is nothing on Matsuya's menu I have not found at other Japanese restaurants, but everything I have tasted is exceptional. You can order à la carte or from special combinations. Either way, it is difficult to spend more than $6 to $7 per person. From the appetizer selection, choose spinach in a soy-based sesame sauce for $1. The spinach is cold, the sauce delicately sweet and salty. Matsuya does a fine job with fish, charcoal broiled with crisp skin. Fish varies depending on what is fresh; pike and mackerel are common selections. Broiled eel is for adventurous diners; sashimi, the popular dish of raw tuna, is another tempting offering. Combination dinners offer a taste of this and that, including delicately batter-coated tempura shrimp and vegetables, beef teriyaki and sashimi. All dinners include a small cabbage salad, excellent clear hot broth, rice, light green tea with a delicate wood-like fragrance and dessert.

MATSUYA, 3469 North Clark Street, Chicago. Telephone: 248-2677. Hours: 5 pm-10 pm, Monday-Friday; noon-10 pm, Saturday-Sunday. No cards. Reservations taken. Wine and saki only. Parking on street.

K/Rating 17.5/20 • Food 7/7 • Service 5/6 • Decor 2.5/4 • Value 3/3

Chicago
MILLER'S PUB
American

$$

The Gallios brothers have been in the Loop for more than 30 years and are known to just about every salesman, judge, lawyer, businessman and traffic cop who ever has occasion to amble down Adams Street. The place is famous for its Canadian baby back barbecue ribs, slowly grilled over hickory wood and served with a special sauce and creamy cole slaw. This one makes rib lovers come back for more. Steaks number among the other house specialties. I particularly enjoy the 12-ounce sirloin butt. You will also find a smattering of Greek and Italian dishes on the menu. A special luncheon menu offers some commendable dining for under $4. Miller's Pub is open almost around the clock; it is living proof that the Loop is alive and well.

MILLER'S PUB, 23 East Adams Street, Chicago. Telephone: 922-7446. Hours: 7 am-4 am, daily. Cards: AE, CB, DC, MC, VISA. Reservations taken. Full bar service. Discount parking at nearby garage.

K/Rating 17/20 • Food 6/7 • Service 5/6 • Decor 3/4 • Value 3/3

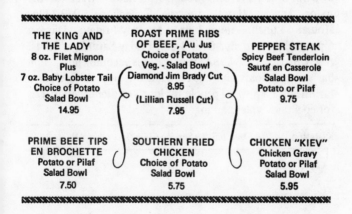

THE KING AND THE LADY
8 oz. Filet Mignon
Plus
7 oz. Baby Lobster Tail
Choice of Potato
Salad Bowl
14.95

ROAST PRIME RIBS OF BEEF, Au Jus
Choice of Potato
Veg. - Salad Bowl
Diamond Jim Brady Cut
8.95
(Lillian Russell Cut)
7.95

PEPPER STEAK
Spicy Beef Tenderloin
Sauté en Casserole
Salad Bowl
Potato or Pilaf
9.75

PRIME BEEF TIPS EN BROCHETTE
Potato or Pilaf
Salad Bowl
7.50

SOUTHERN FRIED CHICKEN
Choice of Potato
Salad Bowl
5.75

CHICKEN "KIEV"
Chicken Gravy
Potato or Pilaf
Salad Bowl
5.95

Chicago
MAXIM'S DE PARIS
French

$$$

Considered by many Chicagoans to be the city's most romantic dining spot, Maxim's offers excellent examples of French cuisine. The dining room is a duplicate of the restaurant's Parisian namesake. Only a decade and a half old in Chicago, Maxim's still manages to suggest a grand patina of *fin de siècle* elegance. Tuxedoed waiters carry themselves with supreme dignity, handling large tables or a special *table à deux* with finesse. A new menu offers some outstanding creations. Consommé of lobster is less filling than the more often served lobster bisque, yet the unmistakable lobster taste adds a certain finish to the delicate clear broth. A scallop mousse in cream sauce with chives makes an excellent second course which could be followed by more robust fare such as steak Dijonnaise or beef with green peppercorn sauce. More unusual is tiny squab in port wine sauce, served on a bed of delicate sweetbreads, all encircled in a demi-crust. Maxim's offers a number of classic French desserts including cold or hot soufflés. The wine list, like the service and food, is impeccably well bred.

MAXIM'S DE PARIS, 1300 North Astor Street (in the Astor Towers Hotel), Chicago. Telephone: 943-1111. Hours: Lunch: noon-3 pm, Monday-Friday; Dinner: 6 pm-midnight, daily; until 1 am, Friday-Saturday. Cards: AE, CB, DC, MC, VISA. Reservations recommended. Full bar service. Coats and ties required for men. Private party facilities for up to 60 people for lunch or dinner; up to 125 for cocktails. Valet parking.

K/Rating 19/20 • Food 6.5/7 • Service 6/6 • Decor 4/4 • Value 2.5/3

LES HORS-D'ŒUVRE

Souffle au Fromage 4.75
Cheese Souffle

Feuillette de Fruits de Mer 6.25
Puff pastry filled with seafood, Lobster sauce

Mousse de Coquilles St. Jacques, sauce Ciboulette 5.75
Mousse of Scallops with a sauce of chives

Toast a la Moelle 4.75
Beef marrow on toast, truffle sauce

Quiche au Saumon 4.25
Quiche with smoked salmon

Escargots au Champagne 5.75
Snails cooked in champagne

LES ENTREES

Supreme de Volaille sous Cloche 11.25
Breast of Chicken served under glass, Sherry sauce

Pigeonneau au Porto sur Ris de Veau 14.75
Squab in Port, served on a bed of sweetbreads

Rognons de Veau en Habit Vert 11.25
Veal kidneys served with spinach

Demi-Canard aux Cerises 12.25
Half of a Roast Duckling, with cherries

Noisettes d'Agneau aux Gousses d'ail 14.75
Noisettes of Lamb with garlic

Mignon de Veau Orloff 15.75
Medallion of Veal; with puree of mushrooms, Mornay Sauce

Cote de Veau poele aux petits legumes 15.25
Veal chop cooked with fresh vegetables

Eminces de Boeuf au Poivre Vert 14.50
Strips of Beef tenderloin with green peppercorns

Entrecote Dijonnaise 15.75
Strip steak with mustard sauce

Tournedos Rossini 16.25
Beef tenderloin served with foie gras

Chicago
MIOMIR'S SERBIAN CLUB
Serbian   **$$**

Miomir Radovanovic knows how to throw a party and you had better have a good time—or else. Miomir's ebullience practically fills the room as he stops to talk, kiss a hand or twirl a female patron across the dance floor. Add to that, good hearty Balkan food, wines and an ethnic floor show with songs in every language from Russian and Hungarian to Yiddish and Hebrew. Serbian food reflects the cross-currents that, over the centuries have passed through this beautiful but sometimes troubled land. Thus you will find influences from Asia Minor such as sarma ($7.25), stuffed cabbage leaves filled with veal, beef and rice, served with sour cream. From Middle Europe comes chicken paprika ($6.95), the Serbian version of weiner schnitzel called becka snicla ($9.95) or gulash ($6.95), born in Hungary but with a Serbian flourish. Among other dinner choices are traditional grilled meats, ćevapčići ($7.75), ground veal and beef in sausage-shaped cylinders or muckalica and pleska-vica, the former a spicy casserole of meat and vegetables, the latter a braised ground round steak. Begin dinner with traditional appetizers such as the cheese spread called kajmak ($1.50) and ajvar ($1.50), the purée of eggplant, green pepper and other ingredients sautéed in olive oil. Dessert treats include strudel, crêpes (palacsintak) and baklava, an influence from the Levant.

MIOMIR'S SERBIAN CLUB, 2225 West Lawrence Avenue, Chicago. Telephone: 784-2111. Hours: 5 pm-2 am, Wednesday-Sunday. Cards: MC, VISA. Reservations required. Full bar service. Casual, neat dress acceptable. Free parking.

K/Rating 19/20 • Food 6.5/7 • Service 6/6 • Decor 3.5/4 • Value 3/3

---

appetizers

CORBA 1.75
Traditional Serbian soup with beef and vegetables.

KAJMAK 1.50
Fermented milk bread-spread originating from the caucasus.

AJVAR 1.50
A mild appetizer, said to be good for long life, consisting of a mixture of grilled egg plant, sweet green pepper and celery in olive oil.

Kajmak and Ajvar are spread on freshly baked
bread and eaten with the aperitif before the Serbian meal.

SERBIAN SALAD 1.75
Mixed vegetable salad prepared from tomatoes, onions, cucumbers and Serbian cheese, lightly sprinkled with olive oil.

COLD PLATE 6.95
Boiled egg, homemade mayonnaise, ajvar, kajmak, cold cuts, Serbian sausage, french cheese, grier and various vegetables.

entrees

SARMA 7.25
Rolled sour cabbage leaves filled with veal, beef, and rice, served in its own sauce, the most popular dish in Serbia.

ROYAL MOUSSAKA 7.25
Alternating layers of egg plant, meat (veal & beef), eggs and vegetables is added to enhance the flavor.

CHICKEN PAPRIKASH 6.95
Chicken cooked in wine sauce.

GULASH 6.95
Serbian gourmet's delight, veal and beef cooked with vegetables and served in a delicious sauce.

LOVACKA SNICLA (huntsman's schnitzel) 7.25
Beef in wine sauce.

BECKA SNICLA (the imperial wiener schnitzel) 9.95
Breaded veal elaborately garnished.

Chicago
MORTON'S
Steak & Lobster

$$$

Arnie Morton's restaurant empire grew by a factor of one in 1979 with the addition of this steak and lobster emporium which bears his family name. Located in what was originally a storage basement of posh Newberry Plaza, Morton's has a decidedly masculine feel to it with its tasteful use of wood beams and stucco. An open grill fronts the restaurant; the prep kitchen is in back and out of sight. Morton's specialties include huge cuts of beef and large lobsters, all served with delicious hash browns or full one-pound baked potatoes. Everything else is extra. There is a chalkboard menu at the front of the room. Recent prices were about $29 for a 3-3/4-pound lobster, $15.95 for a 24-ounce T-bone, $12.95 for a huge double-cut prime rib with bone in and $14.95 for a 20-ounce sirloin. Appetizers and vegetables are basic choices such as shrimp cocktail ($3.95), fresh asparagus with hollandaise ($2.50) and salads ($1.75). If you would like a soufflé for dessert ($2.50 per person) order it well in advance to allow time for preparation. The soufflés come out of the oven with golden crowns and puffy cheeks. Morton's may be its owner's best restaurant; it certainly is his most basic.

MORTON'S, 1050 North State Street, Chicago. Telephone: 266-4820 Hours: 5:30 pm-midnight, Monday-Friday; until 1 am, Saturday. Cards: AE, DC, MC, VISA. No reservations. Parking in Newberry Plaza Garage.

K/Rating 18/20 • Food 7/7 • Service 5.5/6 • Decor 3.5/4 • Value 2/3

Henry B. Clarke House

MY PLACE FOR
American/Greek

$$

To coin a phrase, food is the bread and butter of a restaurant's success. That is the bottom line, no matter what the theme, atmosphere or decor. At My Place For there is no pretense, nothing stunning about the decor, no famous sports or theatre personalities to rub shoulders with. What you will find are friendly waiters and waitresses who actually smile and enjoy what they are doing. Food is abundant and reasonably priced. My Place For is a little bit of a Greek restaurant but without the usual Greek restaurant chauvinism. It also happens to be a spot for some tasty beef, chicken and seafood. Fresh fish is the house specialty whether red snapper or seabass, priced according to size. Barbecued ribs are popular staples. Shish kebab offers large chunks of beef seasoned with oregano, but not overly so to the distraction of the meat's natural goodness. Several other steak cuts round out the beef choices. Duckling in orange sauce, roasted Grecian-style chicken and pork chops complete the menu. Among more unusual selections, try the fried calamari as either appetizer or full dinner selection. Salad lovers will like the Caesar. My Place For is an adult restaurant where children are welcome. Kids can be fed for under $3 and their presence will not be resented.

MY PLACE FOR, 5062 North Lincoln Avenue, Chicago. Telephone: 275-8200. Hours: 4 pm-2 am, daily. Cards: MC, VISA. Reservations recommended. Private party facilities for 10 to 75 people. Parking lot across the street.

K/Rating 17/20 • Food 5/7 • Service 6/6 • Decor 3/4 • Value 3/3

MY PLACE FOR...

BARBEQUED RIBS
Whole slab 7.95
Rib Dinner 6.50
SHISH-KABOB,
  beef tenederloin with onion, green pepper,
    tomato on rice pilaf 5.95

MEAT & FOWL

T-BONE STEAK, *12 oz. U.S.D.A.*
  Prime, broiled 8.75
BUTT STEAK, *10 oz. U.S.D.A. Prime, broiled* 6.75
FILET MIGNON, *10 oz. U.S.D.A.*
  Prime, broiled 7.50
PEPPER STEAK, *with tomatoes & green peppers* 6.95
CHOPPED SIRLOIN, *½ pound*
  of pure ground sirloin, broiled 4.50
PORK CHOPS, *center cut, broiled-served with applesauce* 6.25
ROAST DUCK, *with orange sauce, on rice pilaf* 6.50
CHICKEN, *Grecian style, to perfection* 5.50

all above entrees served with
salad, potato or vegetable

CAESAR SALAD

made for two or more people
$2.00 per person

SIDE ORDERS

Cottage Fries	.75	Rice	.60
Small Salad	.85	Cole Slaw	.60
Onion Rings	1.25	Sliced Tomatoes	1.25
Small Greek Salad	1.35	Feta Cheese	1.45

MY
PLACE FOR...

If you have a taste for deep-dish pizza, Chicago style, here is the place to go it one better. Nancy's serves *the* stuffed pizza. This is certainly an idea whose time has come. Consider the magnitude of this filling feast: Start with a good, rich dough and layer it out thick; turn it up at the sides to contain vast amounts of cheese (four different kinds), an assortment of typical pizza ingredients such as sausage, green peppers, mushrooms, onions; cover this with a thin layer of dough and top it all with a spicy tomato sauce. Now, that's a *stuffed* pizza. The only thing more stuffed at Nancy's are the patrons after they have eaten. Just to look at a stuffed pizza is to quiver with anticipation. When you get a large slice, dripping with cheese, smelling of tomatoes and hot fresh dough, then comes the moment of consummation. Take a forkful, inhale the aromas and taste it all. The cheese oozes around your lips, sauce coats your tongue; you will savor the various ingredients competing for

OUR PRIDE AND JOY
THE ONE AND ONLY STUFFED PIZZA

APPROXIMATELY 45 MINUTE WAIT FOR STUFFED PIZZA

*CHEESE	7.50	8.50	9.50
*SAUSAGE	8.50	9.50	10.50
*MUSHROOM	8.50	9.50	10.50
*GREEN PEPPER	8.50	9.50	10.50
*ONION	8.50	9.50	10.50
PEPPERONI	8.50	9.50	10.50
BACON	8.50	9.50	10.50
SHRIMP	9.00	10.00	11.00
ANCHOVY	8.50	9.50	10.50
*PARTY PIZZA	11.20	12.20	13.10
EXTRA INGREDIENTS – EACH ADD	1.00	1.25	1.50

flavor attention. Eat a stuffed pizza at Nancy's and you know this is a meal, not a snack. Nancy's has a rather broad Italian menu that goes beyond pizza. You will find some genuinely good pasta dishes. Ravioli is stuffed with ground veal, eggs and cheese plus spinach. Manicotti are stuffed with ricotta, then baked and drizzled with sauce. Pizzas range in price from $7.50 to more than $13 and even the smallest will feed at least two people. Pasta dishes are under $4. Meats and fish are $6 to $9. All dinners are served with soup or salad and a side of pasta or baked potato.

Note: Nancy's is also at these locations: 7309 West Lawrence Avenue, Harwood Heights; 940 North York Road, Elmhurst; 1905 North Harlem, Chicago.

NANCY'S, 4256 North Central Avenue, Chicago. Telephone: 736-5828. Hours: 10 am-2 am, daily. Cards: MC, VISA. Reservations recommended. Full bar service. Private party facilities for up to 200 people. Free parking nearby.

K/Rating 17.5/20 • Food 6.5/7 • Service 5/6 • Decor 3/4 • Value 3/3

PASTA

STUFFED SHELLS 3.50
Pasta Shells Stuffed with Ricotta Cheese, Baked in a Rich Tomato Sauce

SPAGHETTI CARUSE 4.00
Chicken Livers, Mushrooms, Tomato, Spices, Sauteed in Red Wine, Over Buttered Spaghetti

BAKED LASAGNA 4.00
Wide Noodles, Special Meat Filling, Parmesan Cheese, Bechamel and Tomato Sauce

RAVIOLI MEAT AND CHEESE 3.75
Hand Made Pasta Pillows Stuffed with Spinach, Veal, Eggs, Parmesan Cheese, In a Delicious Tomato or Meat Sauce

SPAGHETTI WITH MEAT SAUCE 3.00
Served with Bolognesg Style Meat Sauce

MOSTACCIOLI WITH MEAT SAUCE 3.00
Large Hollow Macaroni, Tossed in the Skillet with Meat Sauce

MANICOTTI 3.75
Pasta Muffs Stuffed with Seasoned Ricotta Cheese, Baked in a Rich Tomato Sauce

Chicago
NANTUCKET COVE
Seafood

$$

Seafood restaurants have sprouted up in Chicago in the last few years like mushrooms in the forest after a spring rain. Nantucket Cove has been around long enough to have established roots. The food is generally good, if not great. Flounder stuffed with crab meat is among the better selections. The fish is rich and clean flavored; the crab meat stuffing is accented with wine sauce. Lobster, a house specialty, is reasonably priced here, considering the high price these tasty crustaceans generally command on the wholesale market. From time to time, a special low-priced lobster dinner is featured, but you are best to check on the cost when you visit or make a reservation. Nantucket Cove has a truly distinctive atmosphere and decor, so salty that you might think you should wear a sou'wester to keep high and dry. It is the kind of place Billy Bigelow might go for a schooner of beer and a bucket of steamers after a hard night's work on the carousel. Period accents recall the great whaling days of New England. If our waiter ever introduces himself by saying, "Call me Ishmael," I might not be too surprised.

NANTUCKET COVE, 1000 North Lake Shore Drive, Chicago. Telephone: 943-1600. Hours: 5 pm-11 pm, Sunday-Thursday; until 11:30 pm, Friday-Saturday. Cards: AE, MC, VISA. Reservations taken. Full bar service. Jackets requested for men. Private party facilities for up to 35 people. Parking nearby.

K/Rating 17.5/20 • Food 5.5/7 • Service 5/6 • Decor 4/4 • Value 3/3

Appetizers

OYSTERS ON THE HALF SHELL (6) 2.75	NANTUCKET TURTLE SOUP with Sherry ... 1.60
CHERRYSTONE CLAMS (6) 2.75	CREAMY CLAM CHOWDER Nantucket . 1.25
STEAMED CLAMS 2.75	ONION SOUP au Gratin 1.25
CRABMEAT COCKTAIL.......... 3.25	OYSTERS ROCKEFELLER (4) 2.75

LARGE SHRIMP, Chilled Cocktail or Steamed in Beer 2.95
CEVICHE NANTUCKET: A Spicy Variety of Marinated Fish 1.50

Entrees

SHRIMP FRITTER-FRIED, Sauce Tartare ... 6.95	FILET OF SALMON, HOLLANDAISE 8.95
NEWBURG 7.25	DOVER SOLE................... 9.50
SCALLOPS 7.25	ALASKAN KING CRAB LEGS.......... 9.95
STUFFED DEVILED CRAB 7.75	POMPANO STUFFED WITH
FLOUNDER STUFFED WITH CRABMEAT . 7.75	CRABMEAT HOLLANDAISE 9.95

Lobsters

Ours are not simply alive, but are handled in such a manner that they are their natural ferocious selves.
Pick one from the pond (or watch the waiters do it) and you'll see the difference. We can't divulge our
secret, but it makes such a difference in taste and texture that we serve up to a ton of them a week. All are
steamed unless you tell us otherwise.

ONE CHICKEN LOBSTER: For the Petite Appetite 9.95
MEDIUM SIZE WHOLE LOBSTER.. 14.95
TWO CHICKEN LOBSTERS: For the Hearty Appetite 16.95
BAKED STUFFED LOBSTER SAVANNAH, A Gourmet's Delight 9.95
NANTUCKET PLATTER: One Chicken Lobster, Fried Shrimp and Clams........... 10.95
NEW ENGLAND BEACH PARTY CLAMBAKE (FOR TWO): Two Chicken Lobsters,
Steamed Clams, Shrimp in Shell, Yams, and Corn on the Cob, and Steamed
in Earthern Casserole 21.50

Trout

CHARCOAL BROILED 7.75
SAUTE ALMONDINE 7.95
STUFFED WITH CRABMEAT AND WRAPPED IN VINE LEAVES 8.45

From The Broiler

LAND AND SEAS – Sirloin Steak & Lobster Tail 12.95

WHITEFISH 8.75	CAPTAINS SIRLOIN STEAK ......,,.... 10.50
POMPANO 9.25	MATE'S SIRLOIN STEAK 8.75
REDSNAPPER 9.25	FILET MIGNON 9.25
LOBSTER TAIL 9.50	CHOPPED BEEK STEAK 6.25

(All Entrees are served with Baked Potato or French Fries, Green Tossed Salad, choice of Nantucket Cove
Creamy or other Dressings, Our Own Fresh Baked Cornsticks)

Children Served One Half Order of Shrimp or Chopped Beef, Potato & Salad 3.75

Desserts

ICE CREAM, or Sherbert .... .95	HOT APPLE PIE, Vanilla Sauce .... .95
SPUMONI .... .95	CHEESECAKE .95 WITH STRAWBERRIES 1.25
ECLAIR DE LUXE: An Ice Cream Eclair	CORDIAL PARFAIT................. 1.50
covered with Thick Chocolate Sauce,	STRAWBERRY SNOWBALL: Ice cream
Whipped Topping and Cherries 1.25	covered with shredded coconut and strawberries 1.50

Brews, Beverages and Ferments

Pot of Tea .... .55
Coffee, Special Blend .... .75
Viennese Coffee Briskly Blended, Mocha Ice Cream
and Coffee, Topped with Whipped Topping 2.25
Chocolate Ice Cream Grenada,
with Dark Rum and Nutmeg 2.25

Michelob on Draft 1.25
Heineken on Draft 1.35

WINE adds to the enjoyment of dinner. Our waiters have available a list of our bottled wine selections
and we also have our specially selected California Chablis Wine served by the glass or decanter.

Chicago
NANIWA
Japanese

$

It was in the mid 1960s that Naniwa first opened. This small Japanese restaurant is still in the same location and from the prices, you might think it is still 1966. Although dinner service is à la carte it is not difficult for four people to eat well for little more than $20. For that amount, you could get a double order of tempura, one sukiyaki, a fish teriyaki, an egg and vegetable-rice dish called egg donburi, plus some appetizers and tea. Tempura is probably the easiest introduction for those unfamiliar with Japanese cuisine. One story has it that the cooking method was introduced to Japan by Portugese traders in the 16th century, although little credence has been given the tale by most food historians. In any case, tempura shrimp and vegetables, with their light batter coating are delicious. Another good introduction to Naniwa is sukiyaki. This is a casserole of sliced beef, bean curd, noodles, mushrooms and vegetables in a soup stock. Fish teriyaki, often mackerel, is deep-fried to a dark crisp brown coloring. The bones are easily removed leaving morsels of meat for easy eating. Japanese food at Naniwa offers several choices for more adventurous dining. Eel is cooked with eggs and vegetables. Sashimi, raw tuna belly with horseradish and grated radish is a popular choice. The four-page menu neatly describes each offering so you will not order blindly and come up with something totally unexpected.

NANIWA, 923 West Belmont Avenue, Chicago. Telephone: 348-9027. Hours: 4 pm-9 pm, Monday-Tuesday; noon-9 pm, Thursday-Sunday. No cards. No reservations. No bar service; you may bring your own.

K/Rating 17/20 • Food 6/7 • Service 5/6 • Decor 3/4 • Value 3/3

Chicago
NEW JAPAN ORIENTAL CAFE
Japanese

$

Despite inflation, the "New Japan original egg rolls" are only 45 cents at this neat-as-a-pin small storefront restaurant. A tasteful use of wood and glass creates a hint of Japanese atmosphere just steps away from busy State and Division streets with their clutter of singles' bars. New Japan is tiny; there are only half a dozen or so tables plus a few counter stools. But you don't come here for an authentic tea ceremony. The appeal rather, is some excellent Japanese food at budget prices. Like the egg rolls, the piping hot fried chicken wings are a mere 45 cents. Ramen, typical noodle broth from Japanese kitchens in the $2.15 to $2.65 price range is almost a meal in itself. Large portioned tempura for $3.15 offers a good array of shrimp and vegetables plus a cup of soup, steamed rice and piping hot green tea. The beef teriyaki for $3.50 offers the same. No desserts are served, but you might want to stop into the nearby Ting-a-ling, an old-fashioned ice cream parlor across the street.

NEW JAPAN ORIENTAL CAFE, 45 West Division Street, Chicago. Telephone: 787-4248. Carry-out orders are available for a 10% surcharge. Lunch: 11:45 am-2:30 pm, Monday-Saturday; Dinner: 5 pm-10 pm, Monday-Friday; until 11 pm, Saturday. No cards. No reservations. No bar service; you may bring your own.

K/Rating 15.5/20 • Food 5/7 • Service 4.5/6 • Decor 3/4 • Value 3/3

Two things are usually said about Nick's Fishmarket. First, it is exceptionally good. Second, it is expensive. Both assertions are correct. Thirty dollars per person including a modest wine and tip is not an unusual check. However, portions are large and the menu includes some seafoods not served in Chicago before Nick's opened. For instance, consider abalone in any of four preparations. The basic abalone doré is coated in an egg wash, floured and sautéed in lemon butter. For an added flourish you may have abalone Ricci, the same preparation topped with sautéed asparagus spears, sliced mushrooms and small shrimp. Other preparations offer the abalone with caper-butter or almonds. House specialties include mahi mahi Veronique and good old American catfish. Opakapaka is a fish new to Chicago, thanks to Nick's. It works well with a lemony hollandaise. Bouillabaise à la maison is appropriately seasoned with saffron and includes cut-up chunks of mahi mahi, snapper, mussels and other delectables in its broth. But the soup has a somewhat gelatinous quality which I find unappealing and

Specialities A La Maison

Poached Mahi Mahi Veronique	9.95	Lobster Tail	15.95
Frog Legs, Amandine	10.50	Lobster Thermidor	15.95
Frog Legs, Provençale	10.50	Soft Shell Crab, Meunière (when available)	10.95
Bouillabaisse a la Maison	10.50	Roast Chicken Oregano, Greek Style	9.95
Fresh Catfish, Fishmarket Style	9.95	Calamari Palmerino	9.50
Fresh Catfish, Dill	9.95	Calamari Fritte	9.50
Fresh Hawaiian Ulua, Belle Alliance	10.50	• Fresh Broiled Island Opakapaka, Hollandaise	11.50
Turtle, Teriyaki or Meunière	10.50	Fresh Vegetable Platter	9.95

totally out of character with fish stews. If you like scallops you will love the little morsels of fresh sautéed bay scallops. Not a trace of sand or grit can be found. You can begin dinner at Nick's with such excellent appetizers as soft shell crabs or fried baby squid, which also come in dinner portions. Soups include thick and rich New England clam chowder, consommé and gazpacho. And do not miss Nick's special salad with one of the freshest tasting spinach dressings I have ever enjoyed. Should you want dessert, savor cheesecake or mousse cake for their sweet deliciousness. Nick's Fishmarket is also in Beverly Hills, California and Waikiki, Hawaii.

NICK'S FISHMARKET, 1 First National Plaza, Chicago. Telephone: 621-0200. Hours: Lunch: 11:30 am-3 pm, Monday-Friday; Dinner: 5:30 pm-11:30 pm, Monday-Saturday. Cards: AE, CB, DC, MC, VISA. Reservations required. Full bar service. Jackets requested for men. Private party facilities for up to 14 people. Valet parking after 6 pm at the Monroe Street entrance.

K/Rating 18.5/20 • Food 7/7 • Service 6/6 • Decor 3/4 • Value 2.5/3

Dinners

Fishmarket Clam Chowder or Nick's Special Salad

Fresh Filet of Sole, Meunière or Amandine
Fresh Filet of Sole Fontainbleau
Fresh Stuffed Baked Trout
• Island Mahi Mahi, Amandine
• Fresh Broiled Swordfish, Hollandaise or Duglere
Fresh Catfish, Fishmarket Style
Fresh Catfish, Dill

Seafood Au Gratin
Fried Scallops
Roast Chicken Oregano, Greek Style
Combination Seafood Loui Salad
• Fresh Poached Salmon Crevettes
Fresh Snapper, Hollandaise
Fresh Snapper, Belle Alliance

Fresh Vegetable
Beverage
14.95

Chicago
NORTH STAR INN
Italian $$

The North Star Inn was purchased and taken over in 1978 by Vic Giannotti, former owner of the restaurant that bears his family name in Forest Park, q.v. Giannotti has brought all of his culinary talent to bear in building the Inn into an excellent Italian restaurant. Although kitchen space is limited and the staff was still being trained as of this writing, fans of Giannotti's original restaurant will find perfect solace in such delights as veal piccante, merluzzi, scungill and baked clams. But the real secret of the North Star Inn is often what is not on the menu. Ask about specials, often prepared in limited quantities for long-time customers and friends. You could wind up with such specialties as zucchini marinated in oil and mint, marinated bell peppers or the tangy bitter vegetable, rape. Desserts include one of the best light cheesecakes around; like so many of the other hidden treasures, it is not on the menu: You will have to ask for it. Vic is back in the kitchen and that's some of the best Chicago food news in years.

NORTH STAR INN, 15 West Division Street, Chicago. Telephone: 337-4349. Hours: 5 pm-midnight, Monday-Saturday; bar until 2 am. Cards: AE, DC, MC, VISA. Reservations required. Casual, neat dress acceptable. Valet parking.

K/Rating 18/20 • Food 7/7 • Service 5/6 • Decor 3/4 • Value 3/3

140

Steaks and Chops From the Broiler

Prime New York Cut Sirloin Steak (16 oz.) 10.50

Prime New York Cut Sirloin Steak (22 oz.) 14.50

Filet Mignon 10.50

Prime Butt Steak 9.50

Ladies Cut Prime Sirloin Steak 9.50

Pepper Steak 9.50

Lamb Chops thin (3) 9.50

Center Cut Pork Chops 7.75

Not Responsible for Steaks Well Done

Veal Dishes

Veal Piccante 8.00
Sliced Veal sauted in Butter & Lemon with Special Topping

Veal Scaloppine 7.75
Sliced Veal Sauted with Onions, Mushrooms and Wine Sauce

Veal Parmigiana 7.75
Veal Cutlet topped with Mozzarella Cheese and Sauce

Breaded Veal Cutlet 7.50

Veal Francaise 7.75
Slices of Veal Dipped in Flour and Egg, Fried in Butter, Lemon Rings

Veal Saltimbocca A La Parmigiana 7.75
Veal Cutlet stuffed with Prosciutto and covered with Mozzarella and Baked

Poultry

Chicken Vesuvio 7.75
Chicken sauted in Olive Oil, Garlic, Oregano and White Wine

Chicken A La Cacciatore 7.75
Chicken sauted in Olive Oil, White Wine, Fresh Tomatoes and Mushrooms

Chicken A La Florentine 7.75
Chicken Dipped in Egg Batter, Fried in Olive Oil

Broiled Spring Chicken 7.50

Chicken Oreganato 7.00
Chicken Sauted in Butter, Lemon, Oregano

Chicken Livers and Mushrooms Sauted 6.75

Seafood

Broiled Lake Superior Whitefish 7.75

Broiled Red Snapper 8.50

Red Snapper Livornaise 9.50

Broiled African Lobster Tails, Drawn Butter .... Market Price

French Fried Shrimp 8.00

Shrimp Marinara with Linguini or Spaghetti 8.50

Deep Sea Scallops 7.75

Baked Bacala with Potatoes 7.75
(Above Dinners Include Soup or Salad, Bread & Butter, Coffee or Tea
Spinach, Baked Potato, French Fries, or Boiled Potatoes

Chicago
OTTO'S BEER HOUSE
AND GARDEN CLUB
American/Creole   **$$**

If you ever wondered what happened to the counter culture
of the 1960s, just take a look at Otto's Beer House and
Garden Club. Back in the days when Weathermen trashed
the Gold Coast and yippies were running pigs for elective
office, Otto's was a small bar and outdoor garden café
with a menu of not much more than burgers, brats and
beer. But now, as sure as Rennie Davis is an insurance
salesman, Otto's has blossomed into a full-fledged restau-
rant. Not exactly decadent by any means, Otto's neverthe-
less has gone far beyond the seedy neighborhood it
inhabits. The bar still slugs out draft beer and mixed drinks
but patrons are more likely to be watching the Cubs or the
Bears on TV rather than discussing how the imperialists are
exploiting the Third World. When it comes to the food,
Otto's does things nicely. Despite bentwood chairs that
might give a backache to an India-rubber man, it is an
attractive setting for lunch or dinner. The emphasis is on

CREOLE SPECIALTIES

	A la Carte	Dinner
MRS. THELMA ROBINSON'S CHRISTMAS GUMBO - A seafood, chicken, ham mixture simmered in a dark roux base, made with fresh vegetables, served with steamed rice	4.50	5.50
CORRINE DUNBAR'S SHRIMP & HAM JAMBALAYA - Rich rice dish decended from Spanish Cajun origins. Made with shrimp and ham	4.95	5.95
LOUISIANA SHRIMP CREOLE - Shrimp cooked in a tangy tomato sauce accented with Cajun spices	4.95	5.95
CRABMEAT MORNAY - Crabmeat smothered in a thick cheese sauce slightly spiced with cayenne	5.25	6.25
CREOLE COMBINATION PLATE - A portion each of creole shrimp, jambalaya, and a cup of gumbo	6.25	7.25

FISH

FISH DU JOUR - Steamed vegetable and rice	priced to market	
FRESH SALMON MORNAY - Steamed vegetable and rice	priced to market	
FRESH RAINBOW TROUT - Stuffed with crabmeat, steamed vegetable and rice	5.95	6.95
FRESH TROUT AMANDINE - Rice and steamed vegetable	5.75	6.75
SEAFOOD COMBINATION PLATE - Fresh broiled trout, fried clams, and Alaskan King Crab Legs	6.95	7.95

FRIED FISH

FISH 'n CHIPS - Tempura batter, cottage fries	3.50	4.50
FRIED CLAM STRIPS - Tartar sauce, lettuce and cole slaw	3.95	4.95

(Complete Dinners include Soup and Salad)

142

New Orleans and Creole cookery. For instance, Mrs. Thelma Robinson's Christmas gumbo is chockful of shrimp, ham, crab meat and chicken in a zesty stew of okra and other vegetables. Where you find gumbo, you often find jambalaya, the Creole rice casserole usually made with many of the same ingredients as gumbo, plus Tabasco sauce and whatever other ingredients or seasonings may be at hand. Crab meat mornay is another tasty entrée choice, a bit more elegant than the Cajun style. There is lots of good tasting crab meat topped with a bounty of mildly seasoned cheese sauce. The platter includes a side of rice and vegetable of the day. For small appetites and budget watchers, Otto's serves egg dishes, omelettes and salads as well as some sandwiches. Service has been annoyingly slow on a previous visit, but all else has been outstanding at Otto's.

OTTO'S BEER HOUSE AND GARDEN CLUB, 2024 North Halsted Street, Chicago. Telephone: 528-2230. Hours: 10 am-11 pm, Monday-Thursday; until midnight, Friday-Saturday. No cards. Reservations taken. Full bar service. Casual dress acceptable. Private party facilities for 25 to 100 people.

K/Rating 16/20 • Food 6/7 • Service 3.5/6 • Decor 3.5/4 • Value 3/3

EGGS AND OMELETTES

All omelettes are 3 eggs served with fresh grapefruit at breakfast
or a fresh steamed vegetable at dinner.

OMELETTE FLORENTINE - With creamed spinach 3.25	**SOUR CREAM & ASPARAGUS OMELETTE** ... 3.75
FRESH MUSHROOM OMELETTE 3.25	**FRESH ALFALFA SPROUT & CHEESE OMELETTE** 3.50
TWO CHEESE OMELETTE - Cheddar and Mozzarella 3.25	**CRABMEAT OMELETTE MORNAY** 4.50
CHEESE & MUSHROOM OMELETTE 3.50	**GUACAMOLE OMELETTE** Summer Only................. 3.95
STEAK 'n EGGS - Steak, eggs (scrambled), fresh grapefruit and New Orleans bread pudding 5.95	**IRISH BREAKFAST -** 3 strips of bacon, 3 sausage, eggs (scrambled) fresh grapefruit and New Orleans bread pudding 4.25

FISH 'n EGGS 4.95
Fish in Tempura batter, eggs (scrambled), fresh grapefruit
and New Orleans bread pudding.

Chicago
PATRICE
French

$$$

This one is hard to find, but once you do find it you will know that it was worth the search. Tucked away on Ernest Court, Patrice is a fairly small restaurant with accommodations for only about 50 people. The crowd here seems to be rather sophisticated: The food meets the challenge. The à la carte menu offers such successes as mussels in cream sauce with shallots or the coarse ground pâté maison with cornichons. Onion soup is hot and sweet. The Patrice salad is a symphony of color with sliced tomato, green beans, watercress and other garden delights of the season. Nightly specialties will often include fresh fish such as salmon with Pernod sauce or perhaps quail in red wine sauce. Entrées are full flavored yet still retain much of the lightness of the new cuisine so much favored by French chefs these days. The calves' liver with white seedless grapes (not raisins, as the menu says) is a far different approach from the more common liver and onions. Duckling with apple cider sauce is a house specialty that is not to be missed. And do not neglect the fillets of sole rolled over spinach, garnished with a vegetable julienne and served in a creamy white wine sauce. Desserts include a light caramel custard with a trace of orange liqueur and an incredibly rich vacherin made with fresh strawberries in season and raspberry sauce.

PATRICE, 914 Ernest Court, Chicago. Telephone: 944-0265. Hours: 5:30 pm-11:30 pm, Monday-Saturday. Cards: AE, MC, VISA. Reservations requested. Full bar service. Jackets requested for men. Private party facilities for up to 50 people. Valet parking and garages nearby.

K/Rating 19/20 • Food 6/7 • Service 6/6 • Decor 4/4 • Value 3/3

Les hors d'oeuvres

Le paté maison 2.50
    Homemade country style paté

Les huîtres 3.75
    Oysters on the half shell with red wine vinegar & shallots

Le saumon fumé 3.50
    Smoked salmon

Le cocktail de crevettes 2.75
    Shrimp cocktail

Les escargots en casserole chablisienne 3.50
    Braised snails in brandy and tarragon sauce

Les quenelles de brochet nantua 3.25
    Pike mousse dumplings in crayfish sauce baked with sauce

Les moules-marinière 3.75
    Mussels with white wine, cream and shallots

Le saucisson lyonnais en croute 1.95
    Baked sausage in a crust with truffle sauce

Les Entrées

Le plat du jour 10.50
    Ask your waiter for the specialty of the day

Le tournedos au poivre 11.75
    French style pepper steak in brandy sauce

L'escalope de veau vallée d'auge 10.50
    Veal scallopini in apple brandy cream sauce

L'entrecôte grillée maitre d'hôtel 11.75
    Broiled sirloin steak with seasoned butter

Le canard au cidre (our chef's creation!) 10.25
    Roast duck with apple cider sauce

Le carré d'agneau aux herbs 12.50
    Herb seasoned roasted rack of lamb

Les coquilles St. Jacques (Patrice creation!) 10.25
    Sauteed scallops with white wine mushroom gratinee

Le foie de veau aux raisins 9.75
    Calf's liver sauteed with raisins in sherry sauce

Les filets de sole grande bouffe 10.75
    Fresh filets of sole served over spinach with sauce and vegetable strips

Chicago
PIQUEO
Peruvian   **$$$**

It looks as if the Asturrizaga family has a lock on Peruvian restaurants in Chicago. One branch owns La Llama, q.v., another brother is involved in El Inca and Moises Asturrizaga started it all at Piqueo. Piqueo strikes me as a place caught in a Catch-22 situation: Mr. Asturrizaga wants to serve authentic Peruvian foods at his more than decade-old restaurant. But neighborhood people have not given it proper support, nor have enough serious diners been drawn by car. Thus, the seasonings have been tempered to appeal to a broader cross section of diners. Table d'hôte dinners range in price from $12 to $15, depending upon the main course. There is no printed menu. Instead, items are recited by a waiter who gives full descriptions of what is being served for each course. Ceviche, the lime-marinated fish with a strong onion accent, is an often prepared appetizer. Shrimp in cream sauce is mild; I prefer ocapa, breaded, fried shrimp seasoned with a hot sauce at the table. Other courses fairly well parallel what is served at La Llama. My suggestion is that if you demand authenticity, go there. If you want more Americanized Peruvian food, try Piqueo. On the other hand, a telephone call ahead to Moises Asturrizaga with a request for truly authentic food is likely to work wonders. Because when Piqueo is good, it is very good indeed.

PIQUEO, 5427 North Clark Street, Chicago. Telephone: 769-0455. Hours: 5:30 pm-10:30 pm, Tuesday-Saturday. Cards: AE, CB, DC, VISA. Reservations required. No bar service: you may bring your own. Parking on street.

K/Rating 15.5/20 • Food 5/7 • Service 5/6 • Decor 4/4 • Value 1.5/3

Chicago
THE PRIME HOUSE
Steaks/Ribs/Chicken $$

A large charcoal grill dominates the front of this restaurant, so as soon as you walk inside you can begin anticipating all the good meat to come. Naturally, the barbecue ribs are popular with many diners, but steak is what The Prime House is really all about. Steaks come in several cuts and sizes, including the 17-ounce T-bone for an extremely reasonable $11.25. I also like the smaller nine-ounce butt (always a flavorful cut of meat) and occasionally the shish kebab, for its char-roasted flavor, enhanced by an assortment of skewered vegetables. The salad bar holds a bounty of fresh garden delights and is included with all dinners as are a baked potato, rolls, butter and coffee or tea. For charcoal broiled prime beef, there is hardly a better value around than The Prime House.

THE PRIME HOUSE, 4156 North Kedzie Avenue, Chicago. Telephone: 463-9732. Hours: 11 am-midnight, daily. Cards: MC, VISA. Reservations recommended. Full bar service. Casual dress acceptable. Private party facilities. Ample parking.

K/Rating 17.5/20 • Food 6.5/7 • Service 5/6 • Decor 3/4 • Value 3/3

Piper's Alley

Chicago
PRONTO RISTORANTE
Northern Italian

$$

Pronto is a New York import which seems to have caught the fancy of Chicago diners, despite a shaky start that included brusque service and high prices. Fortunately prices have been cut back a bit and service improved, although I have had experiences in which a waiter or waitress hardly seemed to know from which end of the bottle the wine is poured. But, by and large, Pronto has become a successful entry on the Chicago dining scene. We prefer the back portion of the two-tiered dining room; it is quieter and more intimate than the kitchen-tile ambiance of the front. Pronto makes a big thing of pasta; their pasta kitchen in the front is one of the first things to catch your eye. Tagliatelle verdi alla Bolognese is a tribute to Italian patriotism with its red, green and white colors. Spaghetti frutti di mare is excellent treatment of the ubiquitous noodle. Fettucine Pronto, a chef's suggestion, is overpoweringly bland. Pronto's fish preparations are topnotch. A particular success is fillet of sole served in a light cream sauce with tasty mussels and shrimp. Similarly, veal gets excellent treatment in its various preparations. Good desserts top off dinner.

PRONTO RISTORANTE, 200 East Chestnut Street, Chicago. Telephone: 664-6181. Hours: 11:30 am-11:30 pm, Sunday-Thursday; until midnight, Friday-Saturday. Cards: AE, DC, MC, VISA. Reservations recommended. Full bar service. Casual, neat dress acceptable. Semi-private party facilities available in upper level dining room. Valet parking.

K/Rating 14.5/20 • Food 5.5/7 • Service 5/6 • Decor 2/4 • Value 2/3

PESCE FISH

CONCHIGLIE ALLA SICILIANA (sea scallops with garlic and parsley)	7.45
SOGLIOLA DI ALTO MARE (Filet of sole, mussels and shrimps)	7.45
SCAMPI FRA DIAVOLO (shrimps in spicy tomato sauce)	8.95
SCAMPI DELLA CASA (shrimps in chef sauce)	8.95

CARNE MEAT

ESCALOPE ALLA MILANESE (with rice, spaghetti or vegetable)	7.45
POLLO ALLA CACCIATORE (chicken with fresh tomatoes, mushrooms and wine sauce)	6.95
SCALOPPINE MARSALA (veal, mushrooms in marsala sauce)	7.45
PICCATA DI VITELLO CON LIMONE (veal sauteed in butter and lemon)	7.45
VEAL PAILLARDE (broiled veal cutlet)	9.95
BROILED SIRLOIN STEAK OR ALLA PIZZAIOLA	11.95

SPECIALITA

MELANZANE ALLA PARMIGIANA (eggplant, ham, cheese and tomato)	5.25
CARCIOFINI RIPIENI AL FORNO (stuffed artichokes, veal, mozzarella, tomato sauce, parmesan)	5.25

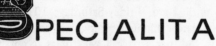

SCALOPPINE PRONTO (veal, prosciutto, mozzarella, egg plant)	7.45

Chicago
R. J. Grunts
American $

The R stands for Rich, the J for Jerry; Grunts just sounded right to Rich Melman and Jerry Orzoff, the two founders of the Lettuce Entertain You, Inc. restaurant empire. R. J. Grunts was their first and still may be the most fun. I am certain it started the trend toward trendy restaurants. Not that it is particularly fancy, but a glance at the huge menu reveals a sense of humor about food, without an insult to taste or pocketbook. The menu notes that all dinners include a free run at the salad bar "where you may choose from our special salad dressings, vegetable toppings, appetizers, lots of things you've never seen before (we're still not sure what that green stuff in the corner is)." Or there is the daily special, which as the menu notes "at press time we didn't know what today's special would be. And furthermore we don't know how much it is. But maybe your waitress will know ... maybe not." With that kind of irreverence, how can you go too far wrong? The truth is, you can't at R. J. Grunts. The food is good and tasty basic USA, served up with a lot of imagination in most cases. By the way, the Sunday brunch for $4.95 is a real bargain; let's hope Rich doesn't find out how much of one it is or he might raise the price. I won't tell if you won't.

R. J. GRUNTS, 2056 Lincoln Park West, Chicago. Telephone: 929-5363. Hours: 11:30 am-midnight, Monday-Thursday; until 1 am, Friday-Saturday; 10 am-midnight, Sunday. No cards. Limited reservation policy for larger parties only. Full bar service. Casual dress acceptable. Private party facilities. Discount parking in nearby garage.

K/Rating 17/20 • Food 5/7 • Service 6/6 • Decor 3/4 • Value 3/3

---

1. HAMBURGER
Juicy chopped Sirloin charbroiled to your taste and served on a lightly toasted sesame bum. (And to add a touch)..it's graced by a heaping portion of cottage fries, our own home made cole slaw and (of course) a dull pickle. **$2⁷⁵**

1a. *CHEESEBURGER
Absolutely the same as above with one gooey exception. Cheese.
* Your choice at no extra charge **$2⁷⁵**

2. GRUNTBURGER ★★★★
The cornerstone of Burgerdom. A charbroiled chopped sirloin topped w/ fried onion and blue cheese dressing. Plus.. cottage fries, cole slaw & pickle. **$2⁷⁵**

3. GOURMET BURGER
This burger is topped with mushrooms, chives, Swisss cheeeze, a rich brown sauce, and served on a toasted sesame bun with cole slaw, cottage fries and a pickle. **$2⁹⁵**

4. SORRY HUN · NO BUN
Sauteed vegetables nestled upon a burger with Italian seasonings, sprinkled w/ parmesan and covered with mozarella cheeze. **$2⁸⁰**

5. ROAST BEEF AW JUICE ★★
Thinly sliced roast beef brisket steeped in its own natural gravy and piled high on a toasted sesame bun.. complimented by tasty fried onion slices, cottage fries and a very dill pickle. **$2⁹⁰** Try this on Italian bread. mmm

6. ROAST BEEF BE QUE ★★★
Very much (exactly) as #5 with R.J.s own B.B.Q sauce. **$2⁹⁵**

7. STEAK TERIYAKI WICH
Charcoal broiled steak that's served on Italian (?) bread with a side of teriyaki sauce. **$3²⁵**

8. TUNA TERRIFIC
Tuna w/ tomato, mushrooms, melted cheese & a side of vegetables open faced n' cold **$2⁸⁵** *available in casserole.

12. LOVE OMLETT REVISED
Sauteed mushrooms bedded down in a frothy mat of freshly beaten (?) eggs.. Slowly pan fried.. and covered w/ creamie mushroom and Sherry sauce. **$2⁶⁵**

Constant testing and endless research personally conducted by Himself."

LUNCHEON SALAD BAR ★★★★
From 11:30 til DINNER. Monday through Saturday you may help yourself to the Salad table w/your sandwich **$1⁰⁰** Now, if all you want is salad...... **$2⁶⁵**

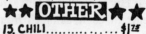

w/onion soup, cuppasoop, or chili salad is $1⁵⁰ extra

★★ OTHER ★★

13. CHILI............... $1⁷⁵

14. FISH SOUP ALA GRUNT
Scalllopps, halibut, clams & shrimps enjoy communal bath in warm spicy tomato base. **$2.95**

17. MEAL IN A BOWL
Large bowl of our homemade vegetable beef soup (w/beef), with crouton and served with cobblestone bread and whipped butter **$2⁹⁵**

18. ONION SOUP EPISODE ★★★
All we can say at this time is.. Home made onion soup covered w/croutons and some melted cheeses and it's served in a crock! **$1⁶⁵**

19. RAFAEL BURGER
R.J.'s Cousin from Vallarta was outraged with the U.S. version of the Jamburger (the national food of Mexico) Similar to Gruntburger but features guacamole, hot sauce, white stuff & tortilla chips **$2⁸⁵**

I have often felt it would be difficult for almost anyone to blind taste food from any number of Greek restaurants and identify from where it came. With very few exceptions the food at Chicago's Greek restaurants is similarly prepared and served. True, one restaurant may prepare fish better than another, or a salad may be more attractive, a soup more pungent. But on balance, there is more similarity than difference among the Greek restaurants I know and enjoy. The differences that do exist are created primarily by the personalities of the owners. They are all in their own way ebullient, gregarious, loquacious hosts who oversee their domains perhaps as much as ancient Greek kings ruled their city-states. At Roditys, the character of the restaurant seems to come as much from the clientele. On a typical evening it may range from orthodox priest to businessman to families with dark-eyed grandmothers and small babies swaddled against an intruding chill. Yet the non-Greek who merely craves good food can find himself in a home-away-from-home at Roditys. Service is flawless. Foods may take some time to reach your table, but that is a sign of fresh

Egg Lemon Soup with Rice	**.35; .50**
Soup of the Day	**.35; .50**
Gyros, Barbequed Beef & Lamb	**2.95**
Saganaki, Kasseri Cheese Flambe	**1.75**
Greek Salad	**1.00**
Greek Village Salad, (No Lettuce)	**1.35**
Taramosalata, Fish Roe Salad	**1.40**
Boiled Dandeloins, Fresh Daily	**1.75**
Spanakotiropita, Spinach-Cheese Pie	**2.95**
Octopus in Wine Sauce	**2.95**
Home-Made Yogurt, Fresh Daily	**1.75**

preparation, not necessarily a lax kitchen staff. Freshness is the mark of fine restaurants. At Roditys I have been impressed by the fresh deliciousness of red snapper hot from the broiler. Lamb, a meat given soul by the Greeks, is braised, broiled, roasted, barbecued. It comes mixed with beef in gyros, on the bone as a chop, roasted and sliced from the loin, leg or shoulder. Order typical Greek casseroles like pastitsio or moussaka, stuffed grape leaves called dolmades or spinach pie with the tongue twisting name spanakotiropita. Another tongue twister to say, but a balm to the tongue is taramasalata. This is a creamy fish roe salad, light pink in color with the sweet saltiness of the sea mixed in with tart seasonings. Old favorites on the menu range from saganaki for an appetizer to baklava and custard for dessert. Then sit back and enjoy a hot draft of strong Greek coffee.

RODITYS, 222 South Halsted Street, Chicago. Telephone: 454-0800. Hours: 11 am-1 am, Sunday-Thursday; until 2 am, Friday-Saturday. Cards: AE. Reservations recommended. Full bar service. Private party facilities for up to 50 people. Free parking lot nearby.

K/Rating 17/20 • Food 6/7 • Service 6/6 • Decor 2.5/4 • Value 2.5/3

MOUSSAKA, Layers of Eggplant & Ground Beef . **2.95**

PASTICHIO **2.95**
Layers of Macaroni, Ground Beef & Bechamel Sauce

DOLMADES. **2.95**
Stuffed Vine leaves with Ground Beef, Rice & Cream Sauce

SPANAKOTIROPITA, Spinach-Cheese Pie . . . **2.95**

BRAISED LAMB **3.50**
With choice of Eggplant, Okra, Squash, Green Beans, Potatoes, Rice Pilaf or Spaghetti

BRAISED STEER **3.50**
With choice of Eggplant, Okra, Squash, Green Beans, Potatoes, Rice Pilaf or Spaghetti

Chicago
SAGE'S EAST
Continental/American

$$

Gene Sage is one restaurateur who takes his food business almost as seriously as he does his saloons. The restaurant is dark and masculine and can be noisy when crowded. While short of haute cuisine, Sage's East offers better-than-good beef and bird as well as nicely done seafoods. Let your mood be your guide as you look over the menu; there are no standouts, nor are there failures. An excellent wine list offers an extraordinarily wide range at fair prices. Desserts will make you fat and happy.

SAGE'S EAST, 181 East Lake Shore Drive, Chicago. Telephone: 944-1557. Hours 11:30 am-2 am, daily. Cards: CB, DC, MC, VISA. Reservations recommended. Full bar service. Jackets required for men. Private party facilities. Valet parking.

K/Rating 17/20 • Food 5/7 • Service 5/6 • Decor 4/4 • Value 3/3

MAN'S MEAT

SIRLOIN STEAK, PROFESSOR MORIARITY Prime Sirloin Steak,
with Mushrooms, Onions sauted in Burgundy Wine with delicate herb seasoning, Garnee   9.95   79/6

STAKE au POIVRE, The Classic Pepper Stake,
with cracked Peppercorns, Heavy Cream, Flambe en Cognac, Onions   9.95   79/6

VEAL in the MANNER of the VIRGIN QUEEN, Medallions of Milk-Fed Veal,
prepared A La Piccata with Marsala Wine, Garnee of the Realm   9.95   79/6

MIXED GRILL, WHITEHALL Double Rib Lamb Chop,
saute Calves Liver, Bacon Dominion of Canada, Mint and Mushrooms   10.95   87/60

TOURNEDOS DE BOUF CHASSEUR,
With Mushrooms, Shallots, Dry White Wine on Toast Rounds, Garnee   11.95   95/6

RACK of LAMB, INNS of COURT, Au Bouquetiers'
with Pommes De Terra and Bacon Dominion of Canada, Garnee — for one   13.50   108/0;   for two   25.00   200/0

PRIME FILET MIGNON, LORD NELSON, with Mushroom Caps, Sauce Bernaise, Crisp Onions Warwick & Garnee of the Realm   11.95   95/6

EYE of the PRIME RIB, LORD MAYOR, Horseradish Sauce Tower of London
Roast in Natural Juices or Bordelaise Sauce. English Cut   8.95   71/6   Commonwealth Cut   9.95   79/6

BABY-BACK-RIBS, Dissertation on Roast Pig, Sauce Charles Lamb   8.95   71/60

SIRLOIN STAKE, PRIME MINISTER, Prime Center Cut of Colonial Beef with Mushrooms, Onions Warwick and Garnee of the Realm   12.95   103/6

CHATEAUBRIAND, SIR ANTHONY EDEN au Bouquetiere Potatoes and Herb butter (for two)   24.00   192/0

Above orders served with Appetizers from Rolling Carts, Salad of the Manor, Potato Du Jour or Pasta and Vegetable Du Jour

BIRDS & BOWLS

ROAST DUCKLING WILLIAM & MARY
Sauce Montmorency, Riz Sauvage, and Garnish Apropos   8.50   68/0

LOBSTER au Whiskey
saute Lobster, bey Shrimp in Whiskey Sauce with Mushrooms, and Riz   12.50   100/0

LE BOUEF of the BURGUNDIAN DUKES
Beef Tenderloin, in Burgundy Wine with Salsify and Mushrooms, and Riz Sauvage   8.95   71/6

Above orders served with Appetizers from the Rolling Carts, Salad of the Manor, Vegetable Du Jour

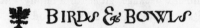

FISH, MOLLUSC & CRUSTACEANS

POACHED SALMON in Chablis Sauce with Mushrooms, Shrimp and Mussels, Rice   8.95   71/60

PRAWNS de Jonghe   8.95   71/60

SCALLOPS and SHRIMP, FOUR SEASONS with Mushrooms, White Wine and Cognac with Sauce of the Dukes, Ring of Rice   8.95   71/60

RED SNAPPER, PRINCE CONSORT, Broiled to Perfection and served with a Dijon Sauce or Almond Butter. Garnee of Citrus   8.95   71/60

KING CRABLEGS from the **BERING SEA** Broiled in the Shell, called King's Council, with Tart Mustard Sauce Cromwell or Drawn Butter   9.75   78/0

CRABMEAT of Our Italian Cousins, en Casserole with a hint of Garlic, Mushrooms and Pasta Andante   8.95

SCAMPI, in Our Own Fashion, Saute with Shallots, Mushrooms, Artichoke hearts, Tomatos, delicately seasoned, Rice   9.96

FILET of DOVER SOLE presented in Thy Choice of Three Modes, Amandine, Ala Meuniere or with Chablis Sauce and Grapes

LOBSTER TAIL from the Waters of the Cape of the South African Colony, Drawn Butter   13.75   110/0

To your advance order LIVE LOBSTER from The Waters of the Wilderness below Newfoundland (Maine) at Market
Served with Appetizers from the Rolling Carts, Salad of the Manor, Rice or Potatoes and Vegetable Du Jour

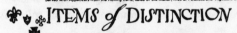

ITEMS of DISTINCTION

BONELESS BREAST OF DUCKLING FITZHUGH
Breast of Duckling rolled in coconut served with a brandied Cherry Sauce,
Riz Sauvage, and Garnee of the Realm   8.95   71/60

SIRLOIN STAKE INNER TEMPLE
Prime Sirloin prepared with a delicate blend of seasonings and Roquefort Sauce of Pitt the Younger, flamed at the table in
Cognac with Garnee of the Realm, Onions Rings and Riz Sauvage   9.96   79/6

VEAL MALAYSIA
Milk fed Provini Veal Saute', breaded with Almonds, done to a golden brown with piquant sauce, Riz Sauvage   9.95   79/6

ICED MAINE LOBSTER, on Nest of Lettuce, with Tomato,
Avocado, Raw Mushroom, Artichoke Hearts, Asperagus Spears, Hard cooked Eggs, Sherried Mayonnaise or Remoulade   9.95   79/6

Above orders served with Appetizers from the Rolling Carts and Salad of the Manor

157

SALLY'S STAGE

$$

If you are ready for a restaurant in which the hostess wears roller skates and zips around a wooden track leading patrons to their tables, then you are ready for Sally's Stage. If you want a little more excitement along with your rolls and butter, there's always the $100,000 Barton Theatre Organ that bellows everything from "Beer Barrel Polka" to "Theme from 2001," depending upon who is at the keyboard. As you might suspect, Sally's Stage is not your everyday sort of diner. What we have here is the quintessential entertainment package, great for a family with loads of kids or adults out looking for a kicky good time. Combine the outrageously corny entertainment, genuinely pleasant service and sometimes more than passable food and you have a formula for success (by Chicago standards, that is). Pizza, ribs, steaks and sandwiches make up the menu. The ribs are prepared with a secret recipe sauce (doesn't everyone have one?) created by the original Sally's Rib Shack, a previous tenant who lives on in some degree of blessed memory between the waitresses turned chorus girls and the Amateur Night every Tuesday. Monday evening brings a pantomimist (plus bargain priced ribs), Wednesday is magic night, Thursday they play Let's Make a Deal. I am not making it up, folks. This is a restaurant fact, not fiction. It is outrageous good fun and probably the only time you will get your glass of Perrier from someone on roller skates.

SALLY'S STAGE, 6335 North Western Avenue, Chicago. Telephone: 764-0990. Hours: 5 pm-11 pm, Monday-Thursday; until 1 am, Friday-Saturday; noon-11 pm, Sunday. No cards. Reservations taken only on Sunday, noon-4 pm. Full bar service. Parking lot next door.

K/Rating 18/20 • Food 5/7 • Service 6/6 • Decor 4/4 • Value 3/3

Marshall Field Clock

Chicago
SALVATORE'S
Northern Italian

$$$

True gourmets search out Northern Italian food with the
same zeal as they do French cooking. After all, need you be
reminded from whom the French learned their art? With
that said, consider Salvatore's. It is not marked from the
street, so you will have to look closely. But there is valet
parking to reward you, once you have found your goal.
Salvatore's occupies the large dining room of a fading hotel.
The room is high ceilinged, lit with porcelain chandeliers
and painted a forest green with white trim. None of this can
disguise the room's age, which is as it should be. If the
printed menu is at all confusing, or should you have any
questions about preparation, your waiter will deftly guide
you through. Begin with antipasto such as scampi Marsala
or elegant prosciutto and figs. Soup varies from day to day;
my samplings have always been excellent. No Italian meal is
complete without the pasta course. Linguini with mussels

ANTIPASTI

Conch Salad	3.50	Scallops Casalinga	3.25
Prosciutto and Melon	2.95	Scampi Marsala	4.95
Prosciutto and Figs	3.50	Mussels Marinara	3.50
Calamari Cacciatore	3.50	Tenserloin Tartar	4 95

ZUPPA

del Giorno	1.50		

PASTA

Fettuccini Carbonara	6.50	Tortellini Salvatore	6.95
Paglia e Fieno	6.50	Linguini with Mussels and	
Linguini with Clams	6.75	Clams Marinara	7.50

and clams is a favorite. Should seafood be your choice for a main course, you are certain to enjoy the zuppa di pesce. No cut-up chunks in this thick broth, instead a small fresh bass or other available fish is cooked in the liquid and brought whole to the table where it is presented after boning. Veal is another Salvatore's specialty. Saltimbocca Florentine and veal with lemon are both nicely done. Chicken gets its due with the spezzatino de pollo. Cut-up chunks are served with red and green peppers along with rice; not only are the colors reflective of Italian patriotism but the chicken and peppers are gustatorially satisfying, too.

SALVATORE'S, 525 West Arlington Place, Chicago. Telephone: 528-1200. Hours: 6 pm-midnight, Monday-Saturday. Cards: AE, MC, VISA. Reservations taken. Full bar service. Casual, neat dress acceptable. Private party facilities for up to 250 people. Valet parking.

K/Rating 16.5/20• Food 6.5/7• Service 5/6• Decor 3/4 • Value 2/3

IL CONSIGLIO DEL CUOCO

Spezzatino de Pollo	7.25	Petto di Pollo Rosamarina	7.50
Saltimbocca Fiorentine	8.25	Petto di Pollo Parmigiana	7.50
Scallopini Limone	7.95	Veal Chop Milanese	8.50
Veal & Eggplant Bella	8.25	Veal Chop Salvatore	8.95
Capriccioso	9.95	Filetto di Manzo	

PESCE

Scampi Villa Sassi	10.95	Scampi alla Marsala	10.95
Zuppa di Pesce	11.25	Scampi & Calamari	
Fresh Fish of the Day	market	mixed Fry	9.95

Chicago
SALZBURGER HOF
Austrian/Continental

$$

Time was when Salzburger Hof was known strictly as an Austrian restaurant, serving delectable schnitzels, flavorful sauerbraten and fantastic nockerl. The schnitzels, sauerbraten and nockerl are still there, but recently Salzburger Hof has expanded to a continental menu. So you will find a beef Wellington, which is really boeuf en croûte with a goose liver pâté and duxelles garnish beneath the heavy pastry crust, all bathed in a red wine-based truffle sauce. You will also find other selections not usually found in Austrian or German restaurants—which only goes to show how some restaurants will change to adapt to what is commonly called "popular demand." I still favor the original Austrian delights and prefer to take my Wellington et al elsewhere. But better veal dishes, goulash or sauerbraten are hard to come by. Desserts are lusciously prepared. The nockerl and the Kaiserschmarren, a baked German pancake with apricot sauce, are house specialties.

SALZBURGER HOF, 4128 North Lincoln Avenue, Chicago. Telephone: 528-6909. Hours: 11:30 am-11 pm, daily. Cards: AE, DC, MC, VISA. Reservations taken. Full bar service. Casual, neat dress acceptable. Private party facilities for up to 45 people. Free parking nearby.

K/Rating 17.5/20 • Food 5.5/7 • Service 5/6 • Decor 4/4 • Value 3/3

Dinners

European Specialties

Wiener Schnitzel   7.95
*Thinly sliced Veal, Breaded and Sauted,
served with German Fried Potatoes
and Assorted Vegetables*

Sauerbraten   7.50
*The Original German Dish served with
Spatzle and Red Cabbage*

Natur Schnitzel   8.50
*Thinly sliced Veal, Sauted in Butter,
served with Asparagus, Carrots
and Croquette Potatoes*

Smoked Thueringer   5.95
*Served with Sauerkraut and
German Fried Potatoes*

Hungarian Beef Goulash   7.00
*Hearty Chunks of Beef, prepared in
a Piquant Paprika Sauce, served with
Spatzle and Green Beans*

Kassler Rib   7.25
*Smoked Pork Loin served with
Sauerkraut and German Fried Potatoes*

Continental Specialties

Veal Cordon Bleu   8.95
*Stuffed Breaded Veal, served with Assorted
Vegetables and German Fried Potatoes*

Entrecote "Cafe de Paris"   10.75
*Prime Sirloin Steak topped with melted
Herb Butter, accompanied by assorted
Vegetables and Croquette Potatoes*

Escalope of Veal aux Champignons   8.50
*Sliced Veal in a Fine Mushroom Sauce,
accompanied by Assorted Vegetables
and Spatzle*

Fresh Calf's Liver   8.00
*Served with Bacon or Onions, German
Fried Potatoes, Beans and Carrots*

Steak au Poivre   10.50
*Prime Sirloin Steak covered with freshly crushed
Black Pepper, Broiled to Taste, served
with Vegetables and Croquette Potatoes*

Veal Kidneys Sautee Madeira
Spaetzle, Peas and Carrots   8.00

Zigeuner Spiess   10.50
*Veal and Beef Tenderloin, Liver, Bacon, Green
Peppers, Onions, Mushrooms, and Chipolata on
a skewer with Broiled Tomato and Risi Bisi*

Prime N.Y. Sirloin   10.50
*Broiled to Your Taste, served with
Assorted Vegetables and Croquette Potatoes*

Fish and Fowl Specialties

Frog Legs Provencale   7.95
*A generous portion of Tender Frog Legs with
a sauce of Garlic and White Wine, Tomato
served with Boiled Potatoes and Carrots*

Broiled Lobster Tails   14.50
*Served with Drawn Butter,
Rice, Peas and Carrots*

Broiled Alaska King Crab Legs
*With Drawn Butter, Vegetables and
Boiled Potato*   9.95

Dover Sole, Veronique   9.50
*Whole or Filet of Dover Sole, Sauted, served
in Brown Butter with Grapes or Almonds
accompanied by Boiled Potatoes and Carrots*

Trout Meuniere   7.25
*Boneless Fresh Water Trout sauted in
Brown Butter, served with Boiled
Potatoes and Carrots*

Surf and Shore   13.50
*Lobster and Filet Mignon, served with
Broiled Tomatoes and Croquette Potatoes*

Roast Long Island Duckling Cumberland
*Crisp Tender Duckling accompanied
by Rice and Red Cabbage*   9.00

Fresh Fish
Ask for our daily Fresh Fish

*All of the above Dinners include a variety of Soup, Fresh Bread and Butter, and a
Chef Salad with your choice of House, Thousand Island, or Garlic Dressing. (Roquefort $.50)*

Coffee .50   Tea .50   Milk .50

Desserts

Salzburger Nockerl   4.50

Apple Strudel   1.00

Kaiserschmarren   3.25

Bavarian Cream   1.00

Pineapple aux Kirsch   1.95

Ice Cream   1.00

Cherry Jubilee   2.50

Chicago
SAUER'S
American/Steaks/Hamburgers $

The echoes of a Strauss waltz may have faded away, but the people at Sauer's still remember the history of their huge building. Nearly a hundred years ago it began as Bournique's Dancing Academy. After World War I, the building languished until its transformation into a trucking garage. Then in 1967, the Sauer brothers opened their restaurant, a huge barn of a place with plain wood tables, bentwood chairs, sandblasted brick walls and an aggregate pebble floor. Skylights and greenery add light and color. The Sauer brothers no longer own the restaurant, but things have not really changed all that much. There are still daily specials, more often than not with a German flair, such as sauerbraten ($3.95) or pot roast ($2.70). Entrées are simple fare and include two steaks, hamburger, beef on rye, a fish platter and spaghetti with meat sauce. Except for the steaks, you will not pay more than $2.70 for a sandwich, spaghetti or fish platter. Side dishes such as slaw or dessert and beverages will cost extra. I don't suggest that Sauer's has the most elaborate food in town, but when you need something fast and inexpensive on the Near South Side, or have to rent a hall for 1000 people and want to wine and dine them inexpensively, Sauer's fills the bill.

SAUER'S, 311 East 23rd Street, Chicago. Telephone: 225-6171. Hours: 11 am-8 pm, Monday-Saturday. No cards. Full bar service. Casual dress acceptable. Extensive private party facilities. Ample parking.

K/Rating 15/20 • Food 4.5/7 • Service 4.5/6 • Decor 3/4 • Value 3/3

	ENTREES	
1	**Charbroiled Sirloin Steak** Fried Potatoes, Salad	**$7.50**
1B	**Charbroiled Top Butt Steak** Fried Potatoes, Salad	**$4.95**
2	**Charbroiled Hamburger** Served on Rye with Fried Potatoes, Cole Slaw and Slice of Raw Onion	**$2.70**
3	**Beef on Rye Bread** Served with Fried Potatoes and Brauhaus Sauce	**$2.40**
4	**Brauhaus Fish Platter** Fried Potatoes, Cole Slaw (Mashed Potatoes on Friday)	**$2.70**
5	**Brauhaus Spaghetti** With Meat Sauce	**$2 40**

6	**DAILY SPECIALS**	
Monday	**Boiled Brisket of Corned Beef** With New Cabbage, Boiled Potatoes	**$2.70**
Tuesday	**Pot Roast a la Deutsch** With Potato Dumplings and Bavarian Red Cabbage	**$2.70**
Wednesday	**Beef Rouladen** With Rice and Grilled Tomato	**$2.70**
Thursday	**Hungarian Goulash** With Noodles and Green Peas	**$2.70**
Saturday	**Sauerbraten** With Spaetzles and Bavarian Red Cabbage, Salad	**$3.95**

Side Orders	Fried Potatoes .65 / Cole Slaw .65 / Salad .65 / Spaghetti $1.20
Desserts	Bavarian Cheesecake .65 / Lemon Ice Box Pie .75
Beverages	Coffee .35 / Tea .35 / Milk .40 / Soft Drinks .40
Beer	Light and Dark Draught Beer, Stein .65 / Pitcher $2.50 (Served only after 2 p.m.)
Wine	Red, White, Rose or Sangria, Glass .75 / Half Litre $2.25 / Full Litre $3.95
Liquor	Bourbon, Scotch, Gin, Vodka, Rum $1.15 / Martini, Manhattan, Cocktails, Blendor Drinks, Bloody Mary, Orange Blossom, $1.35 / Cordials & Cream Drinks $1.50

Chicago/Des Plaines
SAYAT NOVA
Armenian

$

Since the first edition of *Best Restaurants Chicago,* a second Sayat Nova has opened and is equally as fine a restaurant as the original. The new Sayat Nova is not an exact copy however, and in fact, has a more extensive menu than the Chicago location. A glance at the menu will tip you off to the cultures that have influenced Armenian cuisine. Here is a blend that can catch the robust quality of Greek food and the subtle nuance of Turkish. To this, the Armenian people have added their own unique touch. You may want to taste several foods, so come with a group. Six is an ideal number. Enjoy a selection of appetizers. Among them are cold eggplant, tomatoes and onions sautéed in olive oil. Try filo pastries stuffed with spinach or ground meat and pine nuts. Another choice is borek; imagine mild brick cheese lightly seasoned with green onion and the yolk of an egg, then baked in an airy pastry. Or, try sarma, stuffed grape leaves, slightly sweet on the tongue. For dinner you may choose from ten selections. There is a combination platter that offers good taste and texture balance. Shish kebab, lamb or beef, is slowly roasted over charcoal, served on

LAMB MARRAKESH Stewed tender lamb in onions, raisins, almonds and herbs. Served with rice pilaff.	8.95
MAGLUBÉH Spiced rice cooked with lamb, cauliflower and pine nuts. Served with yogurt.	8.95
MEAT BEORAK Spiced meat, onions, tomatoes and walnuts baked in flaky dough. Served with vegetables.	8.95
KIBBÉH Cracked wheat shells stuffed with ground meat, onions and walnuts. Served with vegetables.	7.95
SARMA-KHASHLAMA Stuffed grape leaves, simmered with tender lamb. Served with Yogurt.	8.95
STEAK MADAGASCAR Sautéed tenderloin of beef with green peppercorn in cream and brandy. Served with rice pilaff.	10.95

skewers with tomato, green pepper and a rice pilaf on the side. Entirely different is lula kebab, ground beef or lamb rolled sausage-like, but without the casing. Sautéed lamb is another excellent choice. For dessert, my favorite is atayef with cream. A half-moon-shaped puff pastry, atayef is filled with a most delicate boiled sweet-cream curd; it is somewhere in between a pudding and a chiffon and is topped with warm honey. The Chicago location has a slightly differing menu, but is equally recommended with the new Sayat Nova in Des Plaines.

SAYAT NOVA, 20 West Golf Road, Des Plaines. Telephone: 296-1776. Hours: 11:30 am-11 pm, Tuesday-Friday; 4 pm-midnight, Saturday; until 10 pm, Sunday. Cards: MC, VISA. Reservations required. Full bar service. Casual dress acceptable. Free parking.

SAYAT NOVA, 157 East Ohio Street, Chicago. Telephone: 644-9159. Hours: 11:30 am-midnight, Monday-Saturday; 2 pm-10 pm, Sunday. Cards: MC, VISA. Reservations recommended. Full bar service. Parking nearby.

K/Rating 20/20 • Food 7/7 • Service 6/6 • Decor 4/4 • Value 3/3

ARMENIAN KABAB   8.95
Broiled beef cubes with baked medley of fresh vegetables. Served with pilaff.

LAMB SHISH-KABAB   9.50
Marinated cubes of lamb, broiled with tomato and green pepper. Served with rice pilaff.

BEEF SHISH-KABAB   8.50
Marinated cubes of beef, broiled with tomato and green pepper. Served with rice pilaff.

KIFTAH SHISH-KABAB   7.25
Seasoned ground lamb and beef, broiled with tomatoes and green pepper. Served with rice pilaff.

COMBINATION PLATE   9.50
Sarma, Kibbeh, Imam Bayeldi

Chicago
SPARTA GYROS
Greek

$

Chicago, the great hot dog city by the Lake, is being inundated by gyros. There are gyros stands springing up everywhere, a gift to us from the city's Greek restaurants. Ground beef and lamb are pressed into large rounds which are then cooked on specially designed rotisseries. But not all gyros taste alike and one of the best gyros stands is Sparta, in the heart of the New Town shopping district on the North Side. Order a gyros sandwich for $1.75 and you'll get slices of meat in a pocket of pita, the flat Levantine bread which is enjoying a new-found popularity in Chicago. Fresh slivers of raw onion, a dash of yogurt-based sauce and a couple of tomato slices are all packed into the bread pocket, making a real two-fisted sandwich. A gyros platter gives you a meal, not a snack. Other standard Greek fare such as mousaka, pastitsio and dolmades are well prepared and easy on the finances. Typically sweet Greek baklava and custards highlight the desserts. Sparta offers the hungry traveler through New Town a good haven from junk food.

SPARTA GYROS, 3205 North Broadway, Chicago. Telephone: 549-4210. Hours: 11 am-2 am, daily. No cards. No reservations. Greek wines and brandy only. Parking on street.

Chicago
SU CASA
Mexican

$$

While nothing in the universe is unchanging and, as the philosopher Lucretius tells us, "even stones are conquered by time ... high towers fall and rocks moulder away....", it is comforting to report that Su Casa goes on its way serving consistently delicious Mexican fare. Here is an antique-filled white brick-walled restaurant with the feel of a Spanish colonial hacienda in Old Mexico. There are heavy carved doors, large metal ornamentation and ornate wood statues. Su Casa proves that Mexican cuisine need not be unbearably spicy. To be sure, red pepper sauce and other condiments are placed on your table. But the food of Mexico varies from region to region, as do other cuisines around the world. That at Su Casa is milder, which does not mean less authentic. The combination dinner offers the most varied tastes including Mexican-style grilled steak, stuffed peppers, delicious chicken enchilada, a cheese taco and creamy cool guacamole. Chicken mole is a special treat in an unsweetened chocolate- and spice-based sauce—an altogether wonderful way to prepare chicken. For seafood lovers, try the trout with coriander for an unusual preparation. Desserts include flan, the classic Mexican custard in caramel sauce.

SU CASA, 49 East Ontario Street, Chicago. Telephone: 943-4041. Hours: 11:30 am-2 am, Monday-Friday; 5 pm-3 am, Saturday. Cards: AE, CB, DC, MC, VISA. Reservations required. Full bar service. Coats and ties requested for men. Private party facilities for up to 40 people. Valet parking.

K/Rating 17.5/20 • Food 6/7 • Service 5/6 • Decor 4/4 • Value 2.5/3

Chicago/Lincolnwood
TAMBORINE
American

$

Put together an imaginative menu, an upbeat atmosphere and prices that will not have you scampering for the family jewels and you should have the makings of an attractive restaurant. That is the formula for success at the two Tamborine restaurants. Although one is in a sophisticated Near North setting near Water Tower Place and the other is on a somewhat tacky strip in Lincolnwood, both restaurants offer attractive and similar atmospheres. Tables are graced with a tambourine which serves as way station for salt, pepper and condiments. Dinners are essentially à la carte, although main courses selection includes a salad, vegetable and potatoes. House specialties include Tamborine ribs in a sticky sauce more sweet than sharp or tangy. Lime chicken is a serving of boned, charcoal-grilled breasts brushed with a tart lime sauce and served on its platter with half of a pear. It is a great taste combination: The lime juice is a good flavor enhancer. People who disdain liver should reconsider Tamborine's preparation of liver slices sautéed

...specialties...

Fresh Fish of the Day...The fleet's in with the freshest catch of lake and ocean fish. Deliciously prepared with the Tamborine touch.

Tamborine Ribs...A house specialty. Succulent back ribs prepared in our "Sauce Tamborine." Basted and charbroiled. Then each slab is split, cut in pieces and served to you piled high. 8.95

Chicken 'n Ribs...Two great favorites teamed for extra pleasure. A tender, charbroiled chicken breast shares the platter with a half slab of luscious Tamborine ribs. 8.95

Scallops Kabob...Taste-tempting sea scallops skewered with marinated fresh vegetables and charbroiled to a golden finish. Served with seasoned rice. 6.95

Steak Lover's Steak...A tender New York strip charbroiled to your order. Smothered in sauted mushrooms 11.95

Giant Shrimps...So big and delicious you won't believe your eyes or your palate. Butterflied and deep-fried to a golden brown. Served with hearty red cocktail sauce or our special "Sauce Tamborine" or exotic "Sauce Mattapan." 8.95

Skewered Steak Teriyaki...Cubes of fine tenderloin and fresh vegetables marinated in our special Emperor soy sauce and charbroiled. Just the aromas will start your tastebuds tingling. Served with seasoned rice. 7.95

Steamed Crab Legs...Jumbo King crab legs steamed to a luscious tenderness and split for easy eating. Served with hot drawn butter. 9.95

with mushrooms and served in a casserole-like setting with onions and green peppers. Among appetizers, fried mushrooms or fried zucchini rings served with the house sauce are yummy. And that reminds me of how good the desserts can be. Be sure to save some room and appetite for Hot and Gooey chocolate cake or the fudge pecan pie.

TAMBORINE CHICAGO, 200 East Chestnut Street, Chicago. Telephone: 944-4000. Hours: 11:30 am-midnight, Monday-Thursday; until 1 am, Friday and Saturday; 4 pm-10:30 pm, Sunday. Cards: AE, DC, MC, VISA. Reservations taken. Full bar service. Casual dress acceptable. Private party facilities for up to 36 people. Valet parking.

TAMBORINE LINCOLNWOOD, 6717 North Lincoln Avenue, Lincolnwood. Telephone: 674-0690. Cards: AE, DC, MC, VISA. Hours: 11:30 am-midnight, Monday-Thursday; until 1 am, Friday-Saturday; 4 pm-10:30 pm, Sunday. Reservations taken. Full bar service. Casual dress acceptable. Private party facilities for up to 60 people. Free parking.

K/Rating 17/20 • Food 5.5/7 • Service 5/6 • Decor 3.5/4 • Value 3/3

...specialties...

Seafood Sensation...An Entree salad with generous portions of Jumbo Shrimp and Dungeness Crab, fresh vegetables and fruits of the season, served with a tangy red sauce and Louis dressing. 5.50

Veal Napoli...Lightly breaded, milk-fed veal generously sprinkled with grated parmesan smothered with our own spicy Italian tomato sauce and topped with melted Mozzarella. Baked in a casserole and served bubbling hot. 6.95

Lime Chicken...Boneless charbroiled chicken breasts coupled with a pear half and expertly basted with a tantalizing herb-lime sauce to produce untold taste delights. 6.95

Or Choose, Barbequed or Plain

Steak au Poivre ... Tender, juicy T-bone steak lovingly studded with crushed black peppercorns and charbroiled to your order. 11.95

High Liver...Juicy slices of calves' liver sauteed with mushrooms, onions and green pepper. Even the "Gourmet on the Go" would give this five stars. 6.95

Swellington...We prepare a special dough and fill it with a tasty blend of beef strips, onions, mushrooms and other vegetables; bake it to a golden brown, and then top it all with a light red wine sauce. 6.95

Alicia burger... An inspired treat. First a layer of tantalizing fried eggplant, then a half-pound of delicious, juicy charbroiled chopped sirloin covered with grilled onions and mushrooms, and finally a topping of tangy melted Swiss cheese. 5.00

Chicago
TANGO
Continental/Seafood

$$$

Tango is an extremely modish restaurant with a cocktail lounge that looks like something out of "Clockwork Orange." The restaurant section is less harsh, although its polished tile flooring and hard plaster walls coupled with a high ceiling make the room noisier than I like. If you want more privacy, ask for seating in one of the semi-enclosed booths. Tango's sophistication encompasses an à la carte menu of finely prepared seafoods. For instance, shrimp and scallops Provençal is a fine casserole selection, perfectly seasoned with just the right touches. Fried oysters make a tasty appetizer, as does the ratatouille, either hot or cold. Bouillabaisse is as good as any I know of in Chicago. Each evening Tango also features several selections not on the menu. The variety is extensive, the fish as fresh as is possible. Service is generally pleasant and knowledgeable; waitresses are able to discuss each dish and its ingredients, should you have any questions. There are good wines on the list, reasonably priced.

TANGO, 3170 North Sheridan Road, Chicago. Telephone: 935-0350. Hours: Lunch: 11:30 am-2 pm, Tuesday-Saturday; Dinner: 5 pm-11 pm, Monday-Thursday; until midnight, Friday-Saturday; until 10 pm, Sunday. Cards: AE, MC, VISA. Reservations required. Full bar service. Casual, neat dress; no jeans. Valet parking.

K/Rating 18.5/20 • Food 6/7 • Service 6/6 • Decor 3.5/4 • Value 3/3

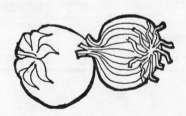

LAKE FISH

served with tureen of soup, salad, rice tango and bread

Fresh Lake Superior Whitefish
    broiled   8.50
    almondine sautéed   9.50

Fresh Brook Trout, *broiled or sautéed*   10.00

Fresh Brook Trout, *sautéed almondine*   11.00

Fresh Brook Trout, *stuffed with*   11.25
    crab meat and sautéed

Fresh Broiled Walleye Pike—*when available*   9.50

OCEAN FISH

served with tureen of soup, salad, rice tango and bread

Fresh Boston Scrod, *sautéed*   8.50

French Turbot
    sautéed   12.50
    almondine   13.50

Dover Sole   12.50
    sautéed and served with sauce albert

SHELL FISH

served with tureen of soup, salad, rice tango and bread

King Crab Legs   13.00
    cold with mustard sauce
    hot with drawn butter

Lobster Tail   *
    with drawn butter sauce steamed or broiled

Shrimp Grenobloise   10.75
    sautéed shrimps with capers and
    croutons in lemon butter sauce

Chicago
THAI LITTLE HOME CAFE
Thai

$$

The food of Thailand has gained wide acceptance among the followers of Chicagoland's scores of ethnic restaurants. Several Thai restaurants have opened since I first visited Thai Little Home Cafe, yet it remains one of my favorites. Although authentic Thai foods are highly seasoned, things can be toned down at your request. À la carte dinners consisting of appetizer, soup, beef, chicken or fish, rice and tea will run about $6 per person. Should you order the excellent deep-fried fish, count on a few dollars more. They use red snapper, tender and easy to bone right at your table. It is covered with bits of onions and small green and red peppers for a visual as well as gustatorial display. (If you have a pepper-sensitive palate you may order the snapper sans its garnish.) Among mild beef dishes, try the meat in oyster sauce or with green pepper and tomatoes. While first impressions might suggest Thai food is nothing but altered Chinese, do not be misled. It has a character all its own, as different from Chinese as New England cooking can be from Cajun.

THAI LITTLE HOME CAFE, 3125 West Lawrence Avenue, Chicago. Telephone: 478-3944. Hours: 11:30 am-9:30 pm, Monday-Tuesday and Thursday-Saturday; noon-9 pm, Sunday. Cards: VISA. No bar service: you may bring your own. Casual dress acceptable. Parking on street.

K/Rating 16/20 • Food 6/7 • Service 5/6 • Decor 2/4 • Value 3/3

SOUP

EGG FLOWERS SOUP................................... .75
WON TON SOUP....................................... .85
TOM YUM KAI OR NUA (Thai style) 1.95
TOM YUM KUNG (Thai style) 2.25

BEEF OR NUA

NUA PUD PRIK 1.85
BEEF CHOP SUEY 1.90
BEEF WITH OYSTER SAUCE 2.15
(Tenderloin Beef with imported Oyster Sauce, Bamboo Shoots,
and Mushrooms)
BEEF WITH GREEN PEPPER AND TOMATO 1.95
(Tenderloin Beef, marinated in Soy and Spices, sauted with
Spring Onion and Bell Pepper)
BEEF CHOW MEIN 1.95
(Tenderloin Beef with Bean Sprouts, Mushrooms, Celery, Bamboo
Shoots and served on Golden Brown Noodles)
KANG NUA 1.85
(Tenderloin Beef cooked and simmered in Thai style Red Curry,
Bamboo Shoots and Coconut Milk)

PORK OR MOO

SWEET AND SOUR PORK 2.50
(Morsels of Pork Tenderloin, marinated in Soya and Rice Wine,
browned in Safflower Oil, then steamed with tantalizing Sweet
and Sour Sauce)
PORK CHOW MEIN 1.90
PORK CHOP SUEY 1.90
PORK PUD PRIK 1.90

CHICKEN OR KAI

CHICKEN WITH ALMOND 2.10
(Diced Chicken with Mushrooms, Bamboo Shoots, with Rice
Broth and covered with Toasted Almonds)
CHICKEN CHOW MEIN 1.90
CHICKEN CHOP SUEY 1.90
CHICKEN PUD PRIK 1.90
(Chicken with Onion, Bamboo Shoots and Hot Pepper)
CHICKEN AND VEGETABLE.............................. 1.90

SEA FOOD

SHRIMP CHOP SUEY................................... 2.20
SHRIMP CHOW MEIN 2.20
SHRIMP PUD PRIK 2.50
(Shrimp with Onion, Bamboo Shoots and Hot Pepper)
SWEET AND SOUR SHRIMP 2.50
DEEP FRIED FISH (Red Snapper) 6.00
DEEP FRIED FISH WITH HOT PEPPER AND SPICES 7.25
SWEET AND SOUR DEEP FRIED FISH (Red Snapper) 7.25
FISH CAKE (Tod Mon) 2.50
(Served with Cucumber, Ground Nut and Vinegar Sauce)

Chicago
THAI VILLA
Thai

$$

Thai food continues to make its mark on Chicago's tastes. One of the better Thai restaurants is the Thai Villa, a storefront setting where imitation walnut paneling, a photograph of the king and queen of Thailand and fresh herbs growing in windowsill flower pots help to set a pleasant tone. In restaurants where the food is less than familiar to all but experienced diners, service is all the more important. Most of the preparations are briefly explained on the menu; those about which you need more information will be detailed by a helpful waiter or waitress. As with other Oriental cuisines, Thai food is best eaten course by course. You can order the standard dinners which average under $6 per person. Or choose à la carte and end up spending about the same. Thai Villa offers four different kinds of egg roll appetizers from among 15 choices. We tried the Thai rolls served cold: A filling of tiny shrimp and bean sprouts are stuffed inside thin rice cakes and drizzled with a honey-like topping. Other appetizers include pork saté on a skewer or a special salad such as pla koong. For $4, four people can get a good sample of mixed Oriental vegetables with whole shrimp in a sharp pepper seasoning. One of my favorite dishes is hot and sour soup. Other broths include a Vietnamese soup, vegetable and wonton. Noodles make up an important part of the Thai diet. After a spicy soup, an order of fried noodles with meat, chicken or shrimp for $2 serves as a real palate refresher. Or try the beef fried rice, which is sweet, not so much as to be cloying, only enough to make you appreciative of the change in tastes from course to course. Main course selections in the $3.50 to $8 price range include several fried fish platters, duck and chicken. Barbecued chicken Thai style is nothing short of delicious. Beef with peanuts and red peppers perk things up while a side vegetable such as fried broccoli helps calm down tastes. The Thai Villa draws a sizable number of Thai diners, a sure sign of its authenticity.

THAI VILLA, 3811 North Lincoln Avenue, Chicago. Telephone: 281-2323. Hours: 4 pm-10 pm, Tuesday-Friday; noon-10 pm, Saturday-Sunday. Cards: DC. Reservations requested. No bar service; you may bring your own. Parking on street.

K/Rating 17/20 • Food 5/7 • Service 6/6 • Decor 3/4 • Value 3/3

PRIK KHING — 2.50
fried chicken or pork in crisp curry

PAD PED — 2.50
fried slice beef in hot taste

MANDARIN PAD PED — 2.75
fried slice beef w/ peanut in hot taste

PAD WOUN SEN — 2.50
fried vermicelli w/ pork or beef (shrimp__ 2.75)

PAD KAI NOR MAI — 2.50
fried chicken and bamboo shutes w/ gravy

FRIED PEA PODS W/ SHRIMP — 3.00

PAD KA NA — 2.50
fried chinese brocoli

SWEET & SOUR — 2.75
choice of pork, beef or chicken

CHOP SUEY — 2.50
w/ pork, beef or chicken

KAI PAD — 3.00
fried chicken w/ yellow bean sauce, ginger and garlic

KOONG TOD PRIK THAI — 4.00
fried shrimp w/ garlic and black pepper

PEPPEP STEAK — 3.60
slice tender beef w/ onions, pepper, tomatoes__
seasoned w/ garlic
and black bean sauce

Chicago
THAT STEAK JOYNT
Steaks

$$

This is without question my favorite steak restaurant in Chicago. It's not that the meat is better, because other steak restaurants have comparable meat. But at That Steak Joynt you can have your steak customized to an almost infinite degree. They'll grill under the gas broiler, charcoal grill, sauté, butterfly, smother in onions—you name it and That Steak Joynt will do it. This also happens to be one of the most pleasant environments around, as well as being a great restaurant. Victorian antiques and bric-a-brac, flocked red wallpaper, an ornate 19th century bar and some of the best service around make a visit here one to remember. An excellent wine list complements the meats, and there are three private-party rooms for special-occasion entertaining.

THAT STEAK JOYNT, 1610 North Wells Street, Chicago. Telephone: 943-5091. Hours: Lunch: 11:30 am-2 pm, Monday-Friday; Dinner: 4 pm-2 am, daily. Cards: AE, CB, DC, MC, VISA. Reservations recommended. Full bar service. Jackets required for men. Private party facilities for up to 100 people. Parking nearby.

K/Rating 19/20 • Food 7/7 • Service 5.5/6 • Decor 3.5/4 • Value 3/3

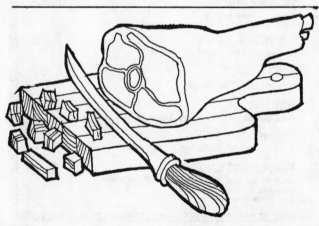

Every JOYNT STEAK is PRIME, AGED and... ..."a cut above the usual"

Enjoy it Your Way:

char-broiled....over the open flame, until the rich natural juices threaten to burst.

sauteed victorian style.... smothered in onions and sautéed in butter sauce until it sizzles with succulence and flavor.

broiled with garlic.... studded with garlic, rich and robust, for the daring gourmet.

broiled with pepper..peppercorns ground in, for those who prefer it spicy.

JOYNT SPECIALTY Rib Eye Steak, Shirlee Sauce*	9.50
PRIME BONELESS SIRLOIN STEAK New York Cut	13.50
PRIME BONELESS MINUTE SIRLOIN Smaller Edition	12.25
PRIME T-BONE King of Steaks	15.25
PRIME FILET MIGNON Bearnaise Sauce*	11.95
PRIME DOUBLE SIRLOIN FOR TWO	24.95
PRIME BUTT STEAK Center Cut	10.50
CHATEAUBRIAND Bouquetiere For Two, Bearnaise Sauce*	25.95
FRESH GROUND SIRLOIN PLANKED STEAK Bouquetiere	8.95
TOURNEDOS OF BEEF Two Petite Filets, Saute en Butter	11.50
TENDERLOIN TIPS with Chef's Wild Rice Dressing	8.95

ONION RINGS 1.95   MUSHROOM CAPS 2.00   BEARNAISE SAUCE .95
*upon request

other delightful delectables

PEPPER STEAK Sauteed, Green Peppers, Wine Sauce	9.95
BAR B QUE BABY BACK RIBS Special Joynt Sauce, Cole Slaw	8.95
TENDERLOIN STEAK EN BROCHETTE Rice Pilaf	8.95
STEAK JOYNT VICTORIA OF BEEF Pink and Tender	8.95
CHICKEN TERIYAKI Rice	8.95
VEGETABLE PLATE All Cooked Vegetables	8.95
STEAK MARINER Butterflied Filet Mignon Topped with Crab Legs, Asparagus and Bearnaise Sauce	12.95
COMBINATION PETITE FILET MIGNON—LOBSTER TAIL	13.95
KING CRAB LEGS Drawn Butter	9.50
SHRIMP SCAMPI Rice Pilaf	10.95
JUMBO SHRIMP Stuffed with Crabmeat	8.95
BROILED TWIN LOBSTER TAILS Lemon or Garlic Butter	16.75
BROILED LAKE SUPERIOR WHITEFISH Bouquetiere	8.95
WHOLE IMPORTED DOVER SOLE Amandine	12.50

$$

Topkapi has been quietly doing its own thing for about 15 years. Now, after a period of indifference, the restaurant seems to be on an ascendancy. As with most ethnic restaurants that offer a combination platter, the one at Topkapi strikes me as the best way to be introduced to what is offered. The shish kebab, lule kebab and lamb chops come in an attractive trio. Stuffed grape leaves filled with a mixture of rice and pignolia nuts, ispanek (a mélange of rice, onion and yogurt) and mucver (vegetables and eggs cooked in olive oil) will please vegetarians. One of my favorite entrées is talesh kebab, chunks of sautéed lamb baked in filo dough pastry. Dinners begin with small bowls of hummous, a chickpea purée, and cacik, cucumbers in yogurt. Pita bread, that flat Levantine staple, is dipped into each or either for delectable taste tantilizers. Next might come a more substantial appetizer such as borek, cheese and spices baked inside of filo dough. Desserts can be exceptional, although the choice is limited to baklava or sometimes telkadayie, reminiscent of honey-sweetened shredded wheat cake.

TOPKAPI, 1909 North Lincoln Avenue, Chicago. Telephone: 642-0522. Hours: 5 pm-midnight, Tuesday-Sunday. Cards: AE, VISA. Reservations recommended. Full bar service. Casual, neat dress acceptable. Private party facilities for 10 or more people. Parking on street.

K/Rating 16.5/20 • Food 6.5/7 • Service 5/6 • Decor 2/4 • Value 3/3

Dinner at Topkapı

Complete Dinner
The Price of Entree is the
Price of Complete Dinner
Choice of Appetizer, Salad, Entree, Dessert

YALANCI DOLMA
Stuffed Grape Leaves

ISPANAK
Spinach with yogurt

CACIK
Cucumber in yogurt

BOREK
Thin leaves of dough filled with Turkish white cheese

SALAD

Choban mixed green salad

ENTREE

SHISH KEBAB 8.00

Choice cuts of lamb or beef marinated in olive oil, onions and spices and charcoal broiled on skewer.
Served with broiled tomatoes.

YOGURTLU PIDELI SHISH KEBAB 8.50

Charcoal broiled tender pieces of beef or lamb. Served with tomato sauce and small pieces of Pide bread
and yogurt.

YOGURTLU PIDELI LULE KEBAB............................ 7.50

Charcoal broiled ground lamb and beef, onions, parsley, spices; rolled and served with tomato sauce and
yogurt and small pieces of Pide bread.

TALASH KEBAB... 7.50

Small pieces of lamb sauteed in butter with onions; wrapped in strudel leaves and baked.

KUZU FIRIN 7.00

Marinated and oven roasted lamb. Extremely succulent, moderately spiced and light.

LULE KEBAB.. 6.50

Ground lamb and beef, onions, parsley and spices, with a touch of cumin; kneaded together and charcoal
broiled. Served with broiled tomatoes.

U. S. CHOICE PRIME BUTT STEAK 6.50

10 ounces of choice prime beef. Served with broiled tomatoes.

PIRZOLA 9.00

Double cut Baby Lamb Chops, seasoned ala Istanbul, served Turkish style.

181

Picture a typical Italian restaurant. Small Christmas lights stud plastic greenery. One wall is decorated with a mural of Venice and the Grand Canal. You'll see romantic couples alongside entire families—all seeking good food at small cost. Toscano is that kind of restaurant. It draws its regulars, but first-time customers are treated to the same cordiality and friendly service. The Tuscan sauces characteristic of northern Italy are thick and meaty, with less tomato acidity than sauces south of Rome. The menu lists the usual pastas—spaghetti, lasagna and ravioli among others. The lasagna is typically meaty; garlic is used sparingly. Among other recommended selections on the menu, Toscano chicken is mildly seasoned in a wine sauce. Veal Toscano is similarly prepared. Like many truly good restaurants, Toscano has one or two specialties which are not listed on the menu. If you like the spice of hot peppers and garlic and the richness of olive oil, ask for their special sauce. Freshly chopped parsley and anchovy add some complexity, but order this sauce on a side pasta only, unless you really like your food hot. Let your appetite and your waitress be your guide.

TOSCANO, 2439 South Oakley Boulevard, Chicago. Telephone: 376-4841. Hours: 11 am-11 pm, Tuesday-Sunday. Cards: CB, MC, VISA. Reservations taken only for groups. Full bar service. Casual dress acceptable. Private party facilities for up to 50 people. Ample parking.

K/Rating 17/20 • Food 6/7 • Service 5/6 • Decor 3/4 • Value 3/3

Our Italian Specialties

"Par Excellence"

	A la Carte	Table d'Hote
SPAGHETTI		
With Meat Sauce	$2.05	$3.45
With Meat Balls	2.90	4.20
With Mushrooms	3.10	4.45
With Chicken Livers	3.10	4.45
With Italian Sausage	3.10	4.45
Spaghetti Toscano Style Chicken Livers and Mushrooms	3.95	5.45
Side Order of Spaghetti		1.00
RAVIOLI		
With Meat Sauce	$3.00	$4.35
With Meat Balls	3.85	5.10
With Mushrooms	4.05	5.35
With Chicken Livers	4.05	5.35
With Italian Sausage	4.05	5.35
Ravioli Toscano Style	5.00	6.30
Side Order of Ravioli		1.20
HALF AND HALF		
With Meat Sauce	$3.00	$4.35
With Meat Balls	3.85	5.10
With Mushrooms	4.05	5.35
With Chicken Livers	4.05	5.35
With Italian Sausage	4.05	5.35
Half and Half Toscano Style	5.00	6.30
MOSTACCIOLI		
With Meat Sauce	$2.05	$3.45
With Meat Balls	2.90	4.20
With Mushrooms	3.10	4.45
With Chicken Livers	3.10	4.45
With Italian Sausage	3.10	4.45
Mostaccioli Toscano Style	3.95	5.45
Side Order		1.00

SANDWICHES

Beef	$2.05	Lettuce, Bacon and Tomato	1.90
Sausage	2.05	Grilled Cheese	1.50
Meat Ball	1.90	Cheese	1.40
Ham	2.05	Chicken Club	2.75

Chicago
TRUFFLES
French

$$$

Truffles is in the running for the most expensive Chicago restaurant, but it certainly puts to rest the suspicion that all hotel dining rooms serve plastic food to plastic diners. Someone in the Hyatt Regency organization threw away the book when Truffles was planned. The restaurant serves exquisite cuisine in a small and dimly lit dining room. Some of the luxury is overstated but the room is still one of the more sophisticated in Chicago. The restaurant's namesake, that rare Perigourdine fungus we know as the truffle, is outrageously overpriced at $18 as an appetizer, a specialty marinated in cognac and served in puff pastry. Try an assortment of pâtés or the classic quenelles de brochet instead. The à la carte dinner entrées offer handsome preparations of veal, steak, poultry and fish. Many dishes are spectacularly prepared at tableside, as are the vegetable bouquets which accompany the main course. Among recommendations, I like the veal Orloff, Dover sole and turbot with lobster, oysters and mushrooms in a creamy Nantua sauce that only the most jaded diners could ignore. Truffles' pastry cart usually contains some fine fruit tarts; otherwise give your expense account a run for the money and try one of the soufflés.

TRUFFLES, 151 East Wacker Drive (in the Hyatt Regency Chicago), Chicago. Telephone: 565-1000; ext. 1733. Hours: Lunch: 11:30 am-2:30 pm, daily; Dinner: 6 pm-11 pm, daily. Cards: DC, MC, VISA. Reservations recommended. Full bar service. Jackets required for men. Parking in hotel garage.

K/Rating 17.5/20 • Food 7/7 • Service 6/6 • Decor 3.5/4 • Value 1.5/3

Côte de Veau Prince Orloff
Loin of Veal, Prince Orloff
sixteen dollars

Noisettes de Veau
Medallions of milk-fed veal, sauteed to perfection
and crowned with a suprême of apricots
sixteen dollars

Tournedos aux Morilles
Center cut filets, garnished and served
with cream of wild mushrooms
fifteen dollars

Entrecôte Café de Paris
Prime sirloin steak, broiled to your specification,
with a delicate Sauce Foyot
sixteen dollars

Selle d'Agneau à la Réforme
Rack of lamb roasted with herbs and spices,
served with a light, peppered lamb sauce
seventeen dollars

Médaillon de Chevreuil, Grand Veneur
Marinated filets of venison sauteed with
mushrooms, served with wild rice maison
eighteen dollars

Turbot d'Empire aux Truffes
Turbot joined with oysters, lobster,
mushroom caps and laced with Sauce Nantua Glace
seventeen dollars

Deux Cailles en Poêlon
Quails with truffles stuffing
eighteen dollars

Langouste à l'Emeril
Lobster prepared in a delicate herb sauce
seventeen dollars

Sôle de Douvres, Dorée
A whole Dover sole, sauteed in lemon butter
sixteen dollars

Canard Rôti
Crisp roast duckling, served with a delicate
lingonberry sauce, wild rice maison
fourteen dollars

Faisan Souvarov
Boneless breast of pheasant in sauce Salmis,
with goose liver and truffles, wild rice maison
sixteen dollars

Fresh vegetables prepared at your table

Chicago
THE WATERFRONT
Seafood

$$

Batten down the hatches, hoist the mainsail and steer a course for Rush Street. The decor of weathered wood, bare brick and fixtures normally seen aboard a brigantine sailing the seven seas leaves little to the imagination. You'll sit in captain's chairs or church pews at copper-topped tables. All that's missing is the gentle motion of waves and the salt smell of the sea. The Waterfront is the only place in town that I know of for cioppino. Despite its foreign-sounding name, cioppino traces its origin to San Francisco, where seamen would cook a waterfront dinner composed of delicacies from their catch. At The Waterfront, cioppino includes shrimp, oysters, clams and crab meat in a Tabasco-like hot sauce seasoned with bay leaves and spices. Served piping hot in a cast iron skillet, it is highly seasoned, not for the timid. Milder are such entrées as sole almondine, trout or red snapper. Sole en sacque, not often found on local menus, is a beautiful preparation as pleasing to the eye as it is to the palate. All dinners include access to the salad bar. In addition to the regular dinner menu, there is a lower-priced selection of snacks for lunch or weeknight after-theater crowds.

THE WATERFRONT, 1015 North Rush Street, Chicago. Telephone: 943-7494. Hours: 11:30 am-midnight, Monday-Thursday; until 1 am, Friday-Saturday; until 11 pm, Sunday. Cards: AE, MC, VISA. Reservations recommended. Casual dress acceptable.

K/Rating 18/20 • Food 6/7 • Service 5/6 • Decor 4/4 • Value 3/3

SOLE EN SACQUE
Filet of sole on a bed of thin-sliced ham stuffed with
tiny Alaskan shrimp, mushrooms and ripe olives in our creamy
sherry sauce. Baked to perfection, in parchment to preserve the
natural juices and aroma for your dining pleasure .... $ 9.95

DOVER SOLE ALMONDINE
The filet sauteed in pure creamery butter and served
with slivered almonds .... $ 10.25

BAKED RAINBOW TROUT
The whole boneless trout baked with a stuffing of celery,
ripe olives, mushroom and herbs .... $ 8.95

PAN FRIED TROUT
The game fisherman's classic treatment .... $ 7.95

BROILED RED SNAPPER
The whole fish -- au Grecque with oregano and onions .... $ 8.75

LAKE SUPERIOR WHITEFISH
This filet of locally famous freshwater fish is quickly broiled to
perfection in lemon butter only, to preserve its delicate flavor .... $ 8.50

MAZATLAN PRAWNS IN A PAN
Jumbo gulf shrimp sauteed in the shell in a sauce of garlic
butter, wine, mushrooms and savory Mexican spices, served in the
cooking pan. Pick them up with your hands and sop up the
wonderful sauce with our sourdough bread .... $ 9.95

TINY BAY SCALLOPS
Sauteed to perfection in savory butter .... $ 8.75

FROG LEGS MEUNIERE
Sauteed to perfection in savory garlic butter .... $ 8.75

SEAFOOD MARYLAND
Lobster, shrimp, crabmeat with mushrooms in a cream
sherry sauce, baked en casserole .... $ 11.25

SUMMER MENU

Entrees served with salad bar in season

SNOW CRAB SOUP
Chilled creamy crab soup blended with cool cucumbers
and watercress .... $ 1.40

COLD SALMON
Salmon steak poached in court bouillon chilled and served
icy cold with dill mayonnaise .... $ 6.95

COLD DUNGENESS CRAB
Served with mustard mayonnaise sauce .... $ 10.25

COLD CRAB LEGS
Served with mustard mayonnaise sauce .... $ 9.25

WRIGLEY BUILDING RESTAURANT
Continental

$$

Back in the time when Lisbeth Scott was making movies, when Andy Pafko was thrilling Cub fans, when chewing gum was a nickel a pack ... back in those days Chicagoans thought of The Wrigley Building Restaurant as a place for exceptional dining. Today Scott, Pafko and nickel gum may have all changed, but The Wrigley Building Restaurant is still among the finest. Even though dwindling crowds have forced its closing on Saturday and Sunday nights, during the week it is still a stylish way to dine at moderate cost. The building itself is an architectural landmark, the largest terra cotta structure in the world, a striking white-tile, twin-peaked edifice. The restaurant represents uncompromising quality. At lunch a haven for the Boul Mich crowd, evenings will find the cavernous dining rooms less crowded and extremely comfortable. Among dinners I have enjoyed is an exceptional preparation of sweetbreads, challenging for any restaurant kitchen and particularly a surprise in one which depends so heavily on the commercial trade. Beef and other grilled meats are done with finesse. Dinners are complemented by a short but well thought out wine list.

WRIGLEY BUILDING RESTAURANT, 410 North Michigan Avenue, Chicago. Telephone: 944-7600. Hours: Lunch: 11:30 am-2:30 pm, Monday-Friday; Dinner: 5 pm-8:30 pm, Monday-Friday. Cards: AE, CB, DC, MC, VISA. Reservations taken. Full bar service. Parking lot at corner of Rush and Hubbard.

K/Rating 19/20 • Food 6.5/7 • Service 6/6 • Decor 4/4 • Value 2.5/3

Wrigley Building

Chicago
ZANADU
American

$$

"In Zanadu did Kubla Khan a stately pleasure dome decree. . . ." Although Chicago's Zanadu is more 20th century chic than Coleridge probably had in mind when he wrote his 19th-century verse, the restaurant does succeed in creating a pleasurable atmosphere with its skylight, terraced dining areas and adventurous art. And in addition to its ambiance the restaurant serves genuinely good food at reasonable prices. The menu runs the gamut from banana French toast, luscious and flavorfully sweet, to twin fillets with béarnaise. Snackers can find great munchies like French-fried zucchini standing sentinel around a cup of barbecue sauce dip. Omelettes are well-stuffed affairs. Sandwiches include the kind of big, thick and juicy burgers you just do not get in the fast food stands. Vegetarians will find several choices, none particularly expensive. If you want the full dinner, including soup or appetizer, salad, potato, vegetable and corn on the cob, pick a platter of huge barbecued beef ribs. There are the kind of ribs you gnaw on right down to the bone, and then keep going after even more flavor. Although Zanadu is not going to threaten any of Chicago's great seafood restaurants, they do serve a credible steamed Boston scrod among a handful of seafood selections. Desserts will tempt even confirmed non-dessert eaters. Who could resist French-fried ice cream? A scoop of vanilla is encased in doughnut dough and deep-fried, then drizzled with rum and cinnamon sauce, and topped with whipped cream. Strawberry cheesecake looks like a berry-studded brick. Crêpes, floats, shakes and sundaes make up other parts of the dessert selection. Zanadu's is firmly on the Sunday brunch wagon, as are dozens of area restaurants, but Zanadu may have one of the best deals going with their $4.95 all-you-can-eat selection.

ZANADU, 6259 North Broadway, Chicago. Telephone: 338-3700. Hours: 11 am-2 am, Monday-Thursday; until 4 am, Friday; until 5 am, Saturday; 10 am-2 am, Sunday. Cards: MC, VISA. No reservations. Full bar service. Private party facilities. Free parking nearby.

K/Rating 19/20 • Food 7/7 • Service 5/6 • Decor 4/4 • Value 3/3

ZUCCHINI PARMESAN
Definitely OK for vegetarians! Zucchini and a cheesy tomato sauce meet without meat $5.95

GINGER FISH
Filet of sole, sauted with crisp vegetables in a light oriental ginger sauce...................$6.50

ROAST BRISKET OF BEEF
A delicious old time favorite— still served with kishke $6.50

FRENCH FRIED SHRIMP
Served with cocktail sauce $6.95

TERIYAKI-ON-A-SKEWER
Tender cubes of beef, water chestnuts, red peppers and mushrooms, marinated in and served with hot teriyaki sauce. On rice—with chopsticks........$7.50

CHICKEN MONTEREY
Baked in a western style barbecue sauce, served with corn-on-the cob, fresh pineapple and strawberries....................$5.95

VEAL LORENZO
Thin slices of veal sauteed in an Italian sauce with red wine and fresh mushrooms $7.95

BROILED LIVER STEAK
Served with sauteed onions $5.75

SPINACH CHOPPED STEAK
Chopped steak/Spinach Soufflé, melted Swiss cheese and a sprinkle of Parmesan............$5.95

SEAFOOD JAMBALAYA
Shrimp and scallops in a spicy ricy mixture of onions, ham, green peppers and tomatoes.....$6.50

GIANT BARBECUED BEEF RIBS
Served with our special sauce....$6.95

SIRLOIN BUTT STEAK
Broiled with & topped with mushrooms $7.95

FRENCH FRIED SCALLOPS $6.50

STEAMED BOSTON SCROD
Fresh and fileted—served with hot lemony butter $6.95

WHITEFISH
Served lightly broiled with lemon. Broiled longer on request........$6.95

TWIN FILETS—WITH BEARNAISE
Tender filet mignon, with a classic sauce $9.95

All dinners served with soup or appetizer, potato & our Shrimp & Salad Bar. Potatoes are Hashed Brown, French Fried or Baked

191

Chicago
ZLATA'S BELGRADE RESTAURANT
Serbian

$$

The more I sample restaurants the more a common truth is driven home: The best values are found in the ethnic restaurants which dot the city. Zlata's Belgrade is a good example. The food is Serbian, prepared in the old-country way. The dishes are steeped as much in history as in sauces. Serbia has had the misfortune to be a battleground over the centuries, fought over by mighty empires. A positive aspect of this has been a cross-pollination of cultures and cuisines. Thus, you will find influences of Greek food such as musaka, an eggplant and ground beef casserole. A Turkish influence creeps in through the use of rice in some dishes. And, of course, there are the unique Balkan specialties themselves. Pjeskavica is a large chopped steak of ground beef and lamb. Cevapcici are small beef and lamb sausages. Muckalica is another grilled beef and lamb dish accented with sharper seasoning. Don't ignore such appetizers as kajmak and ajvar. Ajvar is made from fried red and green peppers, mashed and seasoned. It is not as fiery as it sounds. Kajmak is a mildly tart butter with the slight taste of cream cheese. If you really want to feel the spirit, start dinner with a glass of Slivovitz, the strong Balkan plum brandy. Don't sip it timidly, but boldy take the glass and down the liquid in one gulp. Then you are ready to feast like a Serb.

ZLATA'S BELGRADE RESTAURANT, 1516 Milwaukee Avenue, Chicago. Telephone: 252-9514. Hours: 5 pm-2 am, Wednesday-Sunday. No cards. Reservations recommended. Full bar service. Casual dress acceptable.

K/Rating 15/20 • Food 6/7 • Service 4/6 • Decor 2/4 • Value 3/3

ZUM DEUTSCHEN ECK

$$

Some of the prices at Zum Deutschen Eck have actually gone down since the first edition of *Best Restaurants Chicago*, but there is no compromise with quality. Somewhat off the beaten path, away from Lincoln Avenue's German-restaurant-row, Zum Deutschen Eck has gone its own way for years as the "German Corner." The restaurant's old-world exterior makes it a neighborhood standout. The interior has a beer hall and rathskeller theme, carried out with dining at comfortable tables or booths. On weekends, at its most crowded, the restaurant is loud and boisterous with peels of laughter and German music. A couple of times during the evening, sing-a-longs help whet the appetite for large steins of foamy beer. On week nights, things settle down to a quieter pace. Food is consistently good. Sauerbraten, a house specialty, is marinated a good two weeks in

red wine, vinegar and spices. Then, just before the beef is about ready to get up and walk away, it is cooked in its own juices and served up hot and spicy with spätzle. Braised beef tenderloin à la Deutsch is another excellent choice; the meat is baked in a red wine sauce and served with cooked fresh mushrooms, green peppers, onions, tomatoes and seasonings. It may sound spicy but it is not. It is a good example of basic Middle European cooking. When available, the veal in a white cream sauce is excellent. Lots of lemon juice helps perk up the weiner schnitzel. Hasenpfeffer is a seasonal favorite. Traditional German cold meat salads and homemade head cheese are among featured appetizers. The wine list includes some rarely seen German reds; one taste indicates why they are rarely seen. Stick to the whites or a mugful of frosty beer. Homemade pastries for dessert include a flaky apple strudel.

ZUM DEUTSCHEN ECK, 2924 North Southport Avenue, Chicago. Telephone: 525-8121. Hours: 11:30 am-11 pm, Monday-Thursday; until 2 am, Friday; noon-3 am, Saturday; noon-11 pm, Sunday. Cards: AE, DC, MC, VISA. Reservations recommended. Full bar service. Private party facilities for 25 to 400 people. Ample parking.

K/Rating 17/20 • Food 5/7 • Service 5/6 • Decor 4/4 • Value 3/3

Suburbs: North

Evanston, Glenview, Highland Park,
Highwood, Lake Bluff, Lincolnwood,
Northbrook, Skokie, Winnetka

Highland Park
AEGEAN ISLES
Greek

$

Tucked away in Highland Park's Ravinia section, Aegean Isles is a small storefront restaurant, attractively decorated and moderately priced. As with other Greek restaurants, it is possible to eat well for not much more than $6 per person, and for substantially less if all you want is a small salad, a gyros sandwich and a bit of baklava. Even a large combination dinner is under $7 and includes specialties such as moussaka, pastitsio, gyros, roast lamb, potatoes, rice and peas. I had a less than perfect experience with an order of baked lamb which was more bone than meat. But if fish is your quest, you should have no complaints about a fresh entrée of snapper or seabass. Seafood will vary from day to day, as will prices. I prefer it charcoal grilled, although you can have it gas broiled should you prefer. Appetizers include the usual selection common to Greek restaurants: saganaki, spinach pie, stuffed grape leaves and fish roe salad. Soups always include avgolemono, the tasty, tart egg-lemon broth with rice. Not on the menu but sometimes available is a delectable mushroom soup as fresh as a Hellenic meadow. Ask for it specifically, you may be there on a lucky night.

AEGEAN ISLES, 561 Roger Williams Avenue, Highland Park. Telephone: 443-5620. Hours: 11:30 am-10 pm, Monday-Thursday; until midnight, Friday-Saturday. Cards: MC, VISA. No reservations. Full bar service. Parking nearby.

K/Rating 15.5/20 • Food 5/7 • Service 5/6 • Decor 3/5 • Value 2.5/3

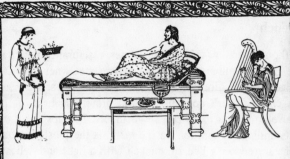

Aegean Specials

COMBINATION PLATE: Pastitsio, Moussaka, Gyros. Lamb, Potatoes, Rice, Peas		6.75
PASTITSIO: Baked Macaroni with Ground Meat. Topped with Cream Sauce		4.75
MOUSSAKA: Sliced Eggplant, Ground Beef, Potatoes, Parmesan Cheese, Cream Sauce		4.75
GYROS PLATE: with Onions, Pita Bread, Rice		4.45
BAKED CHICKEN: with Oregano, Butter Sauce	½ Chicken	4.65
	¼ Chicken	2.75
AEGEAN ISLES CADAMA BEEF		4.85
SHISHKEBAB: Beef Tenderloin, Tomatoes, Peppers, Onions, Mushrooms		7.25
ROAST LEG OF LAMB: Touch of Garlic		6.75
BABY LAMB CHOPS		7.45

From the Aegean Seas

BROILED RED SNAPPER: According to weight (Fresh)	
BROILED SEA BASS: According to weight (Fresh)	
FRIED SQUID: (Calamaria)	4.85

All above served with a Cup of Soup

Beverages

COFFEE, SANKA, TEA	.55	.35
MILK, SOFT DRINKS		.40
GREEK COFFEE		.65

Desserts

BAKLAVA	.85
GALAKTOBOURIKO	.85
CREAM CARAMELE	.85
BOUGATSA FLAMBÉ	1.50

Highwood
ALOUETTE
French

$$$

Without question, this is the best new restaurant to open in the Chicagoland area in the past two years. Owner Christian Zeiger opened Alouette after selling Le Titi de Paris, q.v., to his chef. Zeiger's concept of food brings the best of the nouvelle cuisine to North Shore diners. Perhaps the most outstanding preparation on the menu is the lobster medallions served on a bed of spinach with a light and delicate beurre blanc. The textures and taste are nearly ephemeral yet their memory lingers on. Roast duckling in raspberry sauce is a more robust preparation, as is the superb sliced breast of duck in a deep-flavored green peppercorn sauce. Appetizers are uniformly excellent; the sweet onion tart is a personal favorite. Lobster bisque is close to perfect. Desserts are a pastry triumph. The restaurant has a charming French country decor and a service staff that is second to none.

ALOUETTE, 440 North Green Bay Road, Highwood. Telephone: 433-5600. Hours: from 5 pm, Tuesday-Sunday. Cards: MC, VISA. Reservations required. Full bar service. Jackets required for men. Private party facilities available on week nights. Ample parking.

K/Rating 19/20 • Food 7/7 • Service 6/6 • Decor 3.5/4 • Value 2.5/3

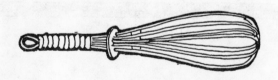

MEDAILLONS DE LANGOUSTE FLORENTINE
medaillons of lobster on a bed of spinach with a light white wine sauce

13.50

TRUITE BRAISEE AU BEAUJOLAIS
rainbow trout braised in a subtle red burgundy with a mousse of lobster

9.75

WHITE FISH GRILLE PROVENCALE OU MEUNIERE
broiled white fish with diced tomatoes, garlic and herbes

9.25

SOLE BRAISEE A LA CIBOULETTE
dover sole braised in a light white wine sauce and chives

12.95

ESCALOPE DE SAUMON A L'OSEILLE
filet of salmon broiled with a sorrel sauce

11.75

CANARD ROTI AUX FRAMBOISES
roast duck in a delicate raspberry and brandy sauce

11.00

POULET AU BASILIC ET CHANTERELLES
boneless chicken braised in white wine, basil and imported mushrooms

8.50

FILET DE BOEUF GRILLE BEARNAISE
broiled tenderloin with bearnaise sauce

11.50

ENTRECOTE BORDELAISE
N.Y. sirloin sauteed with red wine and shallots sauce

13.25

NOISETTE D'AGNEAU A LA MOUTARDE DE MEAUX
eye of rack of lamb broiled with a mustard sauce

12.50

MAGRAI DE CANARD AU POIVRE VERT
sliced breast of duck with a green peppercorns sauce

11.00

ESCALOPE DE VEAU AU CITRON VERT
veal scallopini sauteed with lime

10.50

ROGNONS DE VEAU AUX GOUSSES D'AIL EN CHEMISE
veal kidney sauteed with garlic cloves and madeira sauce

8.25

RIS DE VEAU TREGUAINAISE
sweet breads braised in white wine

11.25

Highland Park
ARNIE'S NORTH
American $$

Arnie Morton's suburban fantasy-come-true is perhaps even more visually dazzling, more sensually assaulting than is his town venture (Arnie's, q.v.). Not only a restaurant, Arnie's North encompasses a full bar and lounge, loft disco, hamburger buffet, salad bar and buffet plus a huge private party room, all under the vaulted roof of a former A & P supermarket. Morton, who is given to aphorisms about his restaurant endeavors, likes to think of himself as the ringmaster of a three-ring circus. If that is so, then Arnie's North is the Barnum and Bailey of restaurants. There is always something going on here. The heart of the restaurant is the Grand Buffet, an immense island which contains dozens of different vegetables, salads, meats, fruit, nuts and tidbits: It comes with most dinners. One of the best bargains since gold was $35 an ounce is the Grand Buffet, the daily chef's special and the pasta of the day for only $6.95. Among more ambitious dinner entrées, steaks are tender, duckling is crisp and tasty in Cassis, fish is firm and fresh, almost understated compared to everything else with which it must compete. Even if you do not want food, but only a drink, make it a point to stop in at Arnie's North. The decor is overwhelming, from the bright red banquettes and brass railings to the giant silver caryatids à la art nouveau. Gaudy might be the word to describe it all. But I have no complaints; it's all part of the fun.

ARNIE'S NORTH, 1876 First Street, Highland Park. Telephone: 432-1200. Hours: 11:30 am-1 am, Tuesday-Friday; 5:30 pm-2 am, Saturday; 10:30 am-midnight, Sunday. Cards: AE, DC, MC, VISA. Reservations taken. Full bar service. Casual dress acceptable. Private party facilities. Ample parking.

K/Rating 18.5/20 • Food 6/7 • Service 5.5/6 • Decor 4/4 • Value 3/3

Highland Park
THE BIG APPLE
Pancakes / Omelettes $

Give me stacks of buttermilks, layers of flapjacks, an eternity of waffles morning, noon and night. If you, as I, think this is more than breakfast food then zero in on The Big Apple. Here is a cheery place where the two large dining areas have a kitchen-like atmosphere and the apple theme is carried out ad infinitum in the wallpaper. Tables are spacious to accommodate pots of butter, pitchers of syrup, assorted jellies, not to mention plates, cups, saucers, glassware and serving platters. The most that you can spend for a pancake is $3.25, which will buy you either the house namesake, a huge apple dandy or its fraternal sibling, a strawberry-lathered specialty dubbed the Highland Fling. These are both essentially German-style pancakes with creative license allowing for the adaptations. The pancakes are redolent with sugar and cinnamon which caramelizes to a warm bubbly glaze. The Big Apple pancake is a ten-inch circle of sweet apple goodness. The Highland Fling is equally bountiful with its berries. For somewhat simpler tastes, try the Dutch Delight for $2.75. It is another big ten incher, sans fruit but dusted with powdered sugar and served with lemon wedges. You will find traditional pancakes such as your basic buttermilks, plus such variations on the theme as blueberries, bananas, pineapple, even pecans and chocolate chips, all for little enough that your $2 bill of payment will yield some change. If you want something different, check out the San Francisco flapjacks.

THE BIG APPLE, 1260 Deerfield Road, Highland Park. Telephone: 831-2490. Hours: 8 am-10 pm, Monday-Thursday; until midnight, Friday; 7 am-1 am, Saturday; until 9 pm, Sunday. No cards. No reservations. Free parking.

K/Rating 18/20 • Food 6/7 • Service 5/6 • Decor 4/4 • Value 3/3

Evanston
CAFÉ PROVENÇAL
French

$$$

The rather brief menu is complemented by evening specialties. Mousseline of bay scallops makes a marvelous appetizer. Cold mussels, stuffed artichoke and the three-layered omelette called Le Crespéou have all been recent appetizer favorites, too. Soup du jour will vary from night to night; classic French onion, baked in the crock, is regularly featured. Although entrée selections are limited, they are not without imagination. Duckling Calvados is prepared in a superb sauce. Veal ragoût, grilled lamb chops and stuffed beefsteak are among meat choices. The latter involves a tartar-like mixture of raw chopped steak bound with shallots, parsley, cognac and Dijon mustard. Fish is always fresh and will vary depending upon availabilities. Desserts tend to be rich and elaborate; chocoholics should be well pleased. Service can sometimes be less than razor sharp but the culinary talents of Cordon Bleu graduate Leslee Ries more than makes up for any minor gaffes in the dining room.

CAFÉ PROVENÇAL, 1625 Hinman Avenue, Evanston. Telephone: 475-2233. Hours: from 6 pm, Monday-Saturday; Cards: MC. Reservations required on weekends. Full bar service. Casual dress acceptable. Private party facilities. Ample parking.

K/Rating 17/20 • Food 7/7 • Service 5/6 • Decor 2.5/4 • Value 2.5/3

Les hors d'oeuvre

Artichaut Farci $2.95
whole stuffed artichoke with
ham and vegetable mireporix

Le Crespéou $2.50
three flavor omelet pâté

Pâté de Campagne $2.50
well seasoned poultry pâté

Poissons du Café Provençal (price varies)
seasonal fish delicacies

Les Potages

Soupe à l'oignon gratinée $2.00
classic onion soup baked with cheese

Soupe du Jour (price varies)

Les Entrées

entrees include salade maison, pommes dauphine, french bread, sweet butter

Poissons du Jour (price varies)
daily fish specialties

Canard au Poivre Vert $9.25
roast duckling in a green peppercorn sauce

Poulet Provençal $7.50
sauteed chicken with tomato, onions, mushrooms

Biftek à la Maison $10.50
stuffed boneless ribeye, red wine sauce

Cassoulet de Castelnaudry $9.95
peasant casserole of pork, lamb, beans, & sausages

Côtes d'Agneau Grillées $9.25
grilled loin lamb chops with garlic & herb purée

Les Desserts

Gâteau de Mousse au Chocolat $2.00
chocolate mousse layered between homemade lady fingers

Les Sorbets aux Fruits $2.00
homemade fruit sorbets

Plat de Fromages $2.50

Dessert Specialités de la Maison (price varies)

Les Boissons

Café $.50   Thé $.50   Café Filtre $1.00

Skokie
DON'S FISH MARKET & PROVISION COMPANY
Seafood

$$

Who would expect to find a really great seafood restaurant in a Howard Johnson's motel, much less in Skokie? Well, folks, that's what we've got. The decor is typical fish restaurant à la Chicago; a re-creation of a New England fish shanty with the usual trappings of weathered board, nautical fittings, polished wood tables and captain's chairs. Yet the food at Don's is so good the decor could be steel mill coffee shop and it would still be sensational. The fish is as fresh as you can get and still be in the Midwest. Pick from a daily catch that often includes snapper, Boston sole, lemon sole, trout, salmon, lake perch, etc. Striped sea bass broiled over charcoal is a real winner. Soft-shelled crabs in butter and almonds practically scream out their succulence. Check the daily chalkboard listing to see what's what. Wonderfully crusty bread and New York bialys, topnotch salad with baby shrimp and crumbled bleu cheese dressing, plus incredibly caloric desserts complete a fine dinner menu.

DON'S FISHMARKET & PROVISION COMPANY, 9335 Skokie Boulevard, Skokie. Telephone: 677-3424. Hours: 5 pm-midnight, daily. Cards: AE, VISA. Reservations recommended. Full bar service. Casual dress acceptable. Private party facilities for 10 to 55 people. Ample parking.

K/Rating 20/20 • Food 7/7 • Service 6/6 • Decor 4/4 • Value 3/3

Glenview
DRAGON INN NORTH
Chinese (Mandarin)

$$

The newest and best of a three-restaurant chain (Dragon Inn and Dragon Seed are the other two), Dragon Inn North offers consistently fine Mandarin, Hunan and Szechwan cuisine. There are more than 50 entrées on the comprehensive menu plus exotic appetizers and simmering soups. Let your waitress make suggestions if you are confused, or call at least a day ahead and order the marvelous Peking duck as a main course to build around. Another great choice is the smoked tea duck with crisp skin and dusky-flavored, dark, rich meat. Incidentally, Dragon Inn is a worthy runner-up if you are on the Far South Side; Dragon Seed has a very good preparation mid-North.

DRAGON INN NORTH, 1650 Waukegan Road, Glenview. Telephone: 729-8383. Hours: 11:30 am-10 pm, Tuesday-Thursday; until midnight, Friday; 6 pm-midnight, Saturday; noon-10 pm, Sunday. Cards: AE, CB, DC. Reservations recommended. Full bar service. Free parking.

DRAGON INN, 18431 South Halsted Street, Glenwood. Telephone: 746-3344. Hours: 11:30 am-10 pm, Tuesday-Thursday; until midnight, Friday; 6 pm-midnight, Saturday; noon-10 pm, Sunday. Cards: AE. Reservations recommended. Full bar service. Free parking.

DRAGON SEED, 2300 North Lincoln Park West (in the Belden Stratford Hotel), Chicago. Telephone: 528-5542. Hours: Lunch: noon-2:30 pm, Tuesday-Friday; until midnight, Friday-Saturday; noon-10 pm, Sunday. No cards. Reservations taken. No bar service: you may bring your own.

K/Rating 18.5/20 • Food 5.5/7 • Service 6/6 • Decor 4/4 • Value 3/3

Evanston
FANNY'S
Italian/American   **$$**

Why does Fanny's have to keep reminding everyone of how good it is by posting awards, letters, photographs and testimonials not only on its walls, but in its advertising and even on the menu? Everyone who goes there knows how good it is. The food speaks for itself. Fanny's is one of the best places I know of for family dining. When it comes to spaghetti, which every kid loves, there is no such thing as portion control at Fanny's; as soon as a platter is nearly emptied, a waiter comes around with fresh tubs of spaghetti and meat sauce. It's so butter-rich with goodness you just cannot say "No" to more. As far as I can tell everything that comes out of the kitchen is fresh, from vegetables to seafood. Fanny boasts that hundreds of pounds of butter are used daily in preparation of her dishes and garlic bread. If there is an award for cholesterol, I am sure this restaurant deserves it. But so what! The results sure are good. Who would think of fried chicken in a restaurant otherwise characterized by Italian food. Yet Fanny's chicken is even better than that other guy's with the red and white stripes. The meat practically falls from the bones; the crust has a savory flavor unlike anything I have tasted elsewhere. Fanny's is not for the weight-conscious diner, although there is a fruit platter on the menu for calorie counters in your group.

FANNY'S, 1601 Simpson Street, Evanston. Telephone: 475-8686/273-3344. Hours: 5 pm-9 pm, Monday-Friday; until 9:30 pm, Saturday; noon-8 pm, Sunday. Cards: AE, MC, VISA. Reservations preferred. Full bar service. Jackets required for men on the first-floor dining room; casual dress acceptable upstairs. Private party facilities for 15 to 90 people. Free parking.

K/Rating 17.5/20 • Food 6/7 • Service 6/6 • Decor 2.5/4 • Value 3/3

Appetizers

Herring (in Cream Sauce)	1.65	Radishes and Green Onions	1.00
Ripe Olives	1.35	Pascal Celery	1.00
Italian Salami	1.40	Fresh Fruit Cup	1.40
Pepperoncini	1.00	Tomato Juice	.75

Fanny's Preparation of Cottage Cheese with French Roquefort Cheese 1.50
Fanny's Preparation of Chicken Livers with Imported Sherry Wine 1.50
Fanny's Antipasto served on Lazy Susan Trays, includes a portion of all above
items 1.75 per person at each table, if ordered for fewer than
number being served .... 2.00 per person

Dinners

Buttered Garlic Toast or Plain Buttered Toast,
Tossed Salad with Fanny's Famous Dressing

FANNY'S WORLD FAMOUS SPAGHETTI	4.95
MUSHROOM SPAGHETTI (no meat)	4.95
MOSTACCIOLI Served with Fanny's Spaghetti Sauce	4.95
FETTUCINI (Buttered Noodles with Cheese)	5.75
FANNY'S MEAT RAVIOLI	5.75
FETTUCINI with Fanny's Spaghetti Sauce	6.15
FANNY'S FAMOUS SPAGHETTI	
With ¼ Southern Fried Chicken	5.95
With ½ Southern Fried Chicken	6.95
SOUTHERN FRIED CHICKEN (¼), French Fries	5.75
SOUTHERN FRIED CHICKEN (½), French Fries	6.95
FRESH LAKE SUPERIOR WHITEFISH served with Fanny's Spaghetti	7.50
FRESH LAKE SUPERIOR WHITEFISH served with Fanny's Fettucini	8.50
Fish flown daily from coast to Johnson's Fish Market, Evanston—where Fanny selects and purchases it every day.	
FANNY'S FETTUCINI	
With ¼ Southern Fried Chicken	6.95
With ½ Southern Fried Chicken	7.95
FANNY'S ONE-QUARTER BROILED CHICKEN prepared with Fragrant Herbs, etc., Served with Fanny's Famous Spaghetti	5.95
ONE-QUARTER BROILED CHICKEN with Fettucini	6.95
BROILED CHICKEN (½) with Fanny's Famous Spaghetti	6.95
BROILED CHICKEN (½) with Fettucini	7.95
FANNY'S HOMEMADE LASAGNA	5.75
DELUXE FRUIT PLATE (all Fresh Fruits) with Roquefort Cheese and Finnish Crackers	5.75

You may request a second helping of Spaghetti (gratis).
Birthday, anniversary cakes (gratis) if ordered when reservation is made.

Winnetka
THE INDIAN TRAIL
American   **$**

In the first edition of *Best Restaurants Chicago*, I wrote
that "the Indian Trail proves that in a world filled with
change some things can remain the same." I was wrong. The
Indian Trail has changed for the better; they have added an
outdoor courtyard for dining in warmer months, and they
have a no-smoking section for diners who prefer to be free
of noxious fumes. Otherwise, the Indian Trail continues to
offer outstanding value. Ample portions are served by the
same Klingeman family that has operated this restaurant for
better than four decades. Everything is fresh; I think they
would even churn their own butter if they had the time and
staff to do it. The menu changes daily and ranges from
steaks to fresh fish to special dinner salads. Homemade pies
are outstanding desserts. If you don't have a grandma to go
home to, this is a perfect place for a family Sunday dinner.

THE INDIAN TRAIL, 507 Chestnut Street, Winnetka.
Telephone: 446-1703. Hours: Lunch: 11:30 am-2:30 pm,
Tuesday-Saturday; Dinner: 4:30 pm-8 pm, Monday-Saturday; 11:30 am-7:30 pm, Sunday. Cards: MC, VISA. No
reservations. No bar service; you may bring your own.
Casual dress acceptable. Private party facilities. Ample
parking.

K/Rating 19/20 • Food 6.5/7 • Service 6/6 • Decor 3.5/4 • Value 3/3

Northbrook
JAMES TAVERN
Early American   **$$**

A bicentennial gift to the Chicago area, James Tavern is a
lovely recreation of an old Colonial inn. Replicas of period
furniture are mixed with some genuine artifacts of early
America to create the charming decor. The outstanding
dinner-roll basket includes sticky sweet buns, cornbread
sticks and old-fashioned Sally Lunn bread. Salads are mixed
tableside in a sprightly herb dressing. Although owned and
operated by Stouffer's, which is known for frozen prepack-
aged foods, everything is prepared from scratch in the
James Tavern kitchen. I particularly like the veal birds and
the crab cakes. The wine list is short but offers several
outstanding selections; even Scuppernong, included perhaps
more for authenticity than for taste, is among the potables.

JAMES TAVERN, 1775 Lake Cook Road, Northbrook.
Telephone: 498-2020. Hours: 5:30 pm-10 pm, Monday-
Thursday; until 11 pm, Friday; 5 pm-11 pm, Saturday;
4:30 pm-9 pm, Sunday. Cards: AE, DC, MC, VISA. Reser-
vations required on weekends. Full bar service. Casual dress
acceptable. Ample parking.

K/Rating 19/20 • Food 6/7 • Service 6/6 • Decor 4/4 • Value 3/3

Highwood
SCORNAVACCO'S
Italian

$$

Scornavacco's menu is typical of scores of American-Italian restaurants. Veal Milanese, veal Parmigiana, veal saltimbocca, chicken cacciatore, chicken Vesuvio, broiled chicken in lemon, garlic and butter. But there is a difference that transcends the menu. Scornavacco's has been around Highwood for more than 40 years. There is a special quality which I look for in genuinely attractive and interesting dining spots. Scornavacco's has it. Maybe it is the special devotion the owners demonstrate when they show off their dining rooms, kitchen and elaborate bar and discotheque. Perhaps it is the visible pleasure diners take in their food. Possibly, it is the "I really care about how you like this restaurant and its food" attitude on the part of its waitresses. I think it is some of all this ... and maybe more. I like to go with family groups to Scornavacco's. That way you can order family style and taste from a lot of preparations. Green noodles al forno are made from scratch, baked in garlic butter and grated Parmesan cheese. Homemade raviolis are stuffed with cheese and served butter rich or, if you prefer, in one of the mellowest marinaras I can recall. Even pizza, an afterthought at full-menu Italian restaurants is better than ordinary. This is thin crust, basic pizza with tomato-rich sauce and enough mozzarella for you to know this is not catsup and saltines you are nibbling.

SCORNAVACCO'S, 550 Green Bay Road, Highwood. Telephone: 432-7651. Hours: 11 am-11 pm, daily plus Sunday brunch. Cards: AE, MC, VISA. Reservations taken. Full bar service. Casual dress acceptable. Private party facilities for up to 400 people. Ample parking.

K/Rating 18/20 • Food 6/7 • Service 6/6 • Decor 3/4 • Value 3/3

SATURDAY SPECIAL

Prime Rib

Salad ..... Choice of:
Baked Potato or Spaghetti
8.95

Dinners

Appetizers

Assorted Italian Antipasto   *Minestrone Soup*
Tomato Juice   *Marinated Herring*

A Little Of Old Italy

VEAL MILANAISE 7.50
Breaded veal with marinara sauce.

VEAL PARMIGIANA 7.95
Breaded veal cutlet baked with tomato
sauce and Parmesan cheese.

VEAL SALTIMBOCCA 7.95
Tender veal topped with prosciutto and
sauteed to a golden brown.

VEAL SCALLOPINI 7.95
Tender sliced veal sauteed in white wine,
sauce and mushrooms.

BRACIOLE 7.95
Tender rolled beef filled with Italian
Stuffing and baked.

VEAL PICCANTE 7.95
Sliced breaded veal dipped in eggs,
baked with lemon and fresh parsley and
mushrooms.

CHICKEN A LA CACCIATORE 7.25
Juicy young Spring chicken sauteed in
olive oil and baked with tomato sauce
and mushrooms.

CHICKEN VESUVIO 7.25
Sauteed in garlic and olive oil with
spices, then baked in white wine sauce
with mushrooms and Parsley potatoes.

ITALIAN SAUSAGE WITH
GREEN PEPPERS Spaghetti 6.75
EGG PLANT PARMIGIANA 6.75

ANTHONY'S SPECIAL 8.50
A delectable offering of Chicken
Vesuvio, Veal, Sausage, Meat ball and
Mostaccioli.

Seafood

KING CRAB LEGS 9.75

FRENCH FRIED SHRIMP 7.25
Butterfly cut.

SHRIMP DE JONGHE 7.95
Anthony's own special topping.
Butter and garlic.

BROILED WALLEYE PIKE 7.50
Italian sauce or almondine.

LAKE SUPERIOR WHITE FISH 7.50
Favorite of the fish lovers. (When available).

BROILED LOBSTER .... Market Price
A large succulent beauty.

SHRIMP SCAMPI A LA SCORNAVACCO . 8.50
Baked Scampi in a butter and garlic
sauce.

On The Wing

BROILED CHICKEN ITALIAN STYLE . 6.50
Tender chicken broiled in lemon, garlic
butter. (Please allow 30 minutes.)

Steaks

TENDER RIB EYE STEAK 7.95
SIRLOIN BUTT STEAK 8.95
NEW YORK SIRLOIN STRIP
STEAK, ... 9.95
BARBECUED BABY BACK RIBS .. 8.75
Tender ribs barbecued to a golden
sensation, covered with our famous sauce.
NEW YORK STRIP STEAK
ITALIANO 10.95
BROILED FILET MIGNON 9.95
SURF 'N TURF .... Market Price
Choice steak broiled to perfection and
accompanied by a succulent lobster
tail.

PEPPER STEAK 8.95
Sliced filet mignon sauteed in wine with
green peppers, tomatoes and mushrooms.

Highwood
SHRIMP WALK
American

$$

When the Shrimp Walk opened a few years ago, the stated intention was to create a New Orleans atmosphere. But over a period of time, the emphasis has gotten away from gumbos and shrimp to a broader seafood menu at reasonable prices. The gumbo is still there of course, as are such yummy appetizers as fried mushrooms and shrimp de jonghe. But the real treat is the French onion soup. Almost a meal in itself, the soup has a sweet, onion tang. It is topped with loads of gooey cheese to produce the kind of French onion soup that may be only a Parisian memory of Les Halles on a misted morning. If deep-fried shrimp is your dish, sample the Basin Street butterflies. These are large Gulf shrimp in a thin batter coating. Shrimp steamed in beer is another offering; they are served in the shell which requires you to dig in and peel them yourself. A combination platter gives you a taste of fried oysters, scallops, shrimp, clams and perch. There is more than enough to satisfy an almost bottomless appetite. Most dinners include a side of cole slaw and excellent cottage fries. A few entrées include refillable salad. It is the standard salad bar concept except your waitress does the work of putting the salad together for you. And yes, if someone in your crowd prefers meat, you will find steak, chicken and hamburgers. There are some desserts such as homemade mud pie made from crushed oreos, ice cream, fudge and nuts, topped with whipped cream.

SHRIMP WALK, 405 Sheridan Road, Highwood. Telephone: 432-0500. Hours: 5 pm-10 pm, Tuesday-Thursday; until 11 pm, Friday; 4 pm-midnight, Saturday; 4 pm-9 pm, Sunday. Cards: AE, MC, VISA. No reservations. Full bar service. Casual dress acceptable. Free parking.

K/Rating 20/20 • Food 7/7 • Service 6/6 • Decor 4/4 • Value 3/3

SHRIMP WALK SPECIALTIES

BASIN STREET BUTTERFLIES
Choice Gulf Shrimp, lightly dusted with French Bread Crumbs.
Deep-Fried, Golden Crisp. Cole Slaw and Potatoes   **$ 6.65**

SHRIMPS-ON-TAP
Succulent Gulf Shrimps Steamed in Finest Draft Beer and Spices.
Served in the Shell for you to peel and enjoy. Slaw and Potatoes   **$ 6.50**

DUNGENESS CRAB
Whole Crab, over 2 pounds, Served Hot with Cocktail Sauce and
Drawn Butter Salad and Potatoes Included.   **$10.50**

STUFFED RED SNAPPER
Florida Red Snapper Baked with a Delectable Mixture of Crab Meat,
Bread Crumbs and Seasonings. Salad and Potatoes Included   **$ 7.95**

SEA KABOB
Tender Pieces of Shrimp, Scallops and Cod, Broiled with
Mushrooms, Green Pepper, Onions and Tomatoes on Two
Skewers. Rice Pilaf and Salad   **$ 7.75**

FROM THE SEA

LOBSTER TAIL
Large Lobster Tail, Broiled and Served with
Drawn Butter. Salad and Fries   **$12.50**

STEAMED CRAB LEGS
Selected with care and Steamed. Served
with Drawn Butter and Cocktail Sauce.
Salad and Potatoes Included   **$10.25**

SHRIMP SALAD
Large Salad Bowl with Crisp Lettuce,
Tomatoes, Hard Boiled Egg and Choice
Gulf Shrimp. Your Choice of Dressing
served on the side   **$ 6.95**

RAINBOW TROUT
Boned and Baked with Butter
and Paprika. Served with Tartar
Sauce. Salad and Potatoes   **$ 7.50**

FLORIDA STONE CRAB
Cracked and Served on a Bed of
Ice with Mustard Sauce. Salad and
Potatoes Included   **$10.50**

YELLOW TAIL
The Pride of Florida for
Tenderness and Flavor. Broiled
with Butter and Paprika. Served
with Salad and Potatoes   **$ 8.25**

FROM THE CHAR-BROILER

CENTER CUT FILET
Open-faced — Broiled to Your
Liking. Served with Fries and Salad   **$ 7.50**

BOURBON STREET BURGER
Half-Pound Choice Beef Cooked to your
Liking. Dark Rye or Bun, Lettuce, Pickle,
Cole Slaw and Potatoes   **$ 3.25**

With Cheese - .15 Extra

FRIED SEA FOOD

*Served with Sauce, Cole Slaw
and Cottage Fried Potatoes*

SEA SCALLOPS	**$ 5.95**
OYSTERS	**$ 5.50**
LAKE PERCH	**$ 5.25**
FISH 'N CHIPS	**$ 4.75**
CLAMS	**$ 4.75**

SEAFOOD PLATTER
Combination of Scallops, Oysters,
Lake Perch, Fried Shrimp and
Clams   **$ 7.25**

FRIED CHICKEN
Juicy "Golden Crisp" Half Chicken,
Fried to Perfection in Our Own
Special Butter   **$ 4.25**

FRIED CHICKEN LIVERS
Generous Portion of Tender Livers,
Deep-Fried, Crisp 'n Crunchy   **$ 3.95**

COMBINATIONS

STEAK and CRAB LEGS	**$11.50**
STEAK and LOBSTER TAIL	**$12.50**
STEAK and FRIED SHRIMP	**$10.50**

ASK YOUR WAITRESS FOR OUR DAILY SPECIALS

SALAD BAR

Items noted are served with our REFILLABLE Salad with croutons, tomatoes and green onions. All others are
served with Cole Slaw. Salad can be substituted for Cole Slaw with any dinner for an Additional $ .75.

A La Carte Salads   **$ 1.75**

DRESSINGS

1000 ISLAND	BLUE CHEESE	ITALIAN
CREAMY GARLIC	CREAMY ITALIAN	FRENCH
	OIL AND VINEGAR	

Lake Bluff
THE SILO
American/Pizza

$$

Pizza restaurants come and go, but it took two Swedes named Gene Bergmark and Carl Skoglund to come up with some of the most enduring and best pizza around. The Silo's pizza fame rests on their deep dish special which comes in nine-inch and 14-inch sizes. Load each up with your choice of ingredients and you have enough to feed a regiment of hungries. The base of it all is the rich, egg-dough crust, golden yellow in color and almost pastry-like in texture. Well-seasoned tomato sauce, rich gooey cheeses and the various toppings make this as much of a casserole as a pizza. A good tossed salad might stimulate tastebuds as will such special tidbits as fried mushrooms about as large as a halfback's knuckles. Chili, sandwiches and a $6.95 steak make up the rest of the menu. The Silo is a large barn-like structure with a cheery open-pit fireplace and sunken bar in the center of the room. Downstairs accommodates most any grouping; upstairs is the Loft which is reserved for adults. And that is as good a way as any to run a family restaurant. Service at the Silo takes time because everything is made from scratch. And what you don't eat of your pizza you can take home for later snacking.

THE SILO, 625 Rockland Road (State Route 176), Lake Bluff. Telephone: 234-6660. Hours: 11:30 am-10:30 pm, Monday-Thursday; until 11:30 pm, Friday; 5 pm-11:30 pm, Saturday; 3:30 pm-9:30 pm, Sunday. No cards. No reservations. Full bar service. Casual, neat dress acceptable. Private party facilities. Ample parking.

K/Rating 20/20 • Food 7/7 • Service 6/6 • Decor 4/4 • Value 3/3

Skokie
THE TOWER GARDEN & RESTAURANT
Continental

$$$

If awards were given for steady restaurant improvement, the Tower would win coming and going. This beautiful restaurant in a garden setting (flawed somewhat by the din of conversation reverberating against the floor-to-ceiling glass windows) has developed from a so-so suburban gathering spot into one of the best French dining rooms on the North Shore. Recommended dishes from the expensive, multipaged menu include one of the house specialties, truite au bleu, lovely trout fresh from the tank poached in court bouillon. Turbot is another treat for lovers of the briny deep's storehouse. A huge rack of lamb for two is presented to diners with a gorgeous vegetable bouquet. The tender lamb is good either with a fine bordelaise sauce or the more traditional mint jelly. Among desserts the kirsch-wasser torte is a taste of Bavarian charm; the crêpes à la Markus are flamed tableside and served in a coffee liqueur sauce. The Tower has without question the finest wine list in the suburbs—if not the entire metropolitan area—with emphasis on the great wines of France and Germany.

THE TOWER GARDEN & RESTAURANT, 9925 Gross Point Road, Skokie. Telephone: 673-4450. Hours: Lunch: 11:30 am-3 pm, Monday-Friday; Dinner 3 pm-11 pm, Monday-Saturday; Brunch: 11:30 am-3 pm, Sunday; Buffet dinner: 3 pm-7 pm, Sunday. Cards: AE, CB, DC, MC, VISA. Reservations required. Full bar service. Jackets required for men. Private party facilities for 10 to 200 people. Free parking.

K/Rating 17/20 • Food 6/7 • Service 5.5/6 • Decor 3/4 • Value 2.5/3

Lincolnwood
T. J. PEPPERCORN'S
Duck Specialties/American

$$

Duckling dinners are the heart of the menu in this unique Hyatt Hotel restaurant. You will find the bird in conventional surrounding of bigarade sauce done up in French fashion. Green peppercorn sauce is mildly tangy in a light cream base. Or order the duck in a honey glaze with slivers of almond. If you are really into duck sans everything, order a naked bird with an extra crispy skin. But my way to Nirvana is duckling lingonberry. The berries are usually found on Swedish pancakes; I am glad they made their way to duck sauce. The semi-sweet tartness works beautifully with the rich poultry flavor. Each of the duck dinners comes with a mixture of wild and long grain rice pilaff plus an apple garnish. Should duck not be your bird, check out chicken à la daisy, a boneless breast with crab meat, almonds and a béarnaise glaze. Steak, fish, shrimp and rack of lamb round out the menu. All dinners include a bounty

of salads. The salad bar is loaded with everything from baby shrimp to guacamole, to shreds of icy lettuce, to coleslaw and cottage cheese, although I must report the chopped liver needs more schmaltz. After a pass or two through the salad bar, some hot bread, a sherbet palate refresher and your main course, you can waddle over to the dessert bar. Help yourself to cakes, hot fudge sundaes, frozen custard, even chocolate mousse or maybe some hot cobbler if you have the room.

T. J. PEPPERCORN'S, 4500 West Touhy Street (in the Lincolnwood Hyatt House), Lincolnwood. Telephone: 583-3200. Hours: Lunch: 11:30 am-3 pm, daily; Dinner: 6 pm-11 pm, Monday-Friday; until 11:30 pm, Saturday; 5 pm-10 pm, Sunday; Brunch: 11:30 am-3:30 pm, Sunday. Cards: AE, CB, DC, MC, VISA. Reservations requested. Full bar service. Casual dress acceptable. Private party facilities. Free parking.

K/Rating 17/20 • Food 6/7 • Service 5/6 • Decor 3/4 • Value 3/3

★★★★★ FIVE-STAR DUCKLING ★★★★

$12.75
Duckling Rubbed With Fresh Sage. Anise. Rosemary And Crushed Spices.
Seared On Our Whirling Rotisserie Spits Till Golden Brown And Crisply Tender.

We Offer You A Choice Of:

MADAGASCAR GREEN PEPPERCORN a la CREME

BIGARADE STYLE
(Orange Sauce)

LINGONBERRY FASHION
(The Swedish Cranberry)

HONEY-ALMOND

MONTMORENCY
(Bing Cherries)

Duckling Is Served With A Timbale Of Mixed Rice Pilaf
And A Poached Apple Filled Appropriately

T.J.'S SPECIALTIES

PEPPERCORN'S DUET
T J 's Not-So-Traditional Pairing Of
Broiled N Y Sirloin Steak And Giant
Gulf Shrimp
$14.50

VEAL A LA MAISON
Medallions Of Veal
Served With Succulent Poached Oysters
And A Creamy Seafood Sauce
$13.75

RACK OF LAMB DIJON
Basted With Dijon Mustard And Baked
With Fresh Bread Crumbs
$16.75

•••CHICKEN A LA DAISY•••
Boneless Breast Of Chicken With Crabmeat.
Almonds. Mushrooms. Topped With Sauce Bearnaise
$9.75

PRIME RIB OF BEEF
Au Jus. A Beefeater's Cut
$12.50

T.J.'S CATCH

SCALLOPS PROVENCALE
Sauteed With Green Onions. Tomatoes.
Garlic And Mushrooms. Nestled On
Rice Pilaf
$9.75

SNAPPER MEUNIER
With Aromatic Herb Butter And Lemon Slivers
$10.95

SAUTEED BROOK TROUT
Pecan Butter
$9.75

BAKED STUFFED SHRIMP LINCOLNWOOD
(An Incredible Gastronomical Experience
That Only Our Chef Knows The Recipe)
$12.95

Evanston
UPSTAIRS DOWNSTAIRS
British Commonwealth

$$

Actually, Upstairs Downstairs is all on one floor on one side of the Inner Court at the Main Shopping Plaza. The name comes from the popular BBC television series that ran in this country a few years ago and is a reminder that this restaurant specializes in foods from the United Kingdom and its Commonwealth. Thus, you will find a gamut from beef Wellington to Kashmiri chicken to Killarney steak and mushroom pie. The Cornish pastie dinner is a particular favorite of mine as is the Ceylon curry, a complex Indian dish, rich in flavor. Although this is a relatively inexpensive restaurant, things are done with the sort of panache you might associate with much richer digs.

UPSTAIRS DOWNSTAIRS, 845 Chicago Avenue (inside the Main Shopping Plaza), Evanston. Telephone: 328-4100. Hours: Lunch: 11:30 am-2 pm, Monday-Friday; noon-2 pm, Saturday; Dinner: 5:30 pm-9:30 pm, Monday-Thursday; until 10:30 pm, Saturday; 5 pm-9 pm, Sunday. Cards: AE, CB, DC, MC, VISA. Reservations recommended. Full bar service. Casual, neat dress acceptable. Private party facilities for 15 to 50 people.

K/Rating 19/20 • Food 6/7 • Service 6/6 • Decor 4/4 • Value 3/3

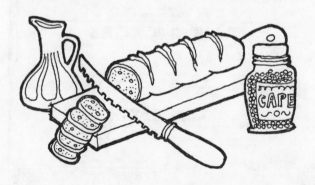

entrees

Kipling's Imperial Steak tenderloin filet of beef, grilled and served
with a unique sauce, oven roasted potatoes and zucchini.   8.50

Ceylon Curry Ceylon Lamb Curry originated in the South of India,   6.50
savored in a mildly spiced cream sauce, served on saffron almond
rice, with chutney and crisp Pappadoms.

Cumberland Trout delicately spiced, served with almond butter   6.50
dressing on a bed of rice, with zucchini.

Killamey Steak and Mushroom Pie flaky pastry over tender   7.00
beef and fresh mushrooms, with oven roasted potatoes and onions,
and zucchini.

Kashmiri Chicken Tikka Boneless chicken marinated in exotic   6.00
spices, served with saffron almond rice, crisp pappadoms and chutney

Pengarron Cornish Pastie rich pastry crust stuffed with seasoned   6.25
minced beef and onions, served with scalloped potatoes
and zucchini.

Khyber Pass Kabab Sirloin cubes of beef, sweet pepper, onions and   6.00
tomatoes, grilled and served on fluffy saffron rice, with chutney.

Breast of Wellington boneless chicken breast simmered in white   7.25
wine, stuffed with mushroom paté and wrapped in a delicate
pastry crust

Quebec Sirloin served with fresh whole mushrooms,   8.95
oven basted potatoes and zucchini.

Commonwealth Convention a sampling of Kashmiri Chicken   8.00
Tikka, Kipling's Imperial Steak, Canadian bacon, with roasted onions,
grilled tomatoes and rice.

Lord Nelson's Respite a delectable fresh fish entree, specially   Market Price
selected on a daily basis. **Please** consult your server for this
evening's variety

Beef Wellington filet of beef wrapped in a delicate pastry, with a   7.50
mushroom and burgundy sauce

Vegetarian Pastie fluffy pastry crust stuffed with seasoned vegetables 5.25

Highland Park
YU LIN'S CHINESE DUMPLING HOUSE
Chinese (Mandarin/Cantonese)

$$

Yu Lin and her husband C. P. Hsieu are the delightful host and hostess in a restaurant which, before they came along, served Texas-barbecued ribs as a specialty. The ribs have been long gone, although the cowboy atmosphere remains in the wagon wheel chandeliers. Since the food is the thing however, you will be well rewarded with page after page of choices from their excellent menu. House namesakes, the steamed or fried dumplings stuffed with ground meat are always a good way to begin. Try some delicately flavored shrimp toast, egg rolls and perhaps wonton or rumaki before moving on to a main course. Moo shu in either beef or pork versions is seasoned ever so simply so as to allow the flavorful hoisin sauce and scallions to make their statements in concert with the meat. Chicken with cashews has always been one of my favorite courses. Smoked tea duck rewards diners with deep dusky flavor. Spicier selections also stud the menu. Among specialties is the ubiquitous Peking duck with its crisp skin and succulent meat. You won't find *omalebanbenhum* anywhere else. It is a Tibetan dish brought here by Mr. Hsieu from his homeland. These steamed ribs are wrapped in a lotus leaf for an unusual flavor. There is even a version of fondue cooking when you order the Tibetan chafing dish. Some specialties require at least a day's advance notice. But it is worth the advance planning on your part.

YU LIN'S CHINESE DUMPLING HOUSE, 1636 Old Deerfield Road, Highland Park. Telephone: 831-3155/831-3166. Hours: 4:30 pm-10 pm, Tuesday-Thursday and Sunday; until 11 pm, Friday; until midnight, Saturday. No cards. Reservations required on Saturday. Full bar service. Casual dress acceptable. Free parking.

K/Rating 18.5/20 • Food 7/7 • Service 6/6 • Decor 2.5/4 • Value 3/3

Dinner for 2 Persons............. $13⁴⁵
Kow Teh
Hot & Sour Soup
Diced Chicken with Bean Sauce
(Eight Wonders)
Sliced Beef with Vegetable
Steamed Rice, Tea and Cookies

Dinner for 3 Persons............. $24⁵⁰
Kow Teh
Hot & Sour Soup
Shrimp with Crispy Rice
Shredded Beef with Green Pepper
Chicken with Cashew Nuts
Fried Rice
Tea and Cookies

Dinner for 4 Persons............. $29⁵⁰
Kow Teh
Hot & Sour Soup
Shrimp Saute
Chicken with Bamboo Shoots and
    Black Mushrooms
Crisy Duck (½)
Shredded Beef with White Onion
Fried Rice, Tea and Cookies

Dinner for 5 Persons............. $36⁵⁰
Kow Teh
Hot & Sour Soup
Moo Shu Pork
Sliced Chicken with Sizzling Rice
Pea Pods Steak
Sweet & Sour Chunk Fish
Shrimp with Bean Curd
Fried Rice
Tea and Cookies

Dinner for 6 Persons............. $45⁵⁰
Kow Teh
Hot & Sour Soup
Shrimp Saute
Shredded Beef with White Onion
Kung Pao Chicken
Sweet & Sour Whole Fish
Smoked Tea Duck
Black Mushroom and Bamboo Shoots
Fried Rice
Tea and Cookies

Dinner for 8 Persons............. $68⁰⁰
Chia Sui
Shrimp Toast
Kow Teh
Egg Roll
Fried Wong Tong
Hot & Sour Soup
Diced Chicken with Cashew Nuts
Double-fried Sliced Pork (Chungking Style)
Shrimp with Green Peas
Honkong Steak
Smoked Tea Duck
Bean Curd with Straw Mushrooms
Fried Rice
Tea and Cookies

221

Suburbs: Northwest

Arlington Heights, Des Plaines, Lake Zurich, Long Grove, Mundelein, Palatine, Wheeling

Mundelein
GALE STREET INN
American $$

You cannot search for the perfect sauce, the lightest soufflé at every meal. There is good basic American food as well and you will find it at the Gale Street Inn. Dinner can run as little as $4.95 for fried chicken or up to about $10 for lobster tails or a combo steak and seafood platter. Frankly I have not had a good seafood experience at the Inn, but other foods have been topnotch. Prime rib of beef is perfect, well marbled and tender. Butt steaks, in small or large portions, are not only excellent values, but taste tempting meal entrées. Ask for beef medium rare and it will be well charred on the outside, juicy, flavorful and pink on the inside. Other recommended entrées include baked veal Parmesan and a whole slab of barbecued baby back ribs slathered in sauce. Nearly a dozen sandwiches are served. Appetizers in generous portions include buttery garlic bread, tangy pizza bread, fried mushrooms and fried onions plus baked onion soup, corn on the cob (when in season) and shrimp cocktail. All dinners include an excellent salad bar. Service is friendly; the restaurant offers pleasant views of Diamond Lake plus some outside terrace dining by the water in warm weather.

Note: The original Gale Street Inn is at 4919 Milwaukee Avenue, Chicago, (725-1300). It has the same menu, no salad bar.

GALE STREET INN, 906 Diamond Lake Road, Mundelein. Telephone: 556-1090. Hours: 11 am-midnight, Tuesday-Sunday. Cards: MC, VISA. Reservations taken only for groups. Full bar service; lounge with dancing and entertainment. Casual dress acceptable. Private party facilities for up to 225 people. Free parking.

K/Rating 16.5/20 • Food 4.5/7 • Service 6/6 • Decor 3/4 • Value 3/3

Palatine
THE GREENHOUSE
Frenchified American

$$

The Greenhouse is a lovely restaurant with a somewhat confused approach to its food. The menu offers a wide variety of foods from egg rolls to baby back ribs to tournedos Beaugency. If the restaurant seems somewhat out of harmony on its menu, there is no question that diners enjoy the beautiful nursery-like surroundings. Leafy plants, wooden walkways and pebble borders set the ambiance for tables covered with white linen cloths. For the not-too-critical diner there are some pleasant encounters. Beachcomber's Skillet ($10.95) combines shrimp, crab meat, bay scallops, and cut-up sole, glazed in the skillet with pineapple and bananas for tropical flair. Roast Long Island duckling ($9.25) is served with an almost honey-like apricot glaze. Poached turbot will not satisfy those accustomed to the finest North Sea fish. This is the less firm Icelandic or Japanese turbot. The Greenhouse is much more successful with an array of red meats including a beautiful rack of

---

ROAST LONG ISLAND DUCKLING
plump duckling roasted in its own natural juices glazed with chefs special apricot sauce and served with wild rice **9.25**

MEDALLIONS OF VEAL OSCAR
young tender veal sauteed in butter, garnished with crabmeat and asparagus spears glazed with a light cheese sauce **11.95**

TOURNEDOS BEAUGENCY
served with artichoke bottom filled with bearnaise sauce and parmesan tomato **11.95**

SHRIMP AND RIBS
barbecued back ribs and shrimp **8.95**

lamb ($14.95), and an acceptable, if not lofty, veal Oscar ($11.95). Dinners include a house salad and potatoes. The Greenhouse will not impress anyone seeking a sophisticated dining experience. But realistically, it is not that kind of a place, menu descriptions to the contrary. Rather, it is an extremely pleasant suburban restaurant where you can get casual, friendly service and a more than 50/50 chance at a good, although not great, dinner.

THE GREENHOUSE, 1200 North Northwest Highway, Palatine. Telephone: 991-2110. Hours: Lunch: 11:30 am-3:30 pm, Monday-Friday; until 3 pm, Saturday; Dinner: 5 pm-11 pm, Monday-Thursday; until midnight, Friday-Saturday; 4 pm-10 pm, Sunday; Brunch: 10:30 am-2:30 pm, Sunday. Cards: AE, MC, VISA. Reservations required. Full bar service; entertainment Tuesday-Saturday evenings. Jackets required for men; no jeans on anyone. Private party facilities for up to 105 people. Free parking lot.

K/Rating 15.5/20 • Food 4.5/7 • Service 5/6 • Decor 4/4 • Value 2/3

Beachcomber's skillet
a glorious assortment of jumbo shrimp, alaskan king crabmeat, bay scallops and sole, gently sautéed in golden butter, served with spanish rice, glazed banana and pineapple in skillet 10.95

Red Snapper
topped with chef's special butter sauce and glazed 9.95

crepes ala Rheine
chunks of lobster and crabmeat sauteed with mushrooms and served in rich thermidor sauce 9.95

poached turbot florentine
the finest imported turbot delicately poached, placed on a bed of spinach, then baked in a creamy sauce laced with white wine 8.95

Crêperies dot Chicago, but La Poêle d'Or is the only one I know of in the suburbs worth its flour, eggs and butter. The Russians call them blintzes, to the Hungarians they are palacsintak, even the Chinese serve Peking duck or moo shu pork in wispy thin pancakes. But the French have elevated crêpe-making almost into an art. At La Poêle d'Or portions are so large you will be hard pressed to clean your plate, whether you choose from the crêpe or the omelette side of the menu. The top of the line Cardinale crêpe ($5.95) offers a luscious creamy blend of scallops, shrimp, and crab meat in a delicate lobster sauce which binds the textures and flavors together in the wrap. The Royale ($4.65) presents another seafood alternative, stuffed with turbot, mushrooms, melted Gruyère and topped with a mornay sauce. For beef eaters, choose the Ambassadeur ($3.85) made from ground beef, tomatoes, rice, green peppers and

OMELETTES

CAMPAGNARDE — 3.65
Tomatoes, artichoke, spinach, mushrooms, garlic.

LYONNAISE — 3.85
Chicken, asparagus, corn, cream sauce, herbs, wine.

FORESTIERE — 3.95
Mushrooms, potatoes, gruyere cheese, garlic butter.

MERVEILLE — 5.45
Crabmeat, lobster sauce, sherry.

CHASSEUR — 3.95
Chicken, liver, mushrooms, brandy, herbs.

BONNE FEMME — 3.95
Bacon, cheese, potatoes.

ANDALOUSE — 3.95
Tomatoes, green peppers, sausage, garlic.

mushrooms with a touch of garlic. Matching the seven crêpe selections are seven different omelettes, most less than $4, although one with crab meat, lobster and sherry is a bit more, at $5.45. Other omelettes include the Forestière with mushrooms, potatoes, Gruyère cheese and garlic butter or the Lyonnaise made with chicken, asparagus and corn in a cream sauce. Should you like an hors d'oeuvre before dinner choose the chicken liver tart ($2.50) accented with a cream sauce and Madeira. After-dinner treats include the house cheesecake ($1.25) with its hint of Grand Marnier blended into the whipped and frozen cheese.

LA POÊLE D'OR, 1121 South Arlington Heights Road, Arlington Heights. Telephone: 593-9148. Hours: Lunch: 11:30 am-2 pm, Tuesday-Friday; Dinner: 5 pm-9 pm, Tuesday-Thursday; until 10 pm, Friday-Saturday; 4 pm-9 pm, Sunday. Cards: AE. No reservations. Full bar service. Casual dress acceptable. Free parking.

K/Rating 17/20 • Food 6/6 • Service 5/6 • Decor 3/4 • Value 3/3

CREPES

CARDINALE   5.95
Scallops, shrimps, crabmeat, lobster cream sauce.

FLORENTINE   3.45
Creamed spinach, american cheese, diced chicken.

AMBASSADEUR   3.85
Ground beef, tomatoes, rice, green peppers, mushrooms, garlic.

PRINCESSE   3.95
Chicken, liver, mushrooms, ham, cream sauce, madeira.

ROYALE   4.65
Turbot, mushrooms, sauce mornay, gruyere.

DUCHESSE   3.95
Chicken, asparagus, gruyere cheese, mushrooms, cream sauce.

BASQUAISE   4.85
Shrimps, tomatoes, green peppers, rice, garlic.

LE FRANÇAIS
French

$$$

Le Français is not to be described; it is to be experienced. This one restaurant has put the small town of Wheeling on the gourmet map of America. Chef Jean Banchet is an ardent student of Brillat-Savarin, Auguste Escoffier and Paul Bocuse. As a result, dazzling carts and trays of foods, from pâtés to pastries, are paraded here before the eyes of gaping diners who ordinarily would not see such artistry outside of gourmet society dinners. Among chef Banchet's proudest accomplishments are his deft preparations of pâtés and terrines, his fish en croûte à la Paul Bocuse, and his mastery of sauces. The fish à la Bocuse may be salmon, turbot or sea bass depending on what is available. The fish is topped with a lobster mousse, baked in a pastry which has been sculpted down to the last gill and fin to resemble the fish it encloses. This creation is served with two, and sometimes three, sauces. You won't find this dish on the printed menu, but it probably will be among the 10 or 12 specialty items offered each night. If fine food is holy, Le Français is its temple and Jean Banchet the high priest.

LE FRANÇAIS, 269 South Milwaukee Avenue, Wheeling. Telephone: 541-7470. Hours: 5:30 pm-10 pm, Tuesday-Sunday. Cards: AE, MC, VISA. Reservations required. Full bar service; extensive wine list. Coats and ties required for men; no jeans. Valet parking.

K/Rating 20/20 • Food 7/7 • Service 6/6 • Decor 4/4 • Value 3/3

Grenadin de Veau aux Chanterelles
Veal Steak Sauté with Chanterelles Mushrooms, Cream Sauce

Aiguillette de Caneton Farcie Rouennaise
Stuffed Breast of Duck with Red Wine Sauce and Goose Liver

Pigeonneau Rôti aux Gousses d'Ail
Roast Baby Squab with Garlic Cloves

Blanc de Faisan Fernand Point
Stuffed Breast of Phaesant Roast with Morels, Cream Sauce

Côte de Veau à la Crème de Ciboulette
Veal Chop Sauté with Chives Cream Sauce

Ris de Veau Poêlé à l'Estragon
Sweet Bread Sauté with Taragon Sauce

Carré d'Agneau Persillé à la Fleur de Thym
Roast Rack of Lamb with Herbs

Tournedos Poêlé à la Graine de Moutarde
Tournedos Sauté with Mustard Sauce

Filet de Bœuf Poêlé au Poivre Frais de Madagascar
Fillet Sauté with Green Pepper Corn Sauce

Pièce de Bœuf à la Moelle au Brouilly
Sirloin Steak Sauté with Marrow and Bordelaise Sauce

Viandes Grillées à Votre Goût
Broiled Steak-Chops to Your Taste

Mille-Feuilles de Saumon Cressonnière
Fresh Salmon Sauté on Layer of Puff dough with Watercress Sauce

Navarin de Homard aux Petits Légumes
Lobster Sauté with Vegetables and Nantua Sauce

Poisson du Lac Beurre Blanc
Fresh White Fish Sauté, with Julienne Vegetables Beurre Blanc

Délice de Sole Tout Paris
Stuffed Fillets of Sole with Lobster Mousse and Two Sauces

Loup de Mer d'après le Marché
Strip Bass when available on the Market

Palatine
LE TITI DE PARIS
French

$$$

In the tradition of some of the finest restaurants in France (or Chicago) Le Titi is now owned by its chef, Pierre Pollin and his wife. The restaurant still retains the freshness which characterized it when it first opened several years ago. Chef Pierre creates some exquisite preparations in the tradition of the nouvelle cuisine. He does wonders with a fresh seafood pâté as an appetizer. Studded with fresh pike, salmon and seabass, and bound in a silky salmon mousse, the fish is balanced with a beurre blanc sauce. In addition to nightly specials, the printed menu regularly offers such treats as pepper steak flamed in cognac and studded with ground black peppercorns. Medallions of veal with apple slices and Calvados is a creamier version of veal Normande than I have encountered elsewhere. Roast duckling in orange sauce is another careful preparation; a garnish of peach halves adds color and sweetness. This menu is so good that it is hard to pick favorites. The only improvement needed is in atmosphere. The restaurant is fairly small and would do well to establish smoking and non-smoking sections. But then, what restaurant wouldn't be better that way?

LE TITI DE PARIS, 2275 Rand Road, Palatine. Telephone: 359-4434. Hours: Lunch: 11:30 am-2:30 pm, Tuesday-Friday; Dinner: from 5:30 pm, Tuesday-Saturday; from 4 pm, Sunday. Cards: AE, MC, VISA. Reservations recommended. Full bar service. Jackets required for men. Free parking.

K/Rating 16/20 • Food 6/7 • Service 5/6 • Decor 2.5/4 • Value 2.5/3

Spécialités Nouvelle Cuisine

Hors D'Oeuvres

Terrine de Poisson Beurre Blanc 3⁷⁵

Mousse de Crevette Sauce Verte 3⁵⁰

Entrées

Filet de Sole Ile de France 10²⁵
Filet of dover sole in white wine sause with julienne of vegetables

Ballotine de Canard aux Noix 10²⁵
Duck with Port wine and walnut sauce

Coquilles St. Jacques "Lucas Carton"
Scallops in white wine and shallots sauce 9⁷⁵

Low Calorie

Filet de Brochet au Citron Vert
Pike with lime sauce 9⁷⁵

Desserts

Sorbets aux Fruits Frais 1⁵⁰

Lake Zurich
A LITTLE TOUCH OF ITALY
Diet Italian

$$

Think about veal Parmigiana and chicken cacciatore, linguine with white clam sauce or lasagna layered with noodles, meat and cheese. Just the thought of that kind of food can put the avoirdupois on some people. But what if there were an Italian restaurant where the calories and carbohydrates were monitored for you, where the food would fill you up but not out. That is the whole idea behind A Little Touch of Italy. There are two menus offered. The regular menu ranges from pizza to Italian-style sandwiches to pasta and other entrées. For instance, lasagna is layered with a thick meat sauce, melted cheeses and of course, broad lasagna noodles. Linguine with clam sauce is delicately seasoned; the sauce is your choice of white or red. I prefer the white and its fresh parsley emphasis which marries so nicely with the subtle flavor of the minced clams. The veal Parmigiana does not fare as well. The meat is a little too burger-like for my taste, although the sauce and cheese topping are acceptable enough. And what do you know! The veal Parmigiana also appears on the separate diet menu, as does the lasagna and the linguine with clam sauce. The diet preparations compare favorably with the regular preparations. I doubt that most people would be able to discern the different styles of preparation in a blind tasting. And the diet items are not only full of flavor, but genuinely light on calories. For instance, chicken cacciatore is only 370 calories and that includes four ounces of chicken, 2/3 cup of pasta plus sauce and seasonings. The restaurant also offers a regular schedule of diet banquets, dubbed Saturnalia Feasts that run an ethnic gamut not limited to Italian.

A LITTLE TOUCH OF ITALY, Route 12 at North Old Rand Road, Lake Zurich. Telephone: 438-2868. Hours: 4 pm-11 pm, daily. Cards: AE, MC, VISA. Reservations recommended. Full bar service. Casual dress acceptable. Private party facilities for luncheons of 20 to 60 people. Diet Saturnalia Feasts held regularly. Free parking.

K/Rating 17/20 • Food 5.5/7 • Service 6/6 • Decor 2.5/4 • Value 3/3

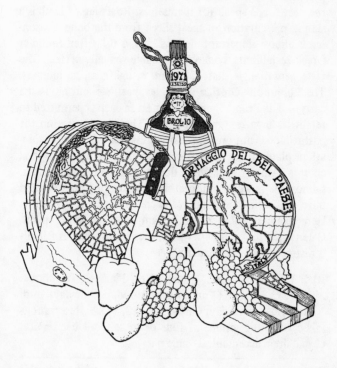

Des Plaines
RIKKI'S
Greek

$$

Even though the menu at Rikki's appears no different from countless other Greek restaurants I know well, there is no mistake that the food is perceptibly different. For one thing it is more subtle. Spices are used with discretion. Cinnamon is not all-consuming of other flavors in the pastitsio; oregano does not dominate in the seasoning of meats. There is a certain refinement, almost a hesitation, as if someone in the kitchen had the good sense to realize that the best foods speak for themselves. Roast leg of lamb is a simple presentation of meat sliced from the bone. Seasoning is almost imperceptible. Sea bass, a fish often found at Greek restaurants, comes to the table virtually perfect. The taste sensation is that of freshness, lightness, naturalness. The ubiquitous Grecian casseroles, pastitsio and moussaka carry out the same theme. The meat in each is permitted to retain its own texture and flavor. The cream sauce on the pastitsio does not drown the other ingredients. The combination plate offers the diner a good sampling of several choices. Among appetizers, do not miss the taramasalata; salmon roe is worked into a blend of mashed potatoes and olive oil until it all achieves a cream cheese-like texture. Here again is another good example of understatement. Often salty to a fault elsewhere, the taramasalata at Rikki's is distinctively well balanced.

RIKKI'S, 8660 Golf Road, Des Plaines. Telephone. 296-6777. Hours: 11 am-11 pm, Monday-Thursday; until 1 am, Friday-Saturday. Cards: AE, MC, VISA. Reservations taken only for groups of four or more. Full bar service. Casual dress acceptable. Ample parking.

K/Rating 17/20 • Food 7/7 • Service 5/6 • Decor 2/4 • Value 3/3

Grecian Specialties

Dinners Include Soup and Greek Salad

	Ala Carte	Dinners
GYROS PLATE	4.25	6.00
A generous portion of Rotisserie Broiled Meat with Onions and Tomato or Rice Pilaf		
SOUVLAKI (Shish Kabob) *Pork Tenderloin with Rice, Peas and Potatoes*	5.95	7.75
BRAISED LAMB *with any two — Rice Pilaf, Potatoes, String Beans, Peas or Spaghetti*	4.50	6.25
ROAST LEG OF LAMB *with any two — Rice Pilaf, Potatoes, String Beans, Peas or Spaghetti* .	5.00	6.75
ROAST LOIN OF BABY LAMB	5.00	6.75
With any two — Rice Pilaf, Potatoes, String Beans, Peas or Spaghetti		
PASTITSIO	4.25	6.00
The pasta lovers delight! Baked Macaroni and Ground Meat topped with a Delicious Cream Sauce and Vegetable		
MOUSSAKA *Thinly Sliced Eggplant, Ground Beef, Parmesan Cheese, White Wine, topped with a Cream Sauce and Vegetable. Baked to perfection*	4.25	6.00
DOLMADES *Ground Braised Beef & Lamb mixed with Rice, wrapped in Grapevine Leaves, with a special Hot Lemon and Egg Sauce and Potato*	4.25	6.00
SPANAKOTIROPITA *Spinach with Feta Cheese topped with Filo and Potato*	3.25	5.00
COMBINATION PLATE *Can't make up your mind? Try this — "You'll like it"*		
A combination of Gyros, Dolmades, Moussaka, Pastitsio & Athenian Potatoes	5.95	7.75
ATHENIAN STYLE ½ CHICKEN *with Rice and Potatoes*	4.75	6.50
ATHENIAN STYLE ¼ CHICKEN *with Rice and Potatoes*	3.75	5.50

Specialties of the Day

DINNERS INCLUDE SOUP AND SALAD

		Ala Carte	Dinners
Monday:	CHICKEN KAPAMA *with Macaroni*	4.50	6.25
Tuesday:	BAKED LAMB *with Rosa Marina (Giovetsi)* — BRAISED LAMB *with Eggplant*	4.50	6.25
Wednesday	BAKED LAMB *with Spaghetti (Giovetsi)* — BOILED LAMB *with Vegetable* ...	4.50	6.25
Thursday:	BAKED LAMB *with Noodles (Giovetsi)*	4.50	6.25
	LAMB *with Artichokes (Avgolemono)*	5.25	6.75
Friday:	BAKED LAMB *with Rosa Marina (Giovetsi)* — BRAISED LAMB *with Squash* .	4.50	6.25
Saturday:	BAKED LAMB *with Spaghetti (Giovetsi)* — BRAISED LAMB *with Okra*	4.50	6.25
Sunday:	BAKED LAMB *with Noodles (Giovetsi)* — BRAISED LAMB *with Eggplant* ...	4.50	6.25
	LAMB *and Artichokes Avgolemono (Egg Lemon Sauce)*	5.25	6.75
	BARBECUED BABY LAMB *with Greek Style Potatoes*	5.25	6.75

Des Plaines
SQUEAKIE'S
American/Seafood $$

Too often, so-called theme restaurants are long on decoration and atmosphere, but short on good food. Squeakie's is an exception: a restaurant where the food is good enough to warrant attention without all the packaging. Essentially, Squeakie's is the re-creation of a typical American commercial street from five or six decades ago. There is a drug store, a bakery, an antique shop, and a barber shop setting. Each of these individual settings serves as a dining room for the presentation of some genuinely attractive seafood and meat dishes. Squeakie's is primarily a seafood restaurant. It is odd to be dining on salmon, brook trout or even fried chicken in what otherwise looks like an old-time barber shop. The re-creations are tastefully done, as is the food. Dinners come with a bountiful salad platter. Instead of going to the salad bar, your waitress brings it to you. Onto a platter of greens she will add copious amounts of whatever you wish from a selection that includes croûtons, alfalfa sprouts, shrimp and bean sprouts. Even blue cheese is yours for the asking, topped off with any of several dressings including the slightly sweet house preparation. Among entrées, I have enjoyed the beer-battered fillet of sole; it combines the clean taste of the white fish with the creamy rich texture of a puffy batter coating. Combination plates are made to order for hearty appetites. You can have a selection of fried fish, clams and shrimp or a platter of broiled seafood that includes an ample assortment of shell- and soft fish. I have not had as good a success with the cioppino. Squeakie's starts with a canned tomato stock, which, though modified by seasonings, I have found a little too raw to marry well with other ingredients in the fish stew. One more note: Squeakie's has a wine sampler available at dinner. You may pick any three wines from their list to sample before you order, thus giving you an idea what your wine will be like.

SQUEAKIE'S, 9225 Golf Road, Des Plaines. Telephone: 298-3510. Hours: Lunch: 11:30 am-3 pm, Monday-Friday; Dinner: 5 pm-11 pm, Sunday-Thursday; until midnight, Friday-Saturday. Cards: AE, MC, VISA. Reservations recommended. Casual dress acceptable. Private party facilities available. Free parking.

K/Rating 17/20 • Food 5/7 • Service 6/6 • Decor 4/4 • Value 2/3

Long Grove
VILLAGE TAVERN
American $$

Depending upon the night you visit, you could run into an auction of antiques, a Dixieland jazz band, a sing-a-long or just a casual party at the Village Tavern. It is that kind of a place. When was the last time a waitress stopped taking your order so she could join in singing "Happy Birthday" to a group of revelers nearby? And chances are, rather than becoming annoyed, you would pitch in and sing, too. The atmosphere is casual and boisterous. You cannot go home hungry. Try the 22-ounce porterhouse steak ($9.75) or a half-pound chopped beefsteak with sautéed onions ($5.50). Chicken is skillet-fried, just like they do in the country ($5.50). Or try some of the barbecued beef ribs ($5.25) for some "get right down to it and dig in" eating. A good lineup of salads and sandwiches helps to round out the menu and although some foods could use a bit more zippy seasonings, the Village Tavern still has enough fun and zesty happenings to make it the fun place it has been for years.

VILLAGE TAVERN, Old McHenry Road, Long Grove. Telephone: 634-3117. Hours: 11:30 am-midnight, Tuesday-Saturday; from 1 pm, Sunday. Cards: MC, VISA. Reservations taken, except Friday and Sunday nights. Full bar service. Private party facilities for up to 125 people.

K/Rating 16.5/20 • Food 5/7 • Service 5/6 • Decor 3.5/4 • Value 3/3

Suburbs: West

**Cicero, Forest Park, Geneva,
Glendale Heights, Naperville,
Oak Brook**

Oak Brook
FOND DE LA TOUR
French

$$$

For businesspeople or others in the Oak Brook area who want to entertain in a fine French atmosphere, Fond de la Tour is the only choice. It also happens to be a good restaurant under any circumstances. There are seats for 72 people in the intimate dining room. Plans call for addition of at least three private dining rooms to accommodate another dozen people each. Best selections from the à la carte menu include extraordinary rack of lamb for two, superb steak Madagascar in a green peppercorn sauce and excellent roast duck in an orange and flamed brandy sauce. Many dishes are beautifully prepared tableside. Wines are reasonably priced although the list does not include vintage designation.

FOND DE LA TOUR, 40 North Tower Road, Oak Brook. Telephone: 620-1500. Hours: Lunch: 11:30 am-2:30 pm, Tuesday-Friday. Dinner: 6 pm-midnight, Tuesday-Saturday; 4 pm-10 pm, Sunday. Cards: AE, DC, MC, VISA. Reservations required. Full bar service. Valet parking.

K/Rating 19/20 • Food 6/7 • Service 6/6 • Decor 4/4 • Value 3/3

Forest Park
GIANNOTTI'S
Italian

$$

Vic Giannotti no longer owns his family restaurant, but the legacy of some of the finest Italian food around lives on. Now owned by businessman-turned-restaurateur, Santo Cinquegrani, the place still is aglow with its somewhat garish atmosphere, bustling waitresses and probably some of the happiest diners this side of an oxygen tent. The same menu prevails as in times past and even though Vic's mother Mary Giannotti does not scurry from table to table urging you to eat more, you will still put away all you can. Seven-course dinners are standards of the place, as is the family-style Fiesta Dinner. However, we prefer ordering à la carte to savor such delicacies as mussels in their black shells, merluzzi salad (cold marinated fish), giant stuffed mushrooms and baked clams. And that's just for openers. Veal piccante is lusciously delicious, sautéed in an egg wash, served in a butter-lemon sauce. Don't overlook the pastas; manicotti and ravioli are particularly special. Beef eaters will enjoy braciola, a rolled steak with stuffing. For dessert the Italian cheesecake is the best in town.

GIANNOTTI'S, 7711 West Roosevelt Road, Forest Park. Telephone: 366-4090. Hours: 4 pm-12:30 pm, Tuesday-Saturday; 2 pm-10:30 pm, Sunday. Cards: AE, CB, DC, MC. Reservations suggested. Full bar service. Private party facilities for up to 90 people. Free parking.

K/Rating 18/20 • Food 7/7 • Service 5/6 • Decor 3/4 • Value 3/3

PRIME NEW YORK CUT SIRLOIN STEAK 11.75
FILET MIGNON 11.75
BUTT STEAK 9.75
LADIES CUT PRIME SIRLOIN STEAK 10.75
PEPPER STEAK 9.50
DOUBLE THICK LAMB CHOPS or Thin (3) 9.50
CENTER CUT PORK CHOPS 8.75
CHOPPED SIRLOIN 6.50
BRAGIOLE A LA NAPOLITANA Rolled Butt Steak with our Special Seasoning 8.00
PRIME STEAK A LA PIZZAIOLO 12.75
Prime New York Cut Sirloin Saute in Olive Oil, Fresh Tomatoes and Oregano

Not Responsibile For Well Done Steak

VEAL PICCANTE 8.50
Sliced Veal sauted in Butter and Lemon with a Special Topping
VEAL SCALOPPINE 8.50
Sliced Veal Steak, sauted in Tomato Sauce, White Wine and fresh Mushrooms
VEAL PARMIGIANA 8.50
VEAL FRANCAISE 8.50
Patties of Veal dipped in Flour and Egg, fried in Butter, Lemon Rings
BREADED VEAL CUTLET 8.50
VEAL SCALOPPINE MARSALA Sliced Veal Steak, sauted in Butter, Marsala Wine 8.50
VEAL SALTIMBOCCA A LA PARMIGIANA 8.50
Sliced Veal Cutlets, stuffed with Prosciutto and covered with Cheese and Baked
VEAL SCALOPPINE A LA GIANNOTTI 8.50
Sliced Veal, sauted in Butter, White Wine, Fresh Mushrooms, Onions, and Fresh Green Peppers

BONELESS CHICKEN A LA PARMIGIANA 8.00
BONELESS CHICKEN FRANCAISE 8.00
CHICKEN A LA CACCIATORE 8.00
Chicken, sauted in Olive Oil, White Wine, Fresh Tomatoes, Mushrooms
CHICKEN VESUVIO Chicken, sauted in Olive Oil, Garlic, Oregano, White Wine 8.00
CHICKEN A LA FLORENTINA Chicken, dipped in Egg Batter, fried in Olive Oil 8.00
PLATTER OF CHICKEN LIVERS, Mushroom Sauce 7.25
CHICKEN OREGANATO Chicken, sauted in Butter, Lemon, Oregano 8.00

COMBINATION LOBSTER AND FILET 13.50
BROILED AFRICAN LOBSTER with Melted Butter 14.75
BROILED RED SNAPPER, Almondine Sauce 8.50
BROILED DOVER SOLE with Almondine Sauce 11.75
FRENCH FRIED SHRIMP 8.50
SHRIMP MARINARA SAUCE 8.50
ZUPPA DI PESCE A LA NAPOLITANA with Linguini 11.50
BAKED BACCALA — Cod Fish 7.50
CALAMARI (Baby Squid) With Linguini or Spaghetti 7.25
LOBSTER FRA DIAVOLO 14.75
Lobster tail, sauted in Tomato, White Wine, served over Linguini or Spaghetti

7 Course Dinners include: Soup — Our Own Special Salad with choice of your favorite Dressing
(our Olive Oil and Vinegar, French, Garlic or 1000 Island — Roquefort Dressing 50¢ extra)
Side Order of Mostaccioli or Ravioli — Assorted Cookies — Fruit — Coffee or Tea

Geneva
MILL RACE INN
American $$

Of the world's cuisines, perhaps the most neglected is American. Fortunately we have a remedy close at hand thanks to the Mill Race Inn. The Inn stands on a site along the Fox River where 125 years ago a blacksmith built his forge. All the smithy's walls are still standing; they now limn out one of the five dining rooms which seat a total of 225 diners. Outside, the Fox flows by; in good weather you can feed the ducks chunks of homemade bread. The Inn produces five-course table d'hôte dinners which include a fine prime rib of beef. Braised lamb shank and baked chicken remain favorite staples. The duckling with wild rice is a lesson in how this often-found entrée should be prepared. Begin dinner with a bowl of fresh homemade soup or perhaps jellied consommé. Among vegetables accompanying your main course, baked acorn squash recalls an older American way to dine. Desserts are all homemade. The Mill Race Inn has undergone some expansion and reconstruction in the past two years, including a new kitchen, but it is still the same country setting along the mill race which it has been for more than 46 years.

MILL RACE INN, 4 East State Street, Geneva. Telephone: 232-2030. Hours: Lunch: 11:30 am-3 pm, Tuesday-Saturday; Dinner: 5:30 pm-9 pm, Tuesday-Thursday; until 10 pm, Friday-Saturday; 11:30 am-9 pm, Sunday. Cards: AE, MC, VISA. Reservations taken only for groups of seven or more. Full bar service. Jackets required for men in the evening. Private party facilities for up to 100 people. Free parking.

K/Rating 20/20 • Food 7/7 • Service 6/6 • Decor 4/4 • Value 3/3

Dinner

Tomato Herb Rice Soup   Jellied Consomme
Apricot Nectar   Tomato Juice
Herring in Sour Cream + 1.25

Roast Prime Rib of Beef   9.75
Oven Baked Chicken   7.25
Braised Lamb Shank   7.95
Sautéed Fresh Rainbow Trout   8.25
Beef Tips in Mushroom Burgundy Sauce   8.25
Braised Pork Tenderloin   7.95
Roast Duck with Wild Rice Dressing   8.75
Brisket of Corned Beef   7.25

Potatoes au Gratin   Herb Rice
Buttered Broccoli   Baked Acorn Squash

Mixed Green Salad
with Mill Race or 1000 Island Dressing
Cottage Cheese and Fruit   Blue Cheese .75

Desserts

Deep Dish Apple or Apricot Pie
with Cinnamon Ice Cream + .75
Baked Custard with Butterscotch Sauce
Rubbarb Creme
Strawberry Meringue
Figs in Wine with Frozen Cream
Fresh Strawberries w/ Sour Cream + Brown Sugar
Queen Elizabeth Cake
Sherbets, Ice Creams and Sundaes

Naperville
NIELSON'S WILLOWAY MANOR
American

$$

Willoway Manor has a history that spans more than a century. Built in the mid-19th century, the mansion is a beautiful example of Greek revival architecture which was so popular in this country at that time. In recent years, the structure has housed a restaurant. While there are some touches of Continental cuisine in such dishes as chicken Kiev or chateaubriand, the emphasis is firmly on fish and steaks. Still there are some surprises such as houbis, the tender mushrooms so popular with Middle Europeans. Some of the entrées try to be a bit too ambitious: wall-eye pike with mozzarella is one example. But by staying with the basic steaks, excellent beef en brochette or brook trout, the Willoway Manor is more successful. You will also find two bars reminiscent of the Victorian era here. While food preparation may be more elaborate elsewhere, it is hard to find another restaurant with the special gracefulness found at Nielson's Willoway Manor.

NIELSON'S WILLOWAY MANOR, Aurora Avenue, Naperville. Telephone: 355-1028/355-1020. Hours: 11:30 am-10 pm, Tuesday-Friday; 5:30 pm-11 pm, Saturday; noon-9 pm, Sunday. Cards: AE, CB, DC, MC, VISA. Reservations recommended. Full bar service. Private party facilities. Ample parking.

K/Rating 17.5/20 • Food 5/7 • Service 6/6 • Decor 4/4 • Value 2.5/3

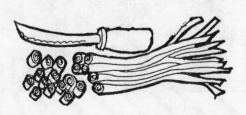

Pork Chops 7.75

Center cut, broiled, served with toast and applesauce.

Cutlet Oskar 9.25

Tender cutlet steak, served with Danish lobster tails and topped with Asparagus Hollandaise.

Filet Mignon 10.25

The most tender cuts of all, taken from prime beef tenderloin, broiled.

Strip Steak 10.95

New York cut of prime meat, the man's steak.

Butt Steak 8.95

New England cut, broiled, the lady's steak.

Beef En Brochette 8.25

Chunk of tenderloin broiled with tomatoes, mushroom, green pepper, served with rice.

Bøf and Hummer 15.95

A petit filet mignon and a single broiled lobster tail.

Ground Sirloin 6.25

Served with sauteed onion.

Chateaubriand Gastronome .... 12.95 each

The finest meat ever, prime tenderloin of beef, vegetable, Sauce Bordelaise and Sauce Bearnaise. For two or more.

The Manor House Chicken 6.25

Served with applesauce.

Chicken Kiev 8.25

Chicken breast stuffed with seasoned butter, breaded, cooked and served with rice.

Chicken Cordon Bleu 8.25

Chicken breast stuffed with ham and cheese served with rice.

Glendale Heights
PEKING MANDARIN
Chinese (Mandarin)

$$

Believe it or not, Mandarin cuisine has ceased to be exotic. That is certainly the case if you consider the literal meaning of the phrase "something that is foreign to us." What this all means is that American diners, at least those in and around Chicago, have broken out of the chop suey and chow mein syndrome; we now look for more than egg rolls and fried rice. Peking duck at $18 to $20 in some restaurants may be financially beyond the reach of many diners, but the taste for it most certainly exists. With all that said, I am rather sorry to see a restaurant as good as Peking Mandarin with a big flashy chop suey neon sign in its front window. At least the sign attracts attention and that is all to the good since it brings folks inside for some fair-to-better-than-middling-foods. Yes, chop suey, chow mein and egg foo yung are on the menu, but so is diced chicken with peanuts or crispy duck or shrimp in red sauce. Prices are

Moo Shu Beef with Mandarin Pancakes	$4.35
Peking Steak	$4.35
Beef with Pea Pods	$4.50
Beef with Black Mushroom and Bamboo Shoots	$4.75
Mongolian Beef	$4.50
Beef with Oyster Sauce	$4.25
Beef with Bar-B-Q Sauce	$3.95
Beef Mandarin with Assorted Vegetables	$4.75
Beef in Garlic Sauce (Hot)	$3.95
Beef with Peanuts (Hot)	$4.25
Steak Chinese Style	$5.95
Beef with Green Pepper and Tomato	$4.25
Beef Kow	$4.25
Chicken with Black Mushroom Bamboo Shoots	$4.50
Chicken with Pea Pods	$4.50
Chicken Mandarin with Assorted Vegetables	$4.75
Chicken with Sizzling Golden Rice	$4.75
Eight Delicious Diced Chicken with Bean Sauce	$3.95
Diced Chicken with Hot and Sour Sauce (Hot)	$4.25
La Tse Chi Din (Hot)	$3.95

generally moderate although Peking duck will set you back
$18. But two or three couples can split it as a course and
still get satisfying taste without spending next month's auto
payment. We love to ravage through appetizers at Chinese
restaurants and Peking Mandarin is no exception. But do
not ignore the 60 or more entrée selections. The aforemen-
tioned chicken with peanuts will add some real spice to
your dinner. Moo shu beef or pork offers delicious shreds
of meat, eggs and seasonings which you can tuck up into
paper-thin pancakes smeared with hoisin, a sauce that
works on Chinese foods the way jelly works on toast.

PEKING MANDARIN, 542 East North Avenue, Glendale
Heights. Telephone: 469-4393. Hours: 11:30 am-10 pm,
Monday-Thursday; until 11 pm, Friday; 4 pm-11 pm, Saturday; 11:30 am-9 pm, Sunday. Cards: MC, VISA. Reservations recommended. Full bar service. Private party facilities
for up to 50 people. Ample parking.

K/Rating 15/20 • Food 5.5/7 • Service 4/6 • Decor 2.5/4 • Value 3/3

Diced Chicken with Peanuts (Hot)	$4.25
Pineapple Chicken	$3.85
Chicken in Garlic Sauce (Hot)	$3.95
Chicken Almond Din	$3.95
Hung Shao Chicken	$3.85
Sweet and Sour Chicken	$3.85
Shrimp with Black Mushroom and Bamboo Shoots	$4.95
Shrimp with Pea Pods	$4.95
Shrimp with Tomato Ginger Sauce	$5.15
Shrimp Mandarin with Assorted Vegetables	$5.95
Shrimp with Sizzling Golden Rice	$5.25
Fancy Shrimp in Red Sauce	$6.25
Shrimp with Peanuts (Hot)	$5.25
Shrimp in Garlic Sauce (Hot)	$4.50
Steamed Fish	$5.95
Hunan Crispy Fish (Hot)	$5.95
Shrimp with Lobster Sauce	$4.50
Hung Shao Shrimp	$4.50
Sweet and Sour Whole Fish	$5.95
Sweet and Sour Shrimp	$4.25

Cicero
THE PELIKAN
Czechoslovakian

$

Although there is a stab at some Middle European decor, you are not likely to loose sight of the fact that The Pelikan is right in the heart of downtown Cicero. This is a basic meat-and-dumplings kind of a place with friendly service, patterned oilcloths covering the tables and a family-style approach to doing things. Although you will find the basic mid-American staples of steak, French fries, fried chicken and hamburger, there are several authentic Bohemian dishes. Svickova, a pickled beef, is similar to the more well-known German sauerbraten, but with a character uniquely its own. The beef is marinated for several days in a brine, then roasted and served in gravy with the mixed flavors of allspice, bay leaf and herbs. Dumplings are bread-like, soaking up the sweet gravy that pools in your platter. Roast duckling with dumplings and sweet red cabbage is a real pleaser. The skin is crisp over the tasty rich meat. A gravy boat brimming over with goodness is brought to your table so you may spoon on as much of the Bohemian nectar-like sauce as you want. The Pelikan reaches across the border into Hungary for beef goulash; it loses nothing in transit. Fresh soup of the day may be excellent liver dumpling or barley mushroom in creamy broth. Those mushrooms, by the way, are old-country houbis shipped to this country by the father of one of the restaurant's owners.

THE PELIKAN, 5639 West Cermak Road, Cicero. Telephone: 652-4105. Hours: 11 am-8 pm, Tuesday-Sunday. Cards: AE, MC, VISA. Reservations taken. Full bar service. Casual, neat dress acceptable. Parking on street.

K/Rating 18/20 • Food 6/7 • Service 6/6 • Decor 3/4 • Value 3/3

Welcome to Pelikan

Included with Dinner:

Soup of the Day or Juice and Dish of Fruit or Salad,
Our Homemade Bakery or Jello

	Regular	Small
T-BONE STEAK with Mushrooms and Onion Rings	5.95	
NEW YORK STRIP STEAK with Mushrooms, Onion Rings and French Fries	5.50	
TOP RIB EYE STEAK with Mushrooms and Onion Rings	5.25	
ROAST DUCK with Dumplings and Sweet-Sour Cabbage	3.75	
FRIED SPRING CHICKEN with Mashed Potatoes, Vegetable ...	3.40	
ROAST HALF SPRING CHICKEN with Mashed Potato, Vegetables	3.40	
BREADED PORK TENDERLOIN with Potatoes, Vegetables	3.60	3.20
ROAST LOIN OF PORK with Dumplings, Sauerkraut	3.50	3.10
PICKLED BEEF with Sour Cream Gravy (SVICKOVA), Dumplings	3.75	3.25
BOILED BEEF with TOMATO GRAVY or DILL GRAVY, Dumplings	3.50	3.10
ROAST SIRLOIN OF BEEF with Mashed Potatoes, Vegetables ..	3.50	3.10
HUNGARIAN BEEF GOULASH with Dumplings	3.50	3.10
THUERINGER SAUSAGE with Dumplings, Sauerkraut	3.30	2.90

Seafoods

	Regular	Small
STUFFED FLOUNDER, Potatoes and Vegetables	3.95	
FRENCH FRIED GULF SHRIMPS, with French Fried Potatoes ...	4.25	
FRENCH FRIED FILLET OF PERCH, Potatoes, Vegetables	3.60	3.20
FILLET OF HADDOCK, Potatoes, Vegetables	3.60	3.20
PAN FRIED TROUT, Boiled Potatoes, Vegetables	3.95	

Suburbs: South

Calumet City, Matteson

Calumet City
THE COTTAGE
Continental

$$$

Who says men make the best chefs? Not Carolyn Buster, and she proves it night after night at The Cottage. With Carolyn busy in the kitchen and her husband Jerry acting the part of genial maître d', this young couple has built their restaurant into one of the brightest lights on the Chicagoland dining scene. The Cottage offers a charming old-world country-inn atmosphere. Jerry and Carolyn are true antique buffs who have gathered hand-rubbed furnishings and authentic period antiques to surround their customers with charm. There is a chalkboard menu posted on one wall, and while items change from night to night, there are certain specialties in the $14.95 to $16.95 price range. They include steak Madagascar, a deliciously seasoned mild pepper steak in wine-based sauce. The Cottage's schnitzel is pork, not veal, my only quibble with what otherwise is an outstanding menu. Rack of lamb has become a popular favorite. Dinners begin with a beautiful appetizer, followed by fresh soup of the day and salad. Vegetables accompany your main course; two dollars more brings you one of Carolyn's dessert specialties. Don't take my word for it. People go there as strangers the first time. They come back again and again as friends.

THE COTTAGE, 525 Torrence Avenue, Calumet City. Telephone: 891-3900. Hours: 5 pm-10 pm, Tuesday-Thursday; until 11 pm, Saturday. No cards. Reservations required. Full bar service. Jackets requested for men. Free parking.

K/Rating 20/20 • Food 7/7 • Service 6/6 • Decor 4/4 • Value 3/3

Matteson
THE LEFT BANK
French

$$$

Matteson is a long trip from the Loop, but The Left Bank is worth the ride. The restaurant, housed in a former suburban bank building, is unusually large for one which produces better French cuisine. There are two dining rooms (plus a disco, thankfully far enough from food service that it does not distract diners), both lavishly decorated with plush seating, crystal chandeliers and enough floor space for captains and waiters to move serving carts and preparation tables about without chaos or distraction. White clothed tables are graced with fresh flowers and appointed with lovely china and servingware. Service is exemplary; watching the preparation of a flamed entrée is a beautiful prelude to the food itself. Among appetizers, you may choose oysters Rockefeller in the classic New Orleans puréed spinach preparation rather than in the cooked broadleaf presentation characteristic of oysters Florentine. The pâté maison here is enhanced by a sweet Cumberland sauce. Many entrées involve elaborate tableside preparation. Roast duckling is as visually spectacular as one could hope; bigarade sauce is excellent with the bird. Seafoods and beef preparations get fine treatment here; chicken Kiev has a dill accent within its buttered goodness. Flaming desserts exploit the magnificent tableside dexterity of the serving staff.

THE LEFT BANK, 21145 Governors Highway, Matteson. Telephone: 747-4545. Hours: Lunch: 11:30 am-2:30 pm, daily; Dinner: 5:30 pm-10:30 pm, Monday-Thursday and Sunday; until 11 pm, Friday-Saturday. Cards: AE, CB, DC, VISA. Reservations recommended. Full bar service. Jackets required for men. Private party facilities for up to 300 people. Valet parking.

K/Rating 16.5/20 • Food 5.5/7 • Service 6/6 • Decor 3/4 • Value 2/3

Prix Fixe Dinner $13.95

Potage

Potage Du Jour

Soupe a l' Oignon Gratinee . . ($1.00)
Hearty onion soup prepared with   (Extra)
Gruyere and Parmesan cheese

Salades

Salade Verte
Crisp Romaine garnished with
fresh garden vegetables

Caesar Salade . . . . ($1.50)
America's most famous contribution   (Extra)
to the salad bowl, prepared tableside

Entrees

(Includes Garden Fresh Vegetables Du Jour)

Brochette De Boeuf Flambé
Cubed beef broiled on a skewer, with onions,
mushrooms and tomatoes, flamed at tableside

Veau Saute aux Fines Herbes
Tender milk fed veal sauteed with
white wine, demi-glaze and fine herbs

Pike Meuniere
Fresh pike sauteed and served with a
lemon butter sauce

Truite Grenobloise
Your trout will be sauteed in butter and served with
a sauce of supreme of lemon and capers

Supreme de Poulet au Porto
Tender breast of chicken is sauteed and enveloped
in a rich port wine sauce, served with wild rice

Entrecote Colbert
A grilled sirloin steak served with maitre d'hotel
butter with the addition of meat glaze and tarragon

Entrecote Maitre D' Hotel
A grilled sirloin steak served with
maitre d'hotel butter

Filet Mignon Bearnaise
A juicy tenderloin steak served with
a bearnaise sauce

Salades

Salade Rive Gauche . . . . $ 2.95
Spinach salad with sliced mushrooms,
chopped eggs and hot bacon dressing

Salade Quatre Saisons . . . . . . $ 2.95
Hearts of palm and tomato wedges
served on Romaine with choice
of dressing

My Lai Salade . . . . $ 2.95
Fresh Limestone Bibb lettuce is
garnished with shrimp and served
with a special chefs dressing

Avacado Salade . . . . $ 2.95
A fresh avocado and Bibb lettuce salad
Choice of dressing

Caesar Salade . . . . $ 5.00
Caesar's famous salad from Southern   (for 2)
California prepared at tableside for two

Les Poissons

Truite Saute Doria . . . . $ 8.95
Your trout sauteed, served with lemon
butter and sauteed cucumbers

Red Snapper en Croute $12.95
Fresh red snapper is first poached, then
wrapped in puff pastry and baked.
Served with sauce mantua

Dover Sole Walewska $12.95
The sole is poached, garnished with
collops of lobster and coated
with mornay sauce

Truite Farcie aux Fruits De Mer $13.25
Baked trout stuffed with lobster,
shrimp, scallops and topped
with a royale glacage

Fresh Seafood Du Jour . . . .
Your waiter will advise you of the fresh
seafood dishes of the day

Homard a La Nage $17.95
Lobster fresh from our tank is sauteed and
prepared with aromatic herbs, brandy, and
cream, garnished with a julienne of fresh
vegetables

Calumet City
PARK AVENUE SPATS
American

$$

From the department of "dining can be fun but not necessarily expensive" comes this far South Side entry. Casual dining in a theme atmosphere is the watchword here, whether you are seated in the Bamboo Room with its terrarium windows, a second dining room with hardwood floors, dark wood trim and bentwood chairs, or a carpeted dining area with a bit more sumptuous atmosphere. Or there is the cocktail lounge with its turn-of-the-century exultation and a most spectacular mechanical fan overhead that is likely to have you gaping like a visiting tourist. In the midst of all this is a menu that ably runs the gamut from sandwiches, salads and omelettes, to steaks, fish, ribs and even duck. About that duck ... it is half of the bird, hickory smoked and barbecued. It takes a good appetite plus a couple of napkins and a hot after-dinner towel to get through it all. If chicken is your thing, you can get that, awash in barbecue sauce and smoky flavor; or there is a slab of ribs which the menu calls the Mercedes Bones of barbecue ribs. Puns, not so incidentally, roll off the menu the way rain runs off a hill. One of the omelettes is called Benedict Omelette (that is almost treasonous). Yet, even as

---

A-Tisket, A-Brisket
Tender hickory smoked beef brisket, sliced thin, piled on sourdough bread with tangy barbeque sauce and butter grilled. ... $2.95

Bronx Bratwurst
Smoked German sausage, grilled and stuffed in a poppy seed bun, topped with Dusseldorf mustard and smothered with sauteed onions $2.55

Stromboli Sandwich
Ground seasoned sausage topped with chopped onion, mozzarella cheese and pizzeria sauce, all in a special Italian loaf and oven baked $3.25

Fifth Avenue Combo
Sliced ham, turkey and Swiss cheese grilled together on sourdough bread $2.95

Sunflower Sandwich
Philadelphia cream cheese generously spread on cracked wheat bread, layered with avocado, alfalfa sprouts, slices of tomato and red onion, walnuts and sunflower seeds $2.50

Italian Sausage Sandwich
A spicy Italian sausage char-broiled, covered with pizzeria sauce and served in a special Italian loaf $2.95

"spatstacular" as puns may be at Park Avenue Spats, the food is uniformly delicious. For instance, a large skewer of beef shish kebab is a hearty portion of the tender meat and succulent grilled flavor. For some imaginative appetizers try meatballs Swellington, an octet of tiny burgers that have been breaded, deep-fried and baked with a mild Cheddar topping. Or try the Ritz Smacker (it is kind of hard to avoid the puns at PAS), a skewer of richly battered and deep-fried vegetables. Should you be willing and eager to splurge on dessert, you will find plenty to keep you grinning if not thinning. Do you remember how good taffy apples were when you were a kid? Try taffy apple pie. You can put on calories just by reading their dessert menu. However, calorie counters can take heart; there is also yogurt, flavored, plain or with fruit.

PARK AVENUE SPATS, 601 River Oaks West (in the River Oaks Shopping Center), Calumet City. Telephone: 891-1115. Hours: 11 am-midnight, Monday-Thursday; until 1 am, Friday-Saturday; until 10 pm, Sunday. Cards: MC, VISA. Reservations taken. Full bar service. Casual, neat dress acceptable. Ample parking.

K/Rating 20/20 • Food 7/7 • Service 6/6 • Decor 4/4 • Value 3/3

East Side, West Side Kabobs

From the east, jumbo shrimp lightly breaded, skewered with fresh vegetables and deep fried ... from the west, tender chunks of choice beef, broiled and skewered with fresh vegetables, mushrooms and pineapple ... both served on a bed of our special rice mixture.

East Side Shrimp	$7.25
West Side Beef	$6.25
All around the town (1 of each)	$6.75

Empire Steak Building

A generous center cut of choice strip steak, char-broiled and covered with sauteed mushrooms ... $7.75

Statue of Liverty

Fresh, milk fed baby calves liver sauteed in butter and smothered with grilled onions, green peppers and mushrooms ... $5.50

Stuffed Rainbow Trout

America's favorite catch, stuffed with a delicious cornbread mixture of Alaskan Crab, shrimp, mushrooms and onions and baked until tender ... $6.25

Index

WHERE TO EAT WHEN YOU COME INTO YOUR INHERITANCE

CHICAGO
Cape Cod Room, 28-29
Chez Paul, 34-35
Cricket's, 42-43
Doro's, 50-51
Dr. Shen's, 48-49
Gordon, 74
Jovan, 88
La Cheminée, 96-97
Le Festival, 110-111
Le Perroquet, 112-113
Maxim's de Paris, 124-125
Morton's, 128
Nick's Fishmarket, 138-139
Truffles, 184-185

SUBURBS
Alouette, 198-199
Fond de la Tour, 239
Le Français, 228-229
The Left Bank, 252-253
Le Titi de Paris, 230-231
The Tower Garden &
    Restaurant, 215

WHERE TO TAKE YOUR CLIENT TO TALK BUSINESS

CHICAGO
Café de Paris, 24-25
Cape Cod Room, 28-29
Chez Paul, 34-35
Nick's Fishmarket, 138-139
Wrigley Building Restaurant,
    188

WHERE TO TAKE YOUR CLIENT TO IMPRESS HIM/HER

CHICAGO
Arnie's, 10-11
Chez Paul, 34-35
Cricket's, 42-43
Doro's, 50-51
Dr. Shen's, 48-49
Jovan, 88
Le Festival, 110-111
Le Perroquet, 112-113
Morton's, 128
Nick's Fishmarket, 138-139
That Steak Joynt, 178-179

SUBURBS
Alouette, 198-199
Le Français, 228-229
The Left Bank, 252-253
The Tower Garden &
    Restaurant, 215

WHERE TO GO TO MAKE AN 8 O'CLOCK CURTAIN

CHICAGO
Arnie's, 10-11
Barney's Market Club, 15
Bastille, 16
Blackhawk, 18-19
Cape Cod Room, 28-29
Dr. Shen's, 48-49
Eli's The Place for Steak, 53
Gene & Georgetti, 66-67
House of Hunan, 82-83
L'Épuisette, 116
Martini's, 118-119
Morton's, 128
Nick's Fishmarket, 138-139
Pronto Ristorante, 150-151
Sage's East, 156-157
Sayat Nova, 166-167
Su Casa, 169
Tamborine, 170-171
That Steak Joynt, 178-179
Wrigley Building Restaurant, 188

DO YA WANNA DANCE?

CHICAGO
Arnie's, 10-11
Maxim's de Paris, 124
Miomir's Serbian Club, 126-127
Truffles, 184-185
Zanadu, 190-191

SUBURBS
Arnie's North, 200

WHERE TO GO FOR A MIDNIGHT RENDEZVOUS

Note: Not all restaurants are open late every evening: Check individual listings for more specific information.

CHICAGO
Cafe Azteca, 23
Chicago Pizza and Oven Grinder Company, 36
D.B. Kaplan's, 44-45
Dae Ho, 46
Dianna's Oppa, 47
Eli's The Place for Steak, 53
Eugene's, 54-55
Family House, 58-59
Garden of Happiness, 61
Geja's Cafe, 64-65
Gino's East, 71
Great Gritzbe's Flying Food Show, 75
Greek Islands, 76-77
Half Shell, 78
La Fontanella, 102-103
Maxim's de Paris, 124-125
Miomir's Serbian Club, 126-127
Morton's, 128
My Place For, 130-131
Nancy's, 132-133
R.J. Grunts, 152-153
Roditys, 154-155
Sage's East, 156-157
Sally's Stage, 158
Sparta Gyros, 168
Su Casa, 169
Tamborine, 170-171

That Steak Joynt, 178-179
The Waterfront, 186-187
Zanadu, 190-191
Zlata's Belgrade Restaurant, 192
Zum Deutschen Eck, 194

SUBURBS
Arnie's North, 200
The Big Apple, 201
Park Avenue Spats, 254-255
Rikki's, 234-235

WHERE TO POP THE QUESTION (or other romantic ideas)

CHICAGO
Gordon, 74
La Cheminée, 96-97
La Fontaine, 100-101
Le Festival, 110-111
Le Perroquet, 112-113
L'Escargot (in the bar), 114-115
Maxim's de Paris, 124-125
Patrice, 144-145
Tango (in a booth), 172-173
Truffles, 184-185

SUBURBS
Café Provençal, 202-203
Fond de la Tour, 239

WHERE TO GO TO EAT IN BLUE JEANS (Levis or Halston)

CHICAGO
Bowl and Roll, 20
Bread Shop Kitchen, 21
Busghetti, 22
Cafe Azteca, 23
Captain Nemo's, 30
Chicago Pizza and Oven Grinder Company, 36
D.B. Kaplan's, 44-45
El Criollo, 52-53
Family Corner, 56-57
French Port, 60
Geja's Cafe, 64-65
Genesee Depot, 70
Gennaro's, 68-69
Gino's East, 71
Great Gritzbe's Flying Food Show, 75
Greek Islands, 76-77
Half Shell, 78
Hamburger Hamlet, 79-80
House of Hunan, 84
Hungarian Restaurant, 85
Jasands, 86-87
Kasztelanka, 90-91
La Choza, 98-99
Lawrence of Oregano, 106-107
Matsuya, 122
Miller's Pub, 123

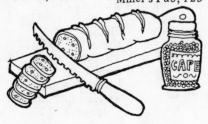

Nancy's, 132-133
Naniwa, 136
New Japan Oriental Cafe, 137
Otto's Beer House and Garden Club, 142-143
R.J. Grunts, 152-153
Sally's Stage, 158
Sauer's, 164-165
Sparta Gyros, 168
Thai Little Home Cafe, 174-175
Thai Villa, 176-177
Zanadu, 190-191

SUBURBS
Aegean Isles, 196-197
The Big Apple, 201
La Poêle d'Or, 226-227
Park Avenue Spats, 254-255
Rikki's, 234-235
Shrimp Walk, 212-213
The Silo, 214
Squeakie's, 236-237
Village Tavern, 237

Great Gritzbe's Flying Food Show, 75
Hamburger Hamlet, 79-80
Kasztelanka, 90-91
La Choza, 98-99
Lawrence of Oregano, 106-107
Lee's Canton Cafe, 108-109
Les Oeufs, 117
Mategrano's, 120-121
My Place For, 130-131
Nancy's, 132-133
The Prime House, 148
R.J. Grunts, 152-153
Roditys, 154-155
Sally's Stage, 158
Sauer's, 164-165
Sparta Gyros, 168
Tamborine, 170-171
Zanadu, 190-191
Zum Deutschen Eck, 193-194

SUBURBS
Aegean Isles, 196-197
The Big Apple, 201
Dragon Inn North, 205
Fanny's, 206-207
The Indian Trail, 208
James Tavern, 209
La Poêle d'Or, 226-227
Mill Race Inn, 242-243
Park Avenue Spats, 254-255
Peking Mandarin, 246-247
The Pelikan, 248-249
Rikki's, 234-235
Shrimp Walk, 212-213
The Silo, 214
Squeakie's, 236-237
T.J. Peppercorn's, 216-217
Tamborine, 170-171
Village Tavern, 237
Yu Lin's Chinese Dumpling House, 220-221

WHERE CAN WE TAKE THE KIDS TONIGHT?

CHICAGO
Bowl and Roll, 20
Busghetti, 22
Captain Nemo's, 30
Chicago Pizza and Oven Grinder Company, 36
The Court House, 38-39
D.B. Kaplan's, 44-45
Dae Ho, 46
Dianna's Oppa, 46
Family Corner, 56-57
Family House, 58-59

WHERE TO GO FOR A LEISURELY BRUNCH

CHICAGO

Abacus, 8-9
Arnie's, 10-11
Dr. Shen's, 48-49
Gaylord India Restaurant, 62-63
Gordon, 74
R.J. Grunts, 152-153
Zanadu, 190-191

SUBURBS

The Greenhouse, 224-225
Scornavacco's, 210-211
T.J. Peppercorn's, 216-217
The Tower Garden & Restaurant, 215

INDEX BY CUISINE

AMERICAN

CHICAGO

Arnie's North, 10-11
Barney's Market Club, 15
Blackhawk, 18-19
Bowl and Roll, 20
Eugene's, 52-53
Genesee Depot, 70
Great Gritzbe's Flying Food Show, 75
Hamburger Hamlet, 79-80
Jasands, 86-87
Lawry's, 105
Mategrano's, 120-121
Miller's Pub, 123

My Place For, 130-131
Otto's Beer House and Garden Club, 142-143
R.J. Grunts, 152-153
Sage's East, 156-157
Sally's Stage, 158
Sauer's, 164-165
Tamborine, 170-171
Zanadu, 190-191

SUBURBS

Fanny's, 206-207
Gale Street Inn, 223
The Greenhouse, 224-225
The Indian Trail, 208
James Tavern, 209
Mill Race Inn, 242-243
Nielson's Willoway Manor, 244-245
Park Avenue Spats, 254-255
Shrimp Walk, 212-213
The Silo, 214
Squeakie's, 236-237
T.J. Peppercorn's, 216-217
Village Tavern, 237

ARGENTINIAN

CHICAGO

El Criollo, 50-51

ARMENIAN

CHICAGO

Casbah, 30-31
Sayat Nova, 166-167

AUSTRIAN

CHICAGO

Salzburger Hof, 162

BRITISH COMMONWEALTH

SUBURBS
Upstairs Downstairs, 218-219

CHINESE

CHICAGO
Abacus, 8-9
Dr. Shen's, 48-49
Garden of Happiness, 61
House of Hunan, 82-83
House of Hunan, 84
Lee's Canton Cafe, 108-109

SUBURBS
Dragon Inn North, 205
Peking Mandarin, 246-247
Yu Lin's Chinese Dumpling House, 220-221

CONTINENTAL

CHICAGO
Arnie's, 10-11
The Bakery, 14-15
Chef Alberto's, 32-33
The Court House, 38-39
Cricket's, 42-43
Gordon, 74
Kenessey's, 92-93
Sage's East, 156-157
Salzburger Hof, 162
Wrigley Building Restaurant, 188

SUBURBS
The Cottage, 251
The Tower Garden & Restaurant, 215

CREOLE

CHICAGO
The Cajun House, 26-27
The Creole House, 40-41
Otto's Beer House and Garden Club, 142-143

CRÊPES

SUBURBS
La Poêle d'Or, 226-227

CZECHOSLOVAKIAN

SUBURBS
The Pelikan, 248-249

DELICATESSEN

CHICAGO
D.B. Kaplan's, 44-45

FONDUE

CHICAGO
Geja's Cafe, 64-65

FRENCH

CHICAGO
Alouette, 198-199
Bastille, 16
Café de Paris, 24-25
Chez Paul, 34-35
French Port, 60
Jovan, 88
La Cheminée, 96-97
La Fontaine, 100-101
Le Festival, 110-111
Le Perroquet, 112-113
L'Épuisette, 116
L'Escargot, 114-115

Maxim's de Paris, 124
Patrice, 144-145
Truffles, 184-185

SUBURBS
Café Provençal, 202-203
Fond de la Tour, 239
Le Français, 228-229
The Left Bank, 252-253
Le Titi de Paris, 230-231

GERMAN

CHICAGO
The Berghoff, 17
The Golden Ox, 72-73
Zum Deutschen Eck,
   193-194

GREEK

CHICAGO
Family House, 58-59
Greek Islands, 76-77
My Place For, 130-131
Roditys, 154-155
Sparta Gyros, 168

SUBURBS
Aegean Isles, 196-197
Rikki's, 234-235

HAMBURGERS

CHICAGO
Hamburger Hamlet, 79-80
Sauer's, 164-165

HUNGARIAN

CHICAGO
Hungarian Restaurant, 85
Kenessey's, 92-93

CHICAGO
Family Corner, 56-57
Gaylord India Restaurant,
   62-63
Khyber India Restaurant,
   94-95

ITALIAN

CHICAGO
Busghetti, 22
Doro's, 50-51
Gene & Georgetti, 66-67
Gennaro's, 68-69
Gino's East, 71
House of Bertini, 80-81
La Fontanella, 102-103
Lawrence of Oregano, 106-
   107
Mategrano's, 120-121
Nancy's, 132-133
North Star Inn, 140-141
Pronto Ristorante, 150-151
Salvatore's, 160-161
Toscano, 182-183

SUBURBS
Fanny's, 206-207
Giannotti's, 240-241
A Little Touch of Italy,
   232-233
Scornavacco's, 210-211

JAPANESE

CHICAGO
Kamehachi, 89
Matsuya, 122
Naniwa, 136
New Japan Oriental Cafe,
137

KOREAN

CHICAGO
Dae Ho, 48
Garden of Happiness, 61

MEXICAN

CHICAGO
Cafe Azteca, 23
El Criollo, 50-51
La Choza, 98-99
Su Casa, 169

OMELETTES

CHICAGO
Les Oeufs, 117

SUBURBS
The Big Apple, 201
La Poêle d'Or, 226-227

PANCAKES

SUBURBS
The Big Apple, 201

PERUVIAN

CHICAGO
La Llama, 104
Piqueo, 146

PIZZA

CHICAGO
Chicago Pizza and Oven
    Grinder Company, 36
Gino's East, 71
Nancy's, 132-133

SUBURBS
The Silo, 214

POLISH

CHICAGO
Kasztelanka, 90-91

SALADS

CHICAGO
Chicago Pizza and Oven
    Grinder Company, 36

SANDWICHES

CHICAGO
Captain Nemo's, 30

SEAFOOD

CHICAGO
Cape Cod Room, 28-29
French Port, 60
Half Shell, 78
Nantucket Cove, 134-135
Nick's Fishmarket, 138-139
Tango, 172-173
The Waterfront, 186-187

SUBURBS
Don's Fish Market & Pro-
    vision Company, 204
Squeakie's, 236-237

SERBIAN

CHICAGO
Miomir's Serbian Club,
126-127
Zlata's Belgrade Restaurant,
192

SOUL FOOD

CHICAGO
Army and Lou's, 12-13

STEAKS

CHICAGO
Eli's The Place for Steak, 51
Gene & Georgetti, 66-67
House of Bertini, 80
Mategrano's, 120-121
Morton's, 128
The Prime House, 148
That Steak Joynt, 178-179

THAI

CHICAGO
Thai Little Home Cafe,
174-175
Thai Villa, 176-177

TURKISH

CHICAGO
Topkapi, 180-181

VEGETARIAN

CHICAGO
Bread Shop Kitchen, 21

INDEX BY GEOGRAPHY

CHICAGO
Abacus, 8-9
Army and Lou's, 12-13
Arnie's, 10-11
The Bakery, 14-15
Barney's Market Club, 15
Bastille, 16
The Berghoff, 17
Blackhawk, 18-19
Bowl and Roll, 20
Bread Shop Kitchen, 21
Busghetti, 22
Cafe Azteca, 23
Café de Paris, 24-25
The Cajun House, 26-27
Cape Cod Room, 28-29
Captain Nemo's, 30
Casbah, 31
Chef Alberto's, 32-33
Chez Paul, 34-35
Chicago Pizza and Oven
    Grinder Company, 36
The Court House, 38-39
The Creole House, 40-41
Cricket's, 42-43
D.B. Kaplan's, 44-45
Dae Ho, 46
Dianna's Oppa, 47
Doro's, 50-51
Dr. Shen's, 48-49
El Criollo, 52-53
Eli's The Place for Steak, 53
Eugene's, 54-55
Family Corner, 56-57
Family House, 58-59
French Port, 60
Garden of Happiness, 61
Gaylord India Restaurant,
    62-63

Geja's Cafe, 64-65
Gene & Georgetti, 66-67
Gennaro's, 68-69
Genesee, 70
Gino's East, 71
The Golden Ox, 72-73
Gordon, 74
Great Gritzbe's Flying Food
    Show, 75
Greek Islands, 76-77
Half Shell, 78
Hamburger Hamlet, 79-80
House of Bertini, 80-81
House of Hunan, 82-83
House of Hunan, 84
Hungarian Restaurant, 85
Jasands, 86-87
Jovan, 88
Kamehachi, 89
Kasztelanka, 90-91
Kenessey's, 92-93
Khyber India Restaurant,
    94-95
La Cheminée, 96-97
La Choza, 98-99
La Fontaine, 100-101
La Fontanella, 102-103
La Llama, 104
Lawry's, 105
Lawrence of Oregano,
    106-107
Lee's Canton Cafe, 108-109
Le Festival, 110-111
Le Perroquet, 112-113
L'Escargot, 114-115
L'Épuisette, 116
Les Oeufs, 117
Martini's, 118-119
Mategrano's, 120-121
Matsuya, 122
Miller's Pub, 123
Maxim's de Paris, 124-125

Miomir's Serbian Club,
    126-127
Morton's, 128
My Place For, 130-131
Nancy's, 132-133
Nantucket Cove, 134-135
Naniwa, 136
New Japan Oriental Cafe,
    137
Nick's Fishmarket, 138-139
North Star Inn, 140-141
Otto's Beer House and
    Garden Club, 142-143
Patrice, 144-145
Piqueo, 146
The Prime House, 148
Pronto Ristorante, 150-151
R.J. Grunts, 152-153
Roditys, 154-155
Sage's East, 156-157
Sally's Stage, 158
Salvatore's, 161-162
Salzburger Hof, 162-163
Sauer's, 164-165
Sayat Nova, 166-167
Sparta Gyros, 168
Su Casa, 169
Tamborine, 170-171
Tango, 172-173
Thai Little Home Cafe,
    174-175
Thai Villa, 176-177
That Steak Joynt, 178-179
Topkapi, 180-181
Toscano, 182-183
Truffles, 184-185
The Waterfront, 186-187
Wrigley Building Restaurant,
    188
Zanadu, 190-191
Zlata's Belgrade
    Restaurant, 192
Zum Deutschen Eck, 193

SUBURBS: NORTH
Aegean Isles, 196-197
Alouette, 198-199
Arnie's North, 200
The Big Apple, 201
Café Provençal, 202-203
Don's Fish Market & Provision Company, 204
Dragon Inn North, 205
Fanny's, 206-207
The Indian Trail, 208
James Tavern, 209
Scornavacco's, 210-211
Shrimp Walk, 212-213
The Silo, 214
T.J. Peppercorn's, 216-217
The Tower Garden & Restaurant, 215
Upstairs Downstairs, 218-219
Yu Lin's Chinese Dumpling House, 220-221

SUBURBS: NORTHWEST
Gale Street Inn, 223
The Greenhouse, 224-225
La Poêle d'Or, 226-227
Le Français, 228-229
Le Titi de Paris, 230-231
A Little Touch of Italy, 232-233
Rikki's, 234-235
Squeakie's, 236-237

SUBURBS: WEST
Fond de la Tour, 239
Gianotti's, 240-241
Mill Race Inn, 242-243
Nielson's Willoway Manor, 244-245
Peking Mandarin, 246-247
The Pelikan, 248-249

SUBURBS: SOUTH
The Cottage, 251
The Left Bank, 242-253
Park Avenue Spats, 254-255

INDEX BY PRICE

CHICAGO
Army and Lou's, 12-13
The Berghoff, 17
Bowl and Roll, 20
Bread Shop Kitchen, 21
Captain Nemo's, 30
Chicago Pizza and Oven Grinder Company, 36
D.B. Kaplan's, 44-45
Dae Ho, 46
Dianna's Oppa, 47
Family Corner, 56-57
Genesee Depot, 70
Gennaro's, 68-69
Half Shell, 78
Hamburger Hamlet, 79-80
Hungarian Restaurant, 85
Jasands, 86-87
Kasztelanka, 90-91
La Choza, 98-99
Les Oeufs, 117
Mategrano's, 120-121
Matsuya, 122
Nancy's, 132-133
Naniwa, 136
New Japan Oriental Cafe, 137
R.J. Grunts, 152-153
Sauer's, 164-165
Sayat Nova, 166-167
Sparta Gyros, 168
Tamborine, 170-171

SUBURBS
Aegean Isles, 196-197
The Big Apple, 201
The Indian Trail, 208
La Poêle d'Or, 226-227
The Pelikan, 248-249

$$

CHICAGO
Abacus, 8-9
Barney's Market Club, 15
Bastille, 16
Blackhawk, 18-19
Busghetti, 22
Cafe Azteca, 23
The Cajun House, 26-27
Cape Cod Room, 28-29
Casbah, 31
Chef Alberto's, 32-33
The Court House, 38-39
The Creole House, 40-41
El Criollo, 52-53
Eli's The Place for Steak, 53
Eugene's, 54-55
Family House, 58-59
French Port, 60
Garden of Happiness, 61
Gaylord India Restaurant,
    62-63
Gene & Georgetti, 66-67
Gino's East, 71
The Golden Ox, 72-73
Great Gritzbe's Flying
    Food Show, 75
Greek Islands, 76-77
House of Bertini, 80-81
House of Hunan, 82-83
House of Hunan, 84

Hungarian Restaurant, 85
Kamehachi, 89
Kenessey's, 92-93
La Fontanella, 102-103
Khyber India Restaurant, 94-95
La Llama, 104
Lawry's, 105
Lawrence of Oregano, 106-
    107
Lee's Canton Cafe, 108-109
L'Épuisette, 116
Martini's, 118-119
Miller's Pub, 123
Miomir's Serbian Club,
    126-127
My Place For, 130-131
Nantucket Cove, 134-135
North Star Inn, 140-141
Otto's Beer House and
    Garden Club, 142-143
The Prime House, 148-149
Pronto Ristorante, 150-151
Roditys, 154-155
Sage's East, 156-157
Sally's Stage, 158-159
Salzburger Hof, 162-163
Su Casa, 169
Thai Little Home Cafe,
    174-175
Thai Villa, 176-177
That Steak Joynt, 178-179
Topkapi, 180-181
Toscano, 182-183
The Waterfront, 186-187
Wrigley Building Restaurant,
    188
Zanadu, 190-191
Zlata's Belgrade Restaurant,
    192-193
Zum Deutschen Eck, 193-194

SUBURBS
Arnie's North, 200
Don's Fish Market & Provision Company, 204
Dragon Inn North, 205
Fanny's, 206-207
Gale Street Inn, 223
Giannotti's, 240-241
The Greenhouse, 224-225
James Tavern, 209
A Little Touch of Italy, 232-233
Mill Race Inn, 242-243
Nielson's Willoway Manor, 244-245
Park Avenue Spats, 254-255
Peking Mandarin, 246-247
Rikki's, 234-235
Scornavacco's, 210-211
Shrimp Walk, 212-213
The Silo, 214
Squeakie's, 236-237
T.J. Peppercorn's, 216-217
Upstairs Downstairs, 218-219
Village Tavern, 237
Yu Lin's Chinese Dumpling House, 220-221

Geja's Cafe, 64-65
Gordon, 74
Jovan, 88
La Fontaine, 100-101
La Cheminée, 96-97
Le Festival, 110-111
Le Perroquet, 112-113
L'Escargot, 114-115
Maxim's de Paris, 124-125
Morton's, 128
Nick's Fishmarket, 138-139
Patrice, 144-145
Piqueo, 146-147
Salvatore's, 160-161
Tango, 172-173
Truffles, 184-185

SUBURBS
Alouette, 198-199
Café Provençal, 202-203
Fond de la Tour, 239
Le Français, 228-229
The Left Bank, 252-253
Le Titi de Paris, 230-231
The Tower Garden & Restaurant, 215

$$$

CHICAGO
Arnie's, 10-11
The Bakery, 14-15
Café de Paris, 24-25
Chez Paul, 34-35
Cricket's, 42-43
Dr. Shen's, 48-49
Doro's, 50-51

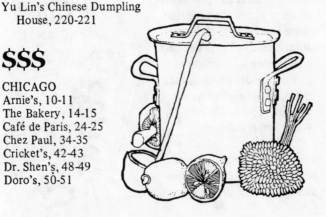

LET THESE GUIDES LEAD YOU TO THE BEST RESTAURANTS OF OTHER AREAS

The best restaurants of Florida, Los Angeles, New York, Philadelphia, San Francisco, Texas and the Pacific Northwest are described in these authoritative guides. Each is written by local food writers and critics. Each is the same size and format as Best Restaurants Chicago & Suburbs.

"This series . . . is designed to bring out the discriminating gourmet in everyone. We've found that many restaurant reviews contain more fancy prose than real meat and potatoes . . . so we're pleased to note that these reports have style *and* substance. . . . There's enough solid dining information in any of these guides to abolish the question 'Where can we eat tonight?' forever."
—*The Travel Advisor*

These books are available at bookstores in their respective areas or may be ordered directly from:
101 Productions
834 Mission Street
San Francisco, CA 94103

RESTAURANT RECOMMENDATION

If you have a favorite restaurant in Chicago, not in this book, please tell us about it in the space below. Send your recommendations and comments to:

Best Restaurant Guides
c/o 101 Productions
834 Mission Street
San Francisco, California 94103

Name of Restaurant _____

Address _____

City _____

Type of Food _____

Your Favorite Dish _____